At the End of Life

TRUE STORIES ABOUT HOW WE DIE

Edited by
LEE GUTKIND

Introduction by Francine Prose

InFACT BOOKS

Requests for permission to reproduce material from this work should be sent to:
Rights and Permissions
Creative Nonfiction Foundation
5501 Walnut Street, Suite 202
Pittsburgh, PA 15232

Cover design by Tristen Knight
Cover art by Mike Perrault
Text design by Tom Dawson

ISBN: 978-1-937163-04-4

Printed in the United States of America on acid-free paper

10 9 8 7 6 5 4 3 2 1

Contents

Editor's Note

Frank at the Piano

LEE GUTKIND

My friend Frank, a teacher, actor, singer, performer, told me once that he volunteers regularly at a nearby hospice, playing the piano for the residents. I was moved by his effort. I said, "You must get great satisfaction knowing you are entertaining these people, soothing them, keeping them comfortable in their final days. More than anything," I added, "you must have wonderful conversations with the folks there—patients, staff, everybody."

Frank looked at me with surprise and perhaps with a bit of horror, as if I'd said something totally outlandish. "Oh, no!" he replied vehemently. "I couldn't."

"You don't go into the patients' rooms or chat with the nurses?"

"No," said Frank. The piano is in one of the front lobby areas. "I just go in and I play, and then I leave when I am tired or feel like they've had enough of my music."

How—why—did he come to do this? A friend had told him there was a piano in the hallway and that the hospice was looking for people to play it, so Frank arrived one day, unannounced, and played.

While he played that first time, a few people walked by to compliment him, and when he was ready to leave, a lady at the front desk thanked him and invited him back, anytime. So Frank, who is retired and in his seventies, appears at the hospice from time to time and plays the piano. He's never "officially" met anyone there, never introduced himself to any of the staff or administration. He appears, plays, and disappears, gliding lightly in and out of this place where people have come to die.

I've asked him a couple of times if this is his way of connecting with the specter of death, facing the inevitable, and he shrugs, laughs, and says he doesn't know what his piano playing and hospice visiting are all about. And I guess it doesn't matter, because he gets something out of it—pleasure, security, reinforcement of his own well-being and health, who knows what else? Perhaps a foreshadowing of what might soon happen to him. Somehow there's a double purpose and benefit—a therapeutic connection for Frank and a tissue of pleasure for the people for whom he is playing.

I am hoping readers of *At the End of Life* will receive that same connection and pleasure—and an added understanding of the challenges of life and death—from the essays collected in this volume.

When one of the editors reviewed the twenty-two essays contained herein, she e-mailed me saying that the combined effect of the book was to her completely depressing. "Of course," I told her, "we are talking about death, the end of the line. What do you expect?"

And then a few weeks later when I began viewing potential cover art for the book jacket this same editor had sent me, all I could think about was how depressing all of the potential visuals seemed to me. And I thought, "Well, of course—what did you tell your editorial colleague?"

But we were both wrong, I think, as I view the entire book, edited now, with jacket and art. Okay, yes, the collection contains sadness, as all works dealing with death must. And yet, the messages inherent in these essays are positive, demonstrating that people can die with strength and dignity and, even more to the point, that their loved ones can endure these deaths and go forward in their lives, with strength and dignity and even a sense of confidence and hope.

We often forget that the death of loved ones has a ferocious impact on the survivors—a burden that can continue long after the funeral and mourning period. For readers and for writers, these essays, no matter how sad aspects of each story might be, illustrate the power of the human spirit to heal, to become renewed, and to come to terms with grief and fear. Reading these essays enhances our understanding now as we contemplate the power of the authors' voices and the deep roots of their compassion and will serve perhaps to strengthen us in the future when we're confronted by death and loss ourselves, as Frank's piano playing brings solace to his listeners today and, perhaps just as important, to the performer tomorrow.

Acknowledgments

At the End of Life is part of a series of narrative books on science and medicine supported by the Jewish Healthcare Foundation, whose primary mission is to support health care services, education, and research and to encourage medical advancement and protect vulnerable populations. On behalf of the writers and staff at *Creative Nonfiction* who worked on *At the End of Life,* I would like to thank Karen Wolk Feinstein and her colleagues at the Jewish Healthcare Foundation—particularly Nancy Zionts and Carla Barricella—not only for their support but also for their faith in the power of true stories and bold voices.

I would also like to thank attorney Melissa Irr Harkes for her legal counsel; managing editor Hattie Fletcher for her advice and counsel; and Courtney McCrimmon, Patricia Park, and Sam Gutkind for their editorial assistance. In addition, I'd like to thank Keith Gregory, Kathryn Lang, and George Ann Ratchford at Southern Methodist University Press, as well as Andrew Blauner, our agent and friend, for their wisdom and support; the Juliet Lea Hillman Simonds Foundation and the Pennsylvania Council on the Arts, whose ongoing support has been essential to the Creative Nonfiction Foundation's success; and the entire staff at *Creative Nonfiction*—especially associate editor Stephen Knezovich for his editorial and coordinating skill and dedication.

Some names and identifying details have been changed to protect the identities of people and institutions mentioned in these essays.

Foreword

New Approaches to End-of-Life Care

KAREN WOLK FEINSTEIN

When I was thirty-seven, I watched my sister die of cancer. Her suffering left me with a powerful emotional scar. Shortly after her death, a movie, *Terms of Endearment,* captured the experience precisely. In both the movie and my sister's real life, a young mother was dying in a hospital intensive care unit. Last-minute scans and denials of pain medication were seemingly cruel and certainly pointless. They had no medical or curative meaning except to help the clinical team do something in a sad situation they couldn't reverse.

As awful as it was to relive my sister's death through the movie, it was somehow consoling to know that her hospital ordeal was not exceptionally horrible; it was the norm.

If you want a meaningful conversation with someone who has suffered a personal loss, ask, "How good was your mother's (father's, husband's, etc.) death?" Far too seldom is the response, "It was sad but beautiful." Most often you'll hear *Terms of Endearment* horror stories about last-minute meaningless interventions or suffering or general confusion. We have all heard them: "My mother wanted to stop treatment; no one would listen," or "We begged for a hospice referral, but it was withheld," or "We suggested to the doctors that it was time to let him rest in peace, but they kept saying 'one more test, one more drug.'"

There is an alternative, however; in the years since my sister's death, hospice care has become more widely available in America. Hospice supports patients and families at the end of life and has done much to make death as pain-free, meaningful, "nonmedical," noninvasive, and comforting as possible. Also new is palliative care, a comprehensive approach to patient care that focuses on symptom management.

I have had family members die in hospitals and under hospice care in their own homes, and I am able to compare both experiences for patient and family. There is no comparison. Hospice and palliative care are remarkable breakthroughs in end-of-life care, one of the important social movements of the last few decades. A good program takes dying from the tragic, unspeakable, and horrifying to a different plane: supportive, tender, peaceful, uplifting. But many patients are denied palliative and hospice care because of physician reluctance to refer, family lack of knowledge, or policy inhibitions. These all could be fixed.

Since its inception in 1991, the Jewish Healthcare Foundation has funded end-of-life and palliative care advances not just in southwestern Pennsylvania but also nationally and abroad. We supported the Leo Criep Chair in Patient-Centered Care at the University of Pittsburgh Medical School. We have funded the development of hospices, pain management innovations, physician orders for life-sustaining treatment directives, caregiver training, education in end-of-life dialogues for health professionals, and anything else we can think of that might improve the end of life. For a project called Closure, we are in the midst of initiating structured community conversations among clinicians, clergy, lawyers, family members, social workers, and others, to understand why people are unable to have a "good" death.

So, the foundation is proud to have helped sponsor this book devoted to beautifully written stories about the end of life. The point was not to produce an academic thesis; it was to extend the community conversation by allowing providers, patients, family members, and others to express themselves and tell their stories. The outpouring of submissions, more than four hundred in all, astounded us and confirmed the value of what you will read here. We want to start community conversations, and this volume is indeed a conversation starter. The stories capture experiences that I know to be true and issues that need to be aired. While there is no "right way" to approach the end of life, patients and families should have their options reviewed and respected by the medical team.

Finally, this volume provides an opportunity to pay tribute to exceptional pioneers who, by example and deed, have done much to improve death and dying. Among them are physicians Linda Emanuel, professor of medicine at the Kellogg School of Management in Chicago, who created the Education for Physicians on End-of-Life Care (EPEC) modules; Joanne Lynn, director of the Center to Improve Care of the Dying (CIDC) at George Washington Medical School in Washington DC, an early crusader for hospice and palliative care; David Servan Schreiber, professor of psychiatry at the University of Pittsburgh School of Medicine and a lecturer in the Faculty of Medicine of Lyon, France, who draws lessons from his own ongoing battle with brain cancer to urge physicians to go beyond medical interventions at the end of life by providing family support; Robert Arnold, holder of the Leo Criep Chair at the University of Pittsburgh, who uses this post to advance end-of-life care systemwide; and Susan Tolle, director of the Center for Ethics in Health Care at Oregon Health and Science University, a leader in promoting state adoption of physician orders for life-sustaining treatment (POLST). They have led and inspired a movement, and I know they will continue to do so.

Karen Wolk Feinstein*, PhD, is president of the Jewish Healthcare Foundation and chair of the Pittsburgh Regional Healthcare Initiative.*

Introduction
Last Days

FRANCINE PROSE

The longer we live, the more of life we experience—youth and age, passion and loss, the beginning and end of a romance, the birth and death of loved ones—the more we may find ourselves distrusting the ability of language to tell us what these life-changing experiences are like. No amount of love poetry can prepare us for the moment when one person starts to matter to us so much more than anyone else. Reading the scene in Chekov's "The Lady with the Pet Dog" in which Gurov looks in the mirror and is shocked to see that he has gray hair cannot really prepare us for the pure weirdness of catching sight of our own reflection—and realizing that *we* are that gray-headed person. Maybe the reason there are so few persuasive scenes of childbirth in literature (I'm excepting the one in which Emma Bovary finds out she has given birth to a girl and turns her head to the wall, or those in which a young woman dies, off screen, in labor) is that it's so hard to convey the amazement of giving birth, of seeing a new human being emerge into the world.

There has never been a shortage of fiction, history, poetry, and memoir concerned with the end of life. Violent death is always a favorite, but many writers seem to have felt they weren't doing their job unless they included plenty of old age and "ordinary" death in the domestic and social panorama they captured on the page. Important and dramatic family deaths punctuate *War and Peace,* Anna Karenina's suicide was a spectacular tour de force, Little Nell's death famously broke the collective heart of London, and what would Balzac's characters have done if they hadn't had all those wills and legacies to incite their schemes and struggles?

I used to think that the eponymous protagonist of Tolstoy's novella *The Death of Ivan Ilych* suffered the worst imaginable death. He realized he'd led his entire life wrong, then screamed for three days and nights until he found some not-very-convincing relief in the healing ministrations of a servant. But after reading the essays in *At the End of Life,* it occurred to me that Ivan Ilych was at least spared the degradations and inhumanities of a modern high-tech death: he wasn't bullied into intubation, hooked up to a ventilator, forced to endure drastic "life-saving" measures after he had resolved to die, had received his family's blessing, and had completed a DNR order.

Remarkable for their honesty, variety, and compression, the essays in this collection tell us what it is like in the early years of the twenty-first century to experience, or to witness, the end of life. As the saying goes, no one who has been there has come back to tell the tale, but the dying appear as characters in many of these pieces, so well rendered that we do get a sense of what their last days, if not the last moments, were like for them.

Obviously, the voices we hear are the voices of the living, of men and women who have survived the deaths of parents and partners and children. We hear, too, from health professionals, doctors, counselors, hospice workers, nurses, a nursing home worker, and an EMT dispatcher, people for whom the end of life—the biological processes and the psychological ramifications—is the basis of what they do, their profession and their calling.

Each writer has a story to tell, an individual perspective on singular characters, incidents, and details. But I would suggest reading the book straight through, or as close to straight through as possible; make no mistake, many of these essays are extremely skillful at recalling and making us feel the pain they describe. What emerges by the end is a larger picture, a jigsaw puzzle assembled from individual pieces, a complete, if disquieting, image of what the end of life is like at this point in our collective history.

You may notice certain elements that recur more often than you'd expect, further testimony to the notion that the end of life involves the soul as well as the body. Apparently, one way to know death is near is that the dying occasionally report visits and conversations with people already dead. Some combination of ritual and instinct prompts the living to open a window in the room where someone has just died, perhaps to enable the spirit to leave the premises in which the husk of the body remains.

But perhaps the most striking theme that recurs in essay after essay is how many *decisions* there are to be made at the end of life. Who will take care of the elderly? What is our obligation to our parents, and how much of our lives must—and can—we give over to their needs? What do we tell the dying, and what do we do with the requests and the information they impart to us? How do we celebrate—or accept—the fact that the dying are often the same people, only sicker, that they were in their prime, the same kindly or difficult parents, the same loving or rejecting relatives? How much should be done to prolong life, when should those efforts stop, and how hard should we struggle for, or against, the wishes of the dying? How do we endure grief, and help others endure it, and how do the living get beyond the feeling that every death is a failure? It would be wrong to suggest that these essays answer these questions; rather, they demonstrate the range and the seriousness of the ways in which the questions have been asked.

The essays by the health professionals are often startling in their honesty, as doctors and nurses and hospice workers remember the first death they witnessed, the most cataclysmic, the most wrenching, the most frustrating, instructive, or simply the saddest. The deaths they handled badly and the ones they handled well. The thoughtfulness of these pieces, the high level of consciousness of their writers, contrasts startlingly, and paradoxically, with the number of essayists—the "civilians," if you will—who remember the ways in which the health care system (staffed by individuals who are less feeling, more doctrinaire, more callous than the contributors to this collection) betrayed and dehumanized loved ones. Occasionally, these two groups overlap, when a doctor writes of the difficulty, the sense of powerlessness, and the confusion of trying to make those very same decisions and deal with the system not as a provider but a consumer: when a parent's life is ending.

In a number of these essays, a professional who has treated or helped the dying is accosted by a relative who wants the doctor to understand who the dead person was in life before age and illness turned a vibrant person into a dying patient. And in a way, these essays perform that same function, resurrecting, if only for a moment, the person who has been lost and making us see what that loss means to those who remain.

What's striking is how many voices make up the chorus that sings to us from these pages, how resonant are the stories they tell, and—by the time we have reached the end of the book—how important we feel it is to listen to the dying and to those who remain. Many of these narratives feel like messages in bottles, washed up on the shore—urgent communications whose authors hope they will reach the land of the healthy and the living. The result is impressive, and we can only feel grateful for having experienced the intensity and the sheer amount of life that has been compressed and contained in a book about its end.

***Francine Prose** is the author of many best-selling books, including* A Changed Man, Reading Like a Writer, *and* Blue Angel, *which was a National Book Award finalist. Her newest nonfiction book is* Anne Frank: The Book, the Life, the Afterlife.

At the End of Life

To Morning

ANNE JACOBSON

Anne Jacobson is nearing the end of her residency, but she's stuck in the midst of a night from hell—three codes in a row—and her free-fall adrenaline response to the alarm that means someone is dying.

A shriek in the darkness drew out my shallow, sleeping breath in a singular gasp. Disoriented in the windowless room, I felt a familiar pounding in my chest that jostled my brain awake. As I fumbled for the light, the small black box continued its ear-splitting siren as it fell off the nightstand and bounced under the bed. I knelt on the gray, stained carpet and fished the beast out from the dusty collection of medical journals and soda cans that lived there. Squinting in the fluorescent light, I saw that the digital numbers coalesced on the pager screen and formed a room number. I grabbed the white coat on the chair and ran.

Three years before, on my very first call in this busy Chicago hospital, the senior resident had directed me in a perky voice to formulate "elevator thoughts" on the way to evaluate a patient. This sort of preplanning worked well on the way to see a child with a fever in the emergency room or an elderly patient who had fallen out of bed. But this particular call came on the code pager, meaning a patient had stopped breathing or had no functional heartbeat or both. This was the third code in the last twelve hours. And so there would be no elevator (the stairs were faster) and no coherent thoughts—except a blistering disbelief that my sleep total for this thirty-hour shift was going to be around twenty minutes.

I knew colleagues who loved the rush of a code, and as a new resident caught up in the action but without real responsibility, I suppose I had loved it also. But now, just months away from finishing residency, I was one of the senior residents in the hospital at night. I dreaded my free-fall adrenaline response to a code that meant someone was dying, apparently against their own or someone else's wishes. At that moment, flying down the dim stairwell in the predawn stillness, I was short on both adrenaline and compassion. Parcels of it had been left all over the hospital—the largest discarded at the bedside of a twenty-year-old woman who was now dead.

Previously young and healthy with no underlying medical conditions, she had arrived in the emergency room earlier in the evening. She was pale and breathing rapidly but joking with her mom and aunt that their girls' night out would have to be postponed. However, the high fever, telltale rash, and initial laboratory tests all pointed to meningococcemia, an uncommon but highly lethal infection that can collapse vital organs in a matter of hours. One of the greatest risks is a condition known as disseminated intravascular coagulation, the bacterial toxins causing the coagulation system to go haywire. Blood clots in all the wrong places, cutting off oxygen supply and causing organ death. Finally, when the body can't clot anymore, it bleeds—from delicate vessels close to the surface and in dark, internal hollows.

I watched and hovered as the young woman's body did exactly this, succumbing to the raging infection. Several hours after her arrival in the emergency room, she was sitting rigid and upright, clutching the bedrails and struggling to breathe. I looked into the wide, panicked eyes of the patient and her family and explained that the medicine we were administering would help relax her before we inserted the tube that would help her breathe. Later in the evening, her heart began to race, trying to compensate for a dangerously low blood pressure. I did my best to communicate to her mother and aunt the severity of her condition and the medications and procedures that might be necessary, all of us peering out from behind the paper gowns and masks required in the rooms of those with serious and contagious infections. They clutched her hands, one on each side, leaving only when the nurse quietly but firmly asked them to step out when the code began. The chaplain guided them away as thick purple blood trickled from her nose and mouth with the chest compressions. My colleagues and I marched down the code protocol, cracking vials of ultrapotent medications, hanging bags of IV fluid and blood, pushing them with a silent prayer through her veins. Her blood pressure continued to fall, and her heart ultimately failed despite our desperate attempts to do something, anything, we could. I looked down at her young, bloated face, the dark eyes so similar to those of the women who had been at her side all night long. Our training had taught us about moments like this, how to tell a family in a compassionate but direct way that someone they loved had died. Looking into the eyes of the dying young woman at that moment, I couldn't imagine what I would possibly say.

A few minutes later, the anxious faces of her family crumpled as I quietly delivered the unthinkable news: "We did all that we possibly could, but Tamara has died. I'm so very sorry."

What had that news cost the patient's mother, her aunt, her grandmother, coming from the mouth of a pony-tailed, bleary-eyed girl not much older than the child they had lost? Did they understand that my quavering voice and lowered eyes came from a place of real compassion? Or that my hasty exit at the sound of the pager was because someone else was now trying to die? The universe had not stopped, had not allowed us a reprieve. I would need to pull myself together in some other dark stairwell, the wails of grief trailing behind me. I prayed consolation would come for her family in time. My own fragile solace came from a deep knowing that her medical care had been correct and thorough and timely. This time the universe didn't cooperate; we were all humbled, face-to-face with our own breakable humanity.

Leaving the young woman's family with the hospital chaplain, I winced at the next room number on the code pager. The area of the hospital known as the skilled nursing facility housed patients who were too sick to go home—or more commonly, back to the nursing home—but not acutely ill enough to qualify for a full hospital admission. Most of the patients were elderly, often in the advanced stages of dementia. Codes in the SNF were rarely successful. The team would go through the motions, cracking frail ribs with chest compressions, unable to locate accessible blood vessels beneath papery, gray skin. I arrived at such a scene in the room of an elderly man; his eyes were open, glazed, and vacant. Another senior resident was at the head of the bed squeezing air into his lungs with an oxygen bag and mask. A wide-eyed medical student pumped rhythmically on his chest, quietly mouthing the number of compressions. The intern was preparing the defibrillator, ready to shock the patient if an appropriate heart rhythm existed. "Do we know his code status?" I asked loudly above the din of activity in the room. The question seemed obvious, but on more than one occasion I had participated in a code while a misplaced chart was discovered with a large "Do Not Resuscitate" the team had overlooked.

The charge nurse informed us the patient was indeed a "full code," despite the fact that the eighty-five-year-old had advanced renal failure and dementia. He had been sent from the nursing home with a fever and was completing a few more days of intravenous antibiotic treatment for a urinary tract infection. "The day shift says no one has been here to see him," continued the nurse. "His nephew is listed as the next of kin, but no one can get a hold of him." I nodded and glanced at the resident with the oxygen bag. "Should we intubate?" she asked quietly. "Let's wait and see if that will be necessary," I responded. She nodded in agreement and redirected the student's hands on the patient's chest. We both had experienced this before—terminally ill patients with family on paper but no one who was involved in their lives. Sometimes the story was as simple as greed, of wanting to keep a monthly disability check alive as long as possible. Other times it was painfully complicated—a now frail and helpless patient had, at some point, ostracized everyone around him through drink or drugs or abuse. Regardless of the circumstances, it was always poignant to be involved in a life-and-death decision for a stranger with no one else to speak for him.

My heart was still heavy with the loss of the young woman in the ICU, the defeat of watching her go in the face of everything we knew how to do. The faces of her family were still with me, grieving the loss of a future that would never be. Now we were keeping a man alive at the other end of life solely because we were medically and legally responsible to do so. His unfocused eyes were turned in my direction as we ran a "soft code"—doing what was required but stopping as soon as our efforts appeared futile. It was not a judgment on the value of his fragile and worn-out body or his worth to society. Rather, at these moments we are called to be our most authentic physician selves, to ease the burden of suffering, to be compassionate unto death. "I will follow that method of treatment which according to my ability and judgment, I consider for the benefit of my patient," states the Hippocratic Oath. I reached for the patient's cold white hand with my own sweating palm and held my other one up in the air. "Enough, that's enough." The team exhaled collectively—we knew this was right. I touched his forehead and whispered, "Rest well." I wondered if anyone would come to his funeral.

Death notes written in the chart are detached and clinical. On paper we physicians stick to stark physical facts: "asystole unresponsive to epinephrine × 2, defibrillation attempted × 3 without success. Pupils fixed and dilated, no palpable pulse or audible breath sounds. Time of death 0253." We reviewed the process of the code with the students and junior residents, making sure they knew what was done and why we had stopped. The paperwork was completed with quick efficiency, the body of the elderly man left to be cleaned and prepared for the morgue. There were new admissions lining up in the emergency room—pneumonia, heart failure, alcohol poisoning, stroke. Most of them would improve with medicine or surgery or time, would live to leave the hospital, would see a daughter's wedding or the birth of another grandchild. By morning the needs of the living would have eclipsed the memory of tonight's losses, the mourning left to families and friends or to no one at all. I spoke some superficial words of encouragement to the weary intern at my side and mentally divided up the work ahead of us.

We worked until our heads were heavy and nodding over admission orders, the first pink rays of dawn breaching the horizon. Two hours remained until rounds would begin on this April Sunday morning. I had fallen into the deep, drooling sleep that was now shattered by code number three. This time it was an elderly woman whose colon had been partly removed several days before for a localized cancer. Aside from some high blood pressure and arthritis, she was otherwise healthy, her surgical recovery fairly uneventful. Because she was in a unit where patients' hearts are monitored continuously, a dangerous rhythm known as ventricular fibrillation was noted immediately, the electrical impulses too uncoordinated to function effectively. The best treatment is early defibrillation, or "shocking" the heart. The nurses had already pushed in the bright red crash cart and were placing rubbery pads on her translucent chest. "Dr. Johnson is on the way. He was coming in early for rounds," breathed the head nurse. "Okay, good," I replied, glancing at the sawtooth pattern on the monitor and welcoming the thought of the older doctor's experience and calm. "Charging . . . all clear . . ." The woman's chest heaved upward as the shock was delivered, the pattern on the screen unchanged.

The room was now overflowing with nursing staff, doctors, students, respiratory therapists, and lab technicians. At some point I noticed a thin, shaking figure in the corner, his blue eyes wide and panicked. Perhaps he had arrived for an early morning visit. Perhaps he had been there all night. In the pressured rush, no one had noticed the quiet little man who was now watching his wife trying to die.

One of my medical school professors frequently reminded us, "You only see what you are prepared to see." When Dr. Johnson arrived, he walked straight through the crowd to the patient's husband, placing an arm around his shoulder. He had been their doctor for over twenty years, attending to them together in the clinic. Undoubtedly, he was prepared to see this man at his wife's side. We continued with cycles of chest compressions, oxygenation, more defibrillation, and medication. The chaotic heart rhythm continued, undeterred by anything we did. Doctor and patient spoke quietly for a few moments, their heads bent together in private conversation. The man nodded in understanding, and the two of them approached the bed together. "Thank you, everyone," called out Dr. Johnson. "That's enough now." The room was silent as activity abruptly ceased. "It's okay," he murmured in the man's ear. "You can hold her hand. She will know that you're here." The man shuffled forward hesitantly, tenderly lifting his wife's hand to his cheek. "Bessie," his voice cracked. "Where are you going without me?"

The breath caught in my chest, twisting open a space that now felt enormous and raw. I exhaled, turned away from the crowd, and gazed out at an exceptional sunrise over Lake Michigan, a soaring skyline watching its city awaken below. The familiar sounds of alarms, telephones, and hospital banter drifted in through the door as the team filed out. Oblivious to all of it, the man held his wife's empty gaze in his own unblinking eyes, the last agonal beats of her heart flickering across the monitor. Suddenly aware that I was an unnecessary presence in this intimate moment, I turned and stepped out into the bustle and chatter of weekend rounds.

"Hey, so what happened in there?" I blinked absently, looking into the bright eyes of my alert and curious colleague who had arrived to take over the next shift. What did happen in there? A man wordlessly said good-bye to the woman he had loved since he was a teen. A soul slipped silently away. The sun rose again, and it was magnificent. I unclipped the code pager from my scrubs and placed it in my friend's outstretched hand. "Oh, one of Johnson's patients, a few days postop. V-fib. Nothing we could do." I recognized the momentary flash of sympathy and panic and relief cross her face, felt it in my own chest as she attached the pager to her hip. The baton had been passed. After rounds she would update the patient list, unceremoniously removing the names of the three who had died, grateful it had not happened on her watch. I finished rounds, attending to lab results, vitals signs, and the usual morning greetings. The needs of the moment required all that was left of my caffeine-fueled attention. The dead would be left where they had fallen.

It was nearly noon when I tossed my stained and rumpled scrubs into the hospital laundry cart. My clothes from the previous day were still folded on the desk in the call room. I didn't feel like the same person who had put them on yesterday morning. Slinging my bag over one shoulder, I leaned against the cool steel wall of the elevator as it hummed its way down eight floors to the hospital lobby. I stopped in front of the long row of glass windows to fumble for my keys. Visitors circled in and out of the revolving door, sweeping in with the fragrant air—the first warm day of a long-awaited midwestern spring. On another day I might have taken the El downtown, found a patch of grass along the lakefront bike path, listened to the waves crash on the graffiti-covered breakwall, and basked in a few vacant, sun-laden hours until it all began again—but not today. Instead, I imagined the moment when I would close the blinds in my tiny apartment a few nondescript blocks away, pull the covers over my head, and sleep away this glorious afternoon. In the darkness it would be easier to forget their faces.

A timid hand on my shoulder startled me. I turned to a face that seemed vaguely familiar, her haggard eyes apologetic. "I'm sorry, Doctor. I didn't mean to bother you. I'm Tamara's aunt, um, from last night?" Her steady gaze drew me back to the bedside of the young woman, the panicked eyes of her family meeting mine, her face bloating, blood pressure dropping, nothing, nothing working. Together we had hovered over her, masked and gloved and gowned, shielding ourselves from infection and death with thin yellow paper. I wished now for a protective mask for the aunt with the broken heart, a papery veil for my own weary spirit. Was there a cool, dark place of rest for the grieving? "We wanted to thank you," she whispered. "We know you did all you could. She was a beautiful girl. She would want you to know that."

Her dark eyes held mine in a long silence, unmasked, both of us beginning to lay an unfinished life to rest. This unexpected compassion would not erase the exhaustion and doubt of a questioning young physician, but her gentle gift would allow a measured peace until morning.

I embraced her, and stepped out into the light.

***Anne Jacobson** is a family physician for the Cook County Health System in Chicago, Illinois. She earned an MD from the University of Wisconsin and a master's in Public Health from the University of Illinois–Chicago. Her work has appeared in* JAMA, *and she lives in Oak Park with her husband, John, and children, Daniel and Maya.*

On Bearing Witness

LAURIE FOOS

After seven years of watching her father battle cancer, Laurie Foos still felt his death seemed sudden. For all the preparation, there was no preparing.

My father called me the day he was going home to die. I remember being surprised that he'd even felt well enough to make the call. In acute renal failure, he'd been admitted to his final hospitalization and had spent the last three weeks in agony from dialysis that left him in painful muscle spasms so intense that he screamed, and never, in the seven years of sickness that had preceded this, had I seen him in so much pain. When he wasn't in agony or asleep, he'd been hallucinating, seeing trains in hallways and children with numbers stamped on their heads jumping up at him from rolling carts. He had finally come to the end. His team of doctors ultimately decided to insert a nephrostomy tube into his cancerous kidney, allowing his body to eliminate enough waste to stop dialysis and allowing us to take him home to die. It had been a battle to get the doctors to admit that was what they were doing, and only when I'd used their medical jargon—"palliative care"—did they concede that the tube was not going to filter poisons and "jump start" the kidney as initially promised.

But on the phone that day, he sounded better. Coherent. Like himself.

"They're letting me go," he said.

"Oh, thank God," I told him. "You're going home. You must be so glad to be getting out of there."

As much as I knew this was the end and had actually been praying for it, I did not want the end to come while he was still in the hospital. In the seven years since his first bowel resection, I'd come to know—and to hate—the small hospital just minutes from my parents' home on Long Island. When he was first diagnosed in 2001, I lived in Massachusetts and would make the drive down to spend the long days in those rooms. But in 2005, I moved back to Long Island to be closer to him. "Semiprivate," they called the rooms, though there is nothing semiprivate about watching another patient retch or vomit just inches away. They all looked the same, no matter which wing, all painted in the crème color that is meant to be calming, all with two beds and two metal chairs for visitors, all with one recliner that denoted the next step out of bed after surgery or serious illness, which would be removed, for space reasons, as soon as the patient was able to walk. All of them with the same dull lighting, all of them cramped with one window we always hoped my father would be closest to, as the heat exacerbated his constant discomfort and the pervasive odors that accompany dire illness. Only in the end did one of the oncologists grant my father the one private room on the floor. For three weeks my mother and two brothers, both of whom lived nearby, gathered around his bedside and struggled to find things to talk about other than illness and dying. For three weeks I spent the long days with my children, then ages three and one, waiting for my husband to come home from work so that I could drive to the hospital and be with my family in that room. When the children napped, I would rest on the couch in preparation for what might have been waiting for me that night. There were few things to be grateful for in that time, but the private room was one. We were grateful for the privacy, for the extra metal chairs, for the private bathroom (for which he no longer had a need, as he was by then fitted with both a colostomy and a catheter until they could insert the nephrostomy tube), for the pale walls and the too-bright light above my father's head. My father's long illness had shown us every wing of that hospital. His last stop was the F wing. *F* for "Foos," I'd think, passing the metal sign as I walked down the long hallway to his room every evening. *F* for "Final."

"Yeah, I am," he said. "I am glad to get out."

And then he paused.

"But what am I really going home to? It's like you're a prisoner in your own body."

That sentence stunned me as I held the phone there in my kitchen that day. Although he'd spoken of dying many times in the last year, he'd been too ill to speak much during those past three weeks in renal failure, and I wasn't sure if he realized this was the end for him. Through all of his hospitalizations—over twenty—he'd always managed to come back. To go back to work, to live much longer than anyone had predicted. As the cancer spread and his quality of life deteriorated, he looked thinner, less robust, but not gravely ill. No one who didn't know him well could guess he was close to death. But in these last three weeks, after seven years of sickness, chemo, radiation, ICU stays, he'd aged twenty years and looked like a man dying. "Look," he'd say, on the one or two times he asked for a mirror, "I look like I'm a hundred years old." The flesh hung off his once heavily muscled arms and folded into wrinkles like the skin of a Sharpei. His body looked oddly gelatinous, and I remember saying to a friend, "I am watching my father melt into a bed." He'd always had hope of hanging on longer, but this time the end was coming.

You have to say something, I thought that day on the telephone. *Say anything. You have to acknowledge what he just said. He's right. He is a prisoner.*

This had been my role for the entirety of his sickness: listening and validating his feelings. Aside from the morphine and fentanyl patches and doses of medication to ease the physical suffering of the terminally ill, when all hope has been lost, when each day is a battle to move through it and into the next, when the dying person knows that each day will be filled with pain and anguish as great as or worse than the day before, there is little we can do but be present and listen, to try to understand how the dying person must feel.

I told him he would be glad to be home, he would be surrounded by his own things, in his own space, and this would make a difference. My mother would take care of him, I said. We would all be there to take care of him.

Then I cried and said, "I know you've been through hell, but I'm glad you're going home. I'm glad you're still here."

I cannot remember what he said, only that he did not say he was still glad to be here, too.

The oncologist refused to offer a time frame when I asked him how long my father could live with that tube. I'd researched it on the Internet and had found no answers. But I told the oncologist that I'd seen what had been happening in those three weeks. In between dialysis treatments, my father grew sicker and sicker until they rushed him in for another emergency treatment. Without dialysis, it seemed clear to me that the poison would overtake him quickly. We didn't want my father to know how much time he had, I explained, but the family needed to be prepared.

"It could be weeks, months," the oncologist said as I pressed him, "depending on how well that tube works."

Months? That doctor had to be kidding. None of us wanted my father to linger for months. There were no longer good days, or even good hours. How could anyone want him to linger for months?

"Have you seen him?" I asked the doctor. "We know this is the end."

But he refused to be pinned down to a time frame.

"There is just no way to tell," the oncologist said. "I don't have a crystal ball."

We knew my father was dying, but we were shocked when, after seven years of battles he'd always managed to win, he was dead in just eight short days.

It is impossible to encapsulate the end of my father's life in those last three weeks in the hospital or even those last eight days at home, because the end had been such a long time coming. My father was diagnosed with colon cancer in February 2001 and died on October 31, 2008, seventeen days after his sixty-ninth birthday. Seven years of sickness. Seven years of abdominal surgeries, colon resections, postsurgical infections that sent him into what the professionals call "the rigors," a spike of fever that results in the spasmodic jerking of the body not unlike a grand mal seizure. Seven years of chemotherapy and radiation cycles, and all of the devastating side effects that go along with treatment, such as vomiting, diarrhea, numbness in the hands and feet, an inability to tolerate very cold or hot food or drinks. In what my family and I deemed a matter of luck in the early stages, the cancer remained in and just outside the colon for four years until it made its first metastasis onto his ureter tube and pelvic bone. In April 2005, during what was supposed to be a routine checkup, doctors found an inoperable mass twisted "like a sheet around a clothesline" on his ureter tube that somehow smashed onto his pelvic bone. And then the waiting for further metastases began.

It was Easter and I was eight months pregnant with my daughter when he took me in the small paneled kitchen to tell me this news. I'd driven down with my husband for the holiday dinner, and when he called me away, I assumed he wanted to talk about the coming baby, his first grandchild. But as I stood there with him, the ceiling fan spinning above our heads, and my mother slinking out of the room, I knew this was not about the baby. He stood with his back against the counter. His voice was low, his face anguished. The kitchen, I remember, looked both smaller and larger at once, the way the world would look, I later learned, when my father began to die.

I leaned in closer to him.

"They found a mass," he said, or maybe it was "I have a mass."

It was a word I'd never heard him use. In the beginning he'd said "tumor" or "growth." But never a word this menacing. Mass. The cancer had hung over him and changed him profoundly even then, as it does anyone who battles the disease. He'd always been physically robust, having been a gifted athlete in his teens, but now he was unable to lift weights, something he loved. The multiple surgeries had weakened his abdominal muscles, causing the muscle mass to split in two. He'd been depressed by his illness in the past, but this time I heard something in his voice I hadn't heard before: fear.

Looking now at the arc of his suffering, which seemed interminable, my family and I say that his strength worked simultaneously in his favor, as well as to his detriment. My father did not want to leave this life—and he said so, time and time again, to my mother, my brothers, and to me. Most of all, he did not want to leave my mother, his bride of forty-five years, who, as the disease progressed, served as both wife and nurse. He did not want to leave us, his grown children, and although he would say with startling matter-of-factness that he knew he would not live to see them grow up, he did not want to leave his grandchildren. (I had had a second child, a son, in 2006.)

I never told him not to say such things, because I knew they were true. As the disease progressed, and his quality of life diminished, we spoke on the telephone every day, sometimes multiple times a day, and I spent every weekend with him, sometimes with my husband and the kids, sometimes by myself. Sometimes he'd talk about his worries about leaving my mother, sometimes about such practical things as the number of insurance policies he had and what they added up to. He needed to talk. The best I could do was to let him.

"I love you so much," he would say at the end of our daily talks on the telephone, as if he knew then that I would need to hold on to those words when he was gone. "I couldn't possibly love you more than I do."

My father underwent the unsuccessful surgery to remove the mass in April 2005, shortly before my daughter's birth in May. For another year and a half, he continued to outrun the cancer as well as he could. Nearly every day, and up until three weeks before his death, he got into his car and went to his postretirement job as a security guard at a local college. Near the end he lived on Percocet and endured the ongoing indignity and deformation of a colostomy bag, but still he went to that job, now I think, as much for us as for himself. The dying must feel, even in the face of hopelessness, some modicum of self-preservation. He did not want to be defined by his disease or by the fact that he was dying. He needed a reason to get up and to move through each day. My father needed to feel useful, and no matter how many times we told him that his usefulness, to us, had nothing to do with going to work, he would hear nothing of stopping.

"I can do it," he'd say. "I can't not work. That's how I am. I'll die if I have to sit around here."

Even at the time, I recognized his need for some semblance of normalcy that was in his mind inextricably tied to working. Now I realize he continued to work not only for himself but for us. I believe he kept working to comfort us as well as himself, to keep his sickness from occupying every thought and conversation.

Only when his body would no longer allow it, when the inoperable cancer had moved into his kidney and caused it to fail, was he forced to give up his job. And when he did, he was right: he died.

• • •

What I had expected to be a clear trajectory toward death—cancer in the colon metastasizing to the liver, the most common way the disease progresses—did not happen at all. The inoperable tumor choking his ureter tube, the tube running from kidney to bladder, had caused one of his kidneys to atrophy and the other to back up with chronic and painful bladder and kidney stones. "Hydronephrosis," the CT scan read. "Atrophic right kidney."

In July 2007, two years after the appearance of the inoperable tumor and five years after his initial diagnosis of colon cancer, he became ill with what appeared to be a stomach flu: vomiting that came and went, chills, and stomach pains. We didn't realize his life was in danger, and even if we had, we could not have forced him to go to the hospital. After the unsuccessful surgery, our understanding of my father's cancer grew murkier, because he had vowed not to have "any more goddamned scans." He knew he was in trouble, but he did not want to know how badly. Although we may have wished to know more than we did, we respected my father's decision not to continue having scans. And now, as I see the finality of his long and arduous suffering, would it have mattered to know that other growths were appearing? Would it have changed the grief, anger, or despair he so often felt in those last few months? Would it have had any impact on his final days?

My mother begged him to go to the emergency room, but he refused, even as his abdomen continued to swell and he became sicker and sicker.

"Please, Daddy, at least go to the doctor," I remember saying. "Maybe you have some kind of flu."

A few more days, he said, and if he didn't feel better, then he'd go. He had a seemingly immeasurable tolerance for pain. My mother finally had to elicit help from the oncology office to convince him to go for a scan. She should bring him into the office, they said, if he refused to go to the hospital, which he did. Finally, the one oncology nurse in his doctor's office to whom he felt most connected, scared him enough to go.

"Tell him to go to the hospital," she told my mother. "And tell him that if he doesn't go, he'll start vomiting his own feces."

But even then, hearing this, he refused until the following morning.

"Tom, please," my mother said. "I'm afraid you'll die on this couch."

In another day or two, he would have died, and considering how much more he would suffer in the next fifteen months, my mother now wishes he had.

He did agree to go to the oncologist's office the next day and then was rushed to the emergency room because his bowel had become completely blocked. My younger brother called to tell me that he'd taken my father to the hospital and to meet them there. Somehow, unlike so many of the other visits to that emergency room, I managed to walk in through the back way, avoiding the waiting room. I'd been in that emergency room so many times I knew the layout and walked immediately over to the white board with the list of patient names and locations. I spotted his name and made my way over to his curtained bed, where I found him looking worse than he had even postoperatively, waiting for the results of a CT scan. His face was gray, his stomach swelled to the size of a woman pregnant with triplets. I immediately placed my hand on his forehead, which was beaded with sweat but cold to the touch, and tried to comfort him. I felt helpless standing there stroking my father's hair and had no idea, then, that helplessness would become a permanent state—for him, and for us, who could offer so little comfort.

"Oh my God, Daddy, your stomach," I said, because there was nothing else, just the obviousness of the condition—and because now it was my turn to be afraid.

"I know, I'm so sick this time. This time it's so bad, this one's so bad. This time I'm just so sick."

We waited for over two hours for what had now become a team of doctors—surgeons, oncologists, gastroenterologists—to make their rounds with the CT scan results. The surgeon, whom my father liked, glanced at my brother, my mother, and me before holding up the results of the scan. I suppose he was gauging our reactions, wondering how we'd receive the news before he spoke.

"Well, Mr. Foos," he said, holding the scan up to the light, "it looks here like you have a blockage in the transverse colon, so I'll need to make an incision here and there . . . and you'll have a colostomy."

I remember that he spoke quickly, in a rush, and didn't look directly at my father. By that point my father had received heavy doses of Dilaudid, a potent pain medication given to cancer patients, and yet his eyes rolled up in his head when he heard that word. He closed his eyes and shook his head back and forth slowly.

No.

My father had undergone three abdominal surgeries and had told the attending surgeon each time, "If I have to wake up with a bag, then don't wake me up."

I gripped my father's hand, hard, and then leaned down to kiss his forehead. It was important to me, always, in times of crisis like this, to be strong for him as he had been strong for us. There would be plenty of time for emotion, I thought, but now I had to be his advocate. Later, after the surgery, the surgeon admitted he'd never seen anyone who was still able to speak at all when as septic and close to death as my father was. But he did speak. He said, "No."

My mother cried and put her hands over her face, turning away.

"Please," I said to the surgeon. "You don't understand. This is psychologically devastating for him. This is the one thing he has never wanted. He's made it clear he did not want to live like that; he would rather die."

The surgeon nodded but did not look at me or, to my best recollection, at my mother or brother. He said he understood, but this was the only way; otherwise my father would die, and die within twenty-four to forty-eight hours. He held up the scan and showed us the places in both the bowel and large intestine when the feces lay trapped. Without a colostomy, there would be no way to release the waste, and my father would die from the poisonous waste.

"Then maybe I should just die," my father said.

The surgeon was careful to detail the kind of death my father would suffer, allowing us, if not my father, to understand the vile nature of such a death. He would without question, as the nurse had said earlier, vomit his own fecal matter until the moment of death. Suffocate or choke—on his own waste.

After the surgeon left, my father lay shaking his head and holding one or another of our hands—my mother's, my brother's, mine. We just stood, waiting, talking, and waiting. What should he do? He did not want to live with a bag.

"Maybe I should just check out," he said. "I don't think I could live like that."

"But you can't die like this, Daddy," I said, and I reiterated what the surgeon had said about vomiting fecal matter. "Not like this," I said. "You don't want to go like this."

I do not know now if we did him a disservice or not. I know that my father was never the same after that day. I know he no longer felt whole; he hated the deformation of the colostomy bag; he hated showering because he was forced then to see the holes in his body; he hated relying on my mother to change the colostomy bags every seven days or so. After the colostomy, his raucous humor was gone. His laughter was replaced by a quiet, unabating sadness. A large part of my father died on that day.

What I do remember is that a friend of mine, who was then a nurse in that hospital, took me outside the curtain and looked at me with tears in her eyes. We were holding hands beside a utility sink in the hallway, and I remember looking at the white sink, at our hands, at my father's curtain, now closed behind us, wondering how it would feel when he was really gone.

"You realize this is palliative, right?" she asked me.

I suppose I must have been taken aback by the medical jargon and said, "What?"

"It's palliative," she repeated.

I remember afterward, somewhat sardonically, that it was a good thing I'd had a decent vocabulary. I knew "palliative" meant there was nothing more to be done. Now any treatment would not extend his life, only make him more comfortable.

"Yes," I said, and we hugged and cried there in the middle of the emergency room hallway as I leaned partly against the sink, partly against my friend.

At some point that day my mother said to me, "Is this the way he's going to die? In increments?" through her sobs.

It was.

Before my father's emergency surgery, I knew little or nothing of a colostomy, its placement, the way it allows for the removal of waste. It is a much cruder device than I'd have expected. A colostomy is the surgical removal of tissue to create two holes in the abdomen, known as stomas. The stomas are then covered with a large ring called a wafer, held on by a special paste, and then snapped onto the wafer are two large kidney-shaped bags. The ostomy videos my mother watched, she later said, looked nothing like the actual ostomy my father had. There had been very little tissue left of his colon, and finding enough colon to create the stomas had presented a challenge.

From the day of the emergency colostomy forward, my father's life consisted essentially of his resignation to a life he'd never wished to live, one that revolved around the timing of waste elimination. He learned to gauge when his body would pass the stool—which was no longer stool but pieces of food passed undigested—and to deal with the humiliation he felt in "no longer being a man."

A few weeks later, following a terribly painful and unnecessary colonoscopy by a consultant who went through both the rectum and the stoma to determine that the blockage in the colon was malignant and terminal, it became clear that my father was dying. He'd lost forty pounds in the hospital. The first time I saw him after he'd come home, he was sitting at the dining room table, struggling to eat soup my mother had made for him. He sat staring at the soup bowl, his lip quivering, and said he'd wished he'd died that day, that he considered it "a failure of nerve" that he didn't force them to let him die.

"But then I looked up at you guys," he said, weeping now, "and I knew I couldn't let you have that as your memory."

I reached over and held my arms around his neck—my God, I could feel his bones, I remember thinking—and I told him it was okay to cry, that he should let it out. I can still hear the shaking sounds of his sobs that day and remember my own collapse in the car when I'd left, wondering what I could do to help my father as he moved closer and closer to death.

In many ways, my father became our guide in his own death. Because he was so willing to discuss dying, to tell us how sad he was in having to leave us, it made it easier for us to express our own sadness in saying good-bye to him. Two months before his death, I gave him permission to stop fighting. He'd been hospitalized again, this time following a fall in the bathroom, and had landed in the ICU with an overwhelming infection. Because of the stones in his kidney and bladder, he'd been unable to take morphine, which he needed for the increasing levels of pain, and so the doctors had decided to "irrigate his bladder" by inserting a tube through his penis and into his bladder, flushing the bladder and tube with fluid, another palliative measure that resulted in more agony for him.

He lay in bed that day looking out the window, and I sensed he had things he wanted to say. He hadn't listened to much of anything my mother, brother, or I had said, rubbing his face with his hands and sighing. As he looked over at me, I saw something in his eyes, some shift, some new and deepening defeat.

"What is it, Daddy?" I asked, kneeling down beside him. "What is it?"

He said he'd just grown so tired, so sick of being sick, that this time he'd felt like he just wanted to die. I told him he should stop fighting for us, we would be okay, it was okay to let go. We cried—my younger brother, my father, and I—and we hugged him and told him how glad we were he was our father, but he'd done enough now, and that he should fight only for himself but not for us.

"If I can get home and feel a little better, if I can still do some things for myself, then I think I can hang on a little longer."

And so he did. He hung on for two more months.

In our very last conversation, before he moved into a state of detachment that remained until he could no longer speak at all, he lay in the hospital bed that had been brought into my parents' home by hospice care, the bed where he would die, and held my hand. At least he'd made it out of the hospital, I thought, remembering the phone call on the day of his release. At least he would die in this room with the day bed and the eyelet pillows, my mother's lacy white curtains.

"Who would've ever thought I'd end up like this?" he asked. His voice had become permanently hoarse following his release from the hospital, and I leaned in to hear him.

"Not me, Daddy. I never did." I stroked his thumb. Because of his many years of hard work, the years of sixteen-hour days, of running a floor waxing and cleaning business in addition to his regular job as a mail carrier, his hands had always been calloused, but now they were soft, smooth.

"Are you afraid?" I asked.

He stared out ahead, as if he were seeing something I couldn't.

"No," he said. "No. It's just . . . strange."

Four days later, I kneeled down at his bedside and gave him permission to die. I'd asked my mother if she wanted to be the one, but she was too upset. In all the conversations I've since committed to memory, in all of the interactions I have tried to keep etched into my mind, I cannot recall much of what I said. What I do know is that I told him I loved him and assured him we would be all right, that it was time to go now, that we wanted him to go. I told him I would miss him every single day of my life . . . and I have.

The next morning he died with my brother at his side. My mother had to leave the house for emergency medical supplies, and in the ten minutes she was gone, he took his leave. I believe he spared her, and perhaps me, too. Seven years of sickness, and yet his death still felt sudden. For all of the preparation, there was no preparing.

I wish now I'd been able to ask him how it felt that day he told me how strange it was. In those last eight days he had the look the dying always seem to have, the wide-eyed look of permanent surprise, of the haunted—or perhaps it is of the hunted. All my life I've believed in knowledge, in understanding. But there is no understanding death.

Recently I had a dream of my family that symbolizes for me the act of taking care of my father. My mother, my brothers, and I are in a river, and we are covered in heavy plaster-cast suits, a kind of body armor. We have our arms above our heads to hold my father's life raft in the current, which is rushing all around us. The water rises to our necks, and my father is buoyant on top of the raft. He yells down to us to let go, and we do, all at once, wading to shore where we stand dripping, shedding our plaster casts of sadness, as my father sails down the river. We have done our part. We have listened, and we have spoken. There is nothing left to say. We have heard him. We have borne witness to all he has been through. We have released him, and he is free. In the face of helplessness, these are the only gifts we have to give until the final letting go.

***Laurie Foos** is the author of the novels* Ex Utero, Portrait of the Walrus by a Young Artist, Twinship, Bingo under the Crucifix, *and* Before Elvis There Was Nothing. *Her short fiction has been published widely in literary magazines and in the anthologies* Wreckage of Reason: An Anthology of Contemporary XXperimental Prose by Women Writers, Chick-Lit: Post-Feminist Fiction, *and others. She teaches in the MFA program at Lesley University and lives on Long Island with her husband and two children.*

Insights in the Rearview Mirror

PHYLLIS GALLEY WESTOVER

When former dean Phyllis Galley Westover saves her 101-year-old father from drowning, she begins to question whether she did the right thing. She cared for him during his last decade of life—giving up her own life to do so—but she "did not reckon with his remarkable stamina." How long is long enough?

Life can only be understood backward; but it must be lived forwards.
—Søren Kierkegaard

When I pulled up my 101-year-old father from the bottom of the swimming pool after he'd given me the slip, did I do him a favor? For what did I save him? Incontinence? Humiliation? Total dependence? If no one else had been home, if his sitter who knew CPR had not arrived as I struggled to hoist my father over the edge of the pool, could I have let him go? Could I have done anything except rescue my father?

Now I think of his death at 103 and along with aging America plot the quality of life in my remaining years—possibly another quarter century if I live close to my father's age. "I've saved a recipe for a lethal dose of Seconal to take with a fine Bordeaux when it's time to toast life good-bye," I tell my family. Truth is, I haven't yet procured the Seconal. Truth is, like my once vigorous father, I, too, always want to see what's around the next bend. Truth is, I'd be loath to cash life in unless I knew tomorrow I'd become senile or be sentenced to suffering and death by irreparable disease or injury. And when I knew—or, worse, was no longer capable of knowing—it would be too late.

Unlike my father, I know in detail what "end of life" means. As an only child with no siblings to help, I cared for him nine of the last ten years of his life. In the seven years since his death, I gnaw the bone of whether the choices I made for both of us were right.

Understanding life backward is one thing; seeing the "right" alternatives in the rearview mirror is another.

One thing I know: the choices I made altered my life as profoundly as my father's. I still search scenes from the caretaking years for answers, signs of how to play that hand again when it's my turn. I confront past decisions, sorting out my father's life along with his final belongings and return to the day I descended the stairs to the basement storage area.

I haul up from our furnace room the plastic clothes hamper labeled in broad, black marking pen, "Fred Westover, Room 407." Loaded with my father's belongings—artifacts I moved from his nursing home room the night he stopped breathing—the hamper and two cardboard boxes of his clothes and toiletries have sat next to the hot water heater for two years. I ponder whether anyone else so literally shoved a task to the basement of awareness.

I take the hamper to the guest room that was my father's room for a decade, the room where I'd hoped he'd die, at home. I think of our friend's jolting telephone call from Tuscaloosa, Alabama, to tell me in Kansas City, Missouri, that my father, a passenger in a car's "death seat," had been injured in an accident. A night flight to Tuscaloosa initiated a three-month stay in which I saw my father through brain surgery and rehabilitation. Clearly, he needed a major change in living arrangements, so I moved him at age ninety-two to live with my husband and me.

I thought one day I'd find him slumped over in his La-Z-Boy rocker, a shock of white hair hanging over his forehead, his talking book machine talking to no one. I did not reckon with his remarkable stamina. I did not know that at 102, even with assistance, his legs would buckle and he would fall, and not I, his other caretakers, or my husband, Lowell, would be strong enough to lift him. It never occurred to me, given his years of daily walks and exercises, that such a thing could happen or that I'd give up taking care of him. But when another caretaker fell and cracked her wrist in her attempt to keep my father from falling, I moved him to a nursing home.

I remove the hamper lid and look into the well. I begin excavating: items to discard, give away, use, keep. I throw out old medications, a half tube of toothpaste, dried shampoo. His electric razor, spool of dental floss, skin lotion, I'll use. I contemplate his hairbrush, a sturdy natural-bristle Fuller brush that once belonged to my mother. I combed the last of my mother's gray-brown hair from it twenty-five years ago. Now I comb out my father's white hair. I don't know what to do with the brush. I put it aside.

Inside a *Smithsonian* magazine that I read aloud to my father after macular degeneration warped his sight, I discover snapshots a physical therapist took at Halloween. My father sits in his nursing home wheelchair wearing a pointed black hat and an orange sweatshirt with a leering black jack-o'-lantern. He holds three-pound weights at shoulder height. I know the therapist thought the pictures cute. I don't. My father looks sad, drawn, and ridiculous, his gaze down, his lips set. I rip up the photos. Throw them into the trash. Photos from his last birthday party I save. In one, my dad in a jaunty wool plaid shirt raises a glass of his favorite Manischewitz raspberry wine and smiles at the table full of friends: the four women who helped me care for him his last four years at home; friends from his Shepherd Center senior current event class; and two buoyant senior stalwarts from our church men's group, the Aging Bulls, who dubbed my dad "the Ancient Bull."

Given my father's perseverance, I should have known he'd become an ancient bull. Born at one and one-half pounds in the winter of 1900, he was discarded by the doctor. His grandmother wrapped him in cloth and placed him in a basket on the lid of the oven set on low and fed him with an eye-dropper of milk she got from his mother. He survived pneumonia three times before he was five. He survived the Spanish flu at eighteen. He worked his way through Hiram College and became captain of the track team, running the demanding half-mile. He taught summer and winter. As president of the American Association of University Professors at the University of Alabama, he helped integrate the university. When state law forced his retirement at age seventy, he taught in Colombia, South America, joined VISTA, and taught a coalminer to read. Quitting the job of productive living was not in his DNA.

Inside a *Unitarian Universalist World* magazine my humanist father valued for its articles on ethics and responsibility, I find birthday cards I'd taped to his room door, some from his former graduate students. Now retired, they still express appreciation for his classes and guidance. "Every person should live as intelligently as they know how," I hear my father repeating. The cards go in the keepsake pile.

In 1992, I cleaned out my father's house of forty-two years and sold his guns, afraid he might find life not worth living after his accident. Intellectually, I grant each of us the right to do with our lives what we decide, but emotionally, I wasn't up to searching his five acres of woods for his body. Not that my father had ever been suicidal: just practical. Once when talking about a friend bedridden with terminal cancer, he'd said, "If ever I'm terminally ill or can't take care of myself, I know how to take care of the problem."

Now I wonder if I removed his options without offering another. While recovering from a hip replacement after a fall in a senior relay race at age ninety-six, my father, disgruntled with nursing home life, announced to his physical therapist that he planned to live until Christmas, then die. She said, "Oh, Fred, you wouldn't do that to your family at Christmastime!"

"Why not?" he asked. "Everyone will be there, and it will save travel expense for a funeral later."

When she asked him how he planned to die, he said, "I won't tell you, because then you'd try to stop me."

I brought him home in October, and Christmas came and went with no dire deeds or dark pronouncements.

Clearly, his mind was sharper then. After his hundredth birthday he lived more frequently in denial—denial of incontinence, legal blindness, poor balance, and especially loss of mental acuity. At 101, he no longer could operate his talking book player he'd used for ten years. He thought by fast rewinding a cassette tape, he would hear the continuation of the story when he pressed "Play" again. In a sense he was right. He often didn't remember what he'd heard before.

Sometimes he got tired of "reading." He wanted to *really* read, to *see* the words on the page—and to write. He had revisions in mind for the reading manual he had completed at ninety-one just as his eyesight faded. He wanted to rake leaves with me in the yard, even though he could not stand without his walker. "Phyllis," he'd say, waving his hand in exasperation, "I'm just waiting around to die!"

I'd tell him he'd worked hard all his life and had earned the right to listen to good books. That's not what he wanted to hear, and I knew it. But what should I say?

What constructive thing to do could I give a legally blind man with poor balance and sketchy cognition? Not stringing beads. I couldn't say what I was feeling: "That's true, Daddy. I'm sorry, but would you please get dying over with so I can get my life off hold and work again?" No one ever tells you that you'll come to think such a thing. The unspoken words made me gag, and I wanted to drive my fist through the wall.

My father once said to me, "Tell me when it's time to die." I cannot imagine saying, "Daddy, it's time to die. Life isn't going to get better." Now I wonder if I wimped out, welshed on my responsibility—even though I never promised to say such a thing. He was always more matter-of-fact than I, and he trusted me to speak the truth.

I thought I knew right from wrong. Now I'm not sure. When my father's mind was as perfect as his heart and lungs remained, I know what he considered the life worth living. That life dissolved. Gone were his guns, and gone was his freedom even to leave the house to stumble and break his neck—or drown. The very rights I claim for me, I removed from him through my meticulous care.

I could never have forgiven myself for being careless with his life. But was I careless with his wishes?

I ponder who or what I protected: my feelings and apprehensions or my father's values and wishes? But did I really know what his wishes were at 98, 99, 100, 101, 102—how long he wanted to live? I did not. His living will spoke only to critical, life-failing turns, not to a grade "D" life-holding pattern. So, along with Joan Didion in that final hand, I just played it as it lay.

I pull up from the hamper a string of brass bells spaced on a red silk cord.

Their sound makes me wince. I strung them to the front bar of my father's walker so I would know through the baby monitor when he was getting up alone at night or attempting to leave the house. Sometimes writing at my computer, I would hear his walker bells near the hall coat closet. I'd check.

"I'm going for a walk, Phyllis," he'd announce.

"Wait for me, Daddy. I'll go, too."

The sidewalk in front of our house is pitched and angled by oak roots, the surface scattered with acorns that roll like marbles. I was glad the front door had a bolt lock, and my father couldn't see the key. My cousin and his wife gave us a pair of mechanical cardinals that sang when a body passed in front of them. I placed them so I knew when my father left his room. The house alarm system beeped if the garage door opened. I barred the sliding glass door to the pool. My father and I were each other's prisoners.

This is not what my father had in mind for the end of his life—my father, who rode his Indian motorcycle from Chicago to Connecticut, who learned to fly a Piper Cub, who even in his mideighties would leave Kansas City at 8 A.M. with a toot of his horn and call at 10:30 that night from Tuscaloosa to say, "I'm home."

A sitter asked me if longevity ran in my family. I startled both of us when I said, "Somewhat, but at least both my father's parents had the courtesy to die at eighty-six."

"Phyllis!" she said.

I walked around my unguarded response and was ruefully bemused. Of those important to me in their eighties, which did I wish to be so "courteous"? None. And when I reached eighty, how "courteous" did I plan to be? I didn't. I looked forward to emulating our eighty-four-year-old friend who enjoyed free lift tickets on the ski slopes.

Friends puzzled why I didn't place my father in a suitable nursing home so I could get a life again. Their experience with "suitable" was not mine. I made screening visits to twelve facilities. During a February ice storm when our power and heat were out for eight days, I found my father a warm room in one of the best nursing homes. We talked with him about a trial stay there for a month. The second Sunday, I arranged transportation to church for him and brought him home for lunch afterward. In ten days he'd lost muscle tone and had become depressed. In helping him to the bathroom, I discovered that on that bitterly cold day, he'd been dressed with no underclothes. I moved him home the next day.

I reach for a triangular shape I know well: my father's talking clock that rested on his bedside table. I replace the battery and press down the pinnacle. The canned voice announces the wrong time. Again, dissonant resentment and sadness stretch me back five years. From the baby monitor button in my ear, I heard the canned voice say, "Five-forty-five A.M." My father was awake. He was checking the time and would get up—no matter how early. I must help my father with his morning ritual. Failing balance made dressing precarious. Failing memory made socks forgotten.

From loss of sleep to loss of career, my life revolved around my father's needs. I heard my father—always proud of my university teaching—ask me in his ninth year living with us, "How is your career coming along?"

I was caught too off guard to parry tactfully, and my suppressed frustration spurted through the opening like lava.

"What career? I gave it up to care for you."

"Oh, you mustn't do that! You'll resent it," he said, frowning.

"I've already done it."

In the silence neither of us knew how to break, I marveled at his instant accuracy and flash of wisdom. If I had known ten years earlier when I left my profession to care for my father that it would be a permanent change, not just a two—or three—year hiatus, would I have done it?

I wondered which of us suffered from dementia. Why hadn't I seen where I was leading myself? I, a dean and sought-after consultant on nontraditional learning programs, had been late in learning that I'd bought into the deepest of traditions: "A son is a son until he takes a wife; a daughter is a daughter all of your life." No one ever tells you love and loyalty can turn on you.

I run my finger around the dial of the clock and ache inside that such a rational, independent, and supportive man was brought so low. I ache because instead of feeling only compassion I still feel resentment. "You can get used to anything, even your life," it's said. I've read of an experiment in which a frog was first tossed into hot water; immediately it jumped out. Then the frog was placed in cold water, and, gradually, the water was heated until the frog was cooked without the frog's ever attempting to jump out. My father and I were like the frog. He didn't know that he didn't know, and I kept on keeping on.

I put the talking clock in the giveaway pile and lift out the portable radio/cassette player and a handful of tapes. Finally, only the tape of steam engine train sounds made him smile. One summer, he took a break from teaching at Brooklyn College to work as a fireman on the Long Island Railroad just to be near steam engines.

In his last years my father would fixate on taking a train to Ohio. "Phyllis," he'd announce, "I've been thinking. I want to visit our family in Geneva and Ashtabula and to talk to the president of Hiram College about a teaching position. I could teach educational psychology and statistics again if a student assistant helped me read. I can live in the dorm. It would give you a rest from caring for me."

I countered with all the logical reasons why this wouldn't work, hating myself—and him—for making me play pipe-dream-bursting Hickey in a geriatric version of *The Iceman Cometh.* On one occasion, after hearing my father ask me for the fourth time that week for ticket money, my husband Lowell said in exasperation, "Papa Fred! Who'd change your diapers—the conductor?" I winced. My father didn't answer. Perhaps he didn't get it. Just as well.

I put the radio/cassette player in the use pile and the steam engine train tape in the keepsake pile.

I retrieve an unopened package of Depends and a manila envelope of extra elastic button fasteners, necessities during my father's last four years. Revulsion and sadness prickle and sink in me as I remember the years of toileting my father and the daily brown-smeared laundry. *Please, may no one in my last years have to change my diapers.*

Again I see myself racing for the pool after my friend's frantic call, "Phyllis! Your dad's in the pool and in trouble!" I see my father lying peacefully on his side under seven feet of water and dive to pull him up. But would it not have been better for him to die there with his dignity and self-respect intact, believing he could still swim alone without his lifebelt, having at least attempted for the last time to do something he loved?

Please, may I have enough wits to swig down a lethal dose of Seconal in time. But how does one know when one's brain will turn off?

I put the unopened package of Depends and manila envelope in the give-away pile.

My father's nubby leather wallet, long empty of valuables, lies at the hamper bottom. Even though he could no longer see its contents, he liked having it nearby. I open the wallet and see a photo of my mother from 1968, a Hiram College photo of me from 1953, my father's NYC Air Raid Warden ID card issued by the police department in 1942. The photo shows my father with black hair, alert blue eyes, a strong jaw. I see him leaving our Broadway apartment after dark with a flashlight, eager to rehearse his air-raid patrol with fellow wardens. Too young for World War I and too old for World War II, he served his country this way.

I read the final item in his wallet, the People's Medical Society ID card with Consumers Medical Rights. It informs health care professionals that the undersigned places in their hands his "most precious possessions," his health and life, and counts on their professional care and concern. The card was signed in my father's precise handwriting, something he was not able to do for the last thirteen years of his life. On the back of the card are listed twelve patient rights. The first is "You have the right to considerate and respectful care." Would that I had remembered the card was in his wallet and made a large copy to hang over his bed, ten times the size of the discreet DNR (do not resuscitate) on his door.

I see again my father's swollen right hand at age 102, the deep blue and purple spreading from the base of his ring and little fingers over the bones and veins on the back of his hand. He said it hurt. He didn't know how it happened. I learned from the director of nursing that both the morning physical therapist and a responsible aide also reported it. The injury was not there when I said good night to my father before he went to bed the night before. It happened on the night aide's shift between 11 P.M. and 7 A.M. The night aide denied knowledge of the injury. The nursing director ordered an X-ray that showed no broken bones. She said residents sometimes got their hands caught and sprained in the spokes of wheelchairs. I don't think that happened to my father. Save for assisted trips to the bathroom six feet away, he was in bed all night, not moving around in his wheelchair.

Two months later, my father cautiously flexed the fingers of his then stiff right hand and said with angry conviction, "She meant to do it! She just grabbed my fingers and twisted them back like the police."

"Daddy, why didn't you tell me right after it happened?"

No answer. I knew why. His mind had become Swiss cheese with air-pocket holes randomly hollowing substance. Two months earlier, when he'd sat in silence, barely shaking his head, he'd hit an air pocket. I reported his statement to the nursing director and learned the night aide in question no longer worked there. Even if I tracked her down and pressed abuse charges, it would be the delayed word of an old man with dementia against hers. But I could imagine a tired, underpaid, resentful aide attempting to get my father to the toilet at 3 A.M. with him asserting his stubborn independence in doing it his way. I could imagine her trumping age and fragility with strength and angry frustration.

Now when I think about it at night in bed, I spontaneously jerk. I want to pin the aide to a wall and twist off her fingers. All my screening of nursing homes, all my daily visits at different hours did not prevent what I feared most. And there is nothing I can do about it.

I place the wallet in the keepsake pile. It will join my mother's ostrich wallet with her handwritten ID, my grandfather's pearl penknife, and my father's pocket watch in my jewelry drawer.

I throw out the plastic liner sack and carry the hamper into the backyard's brilliant sun. I attack it with Clorox and detergent. I scrub-brush the smudges. I dissolve with label remover my father's name and room number written in indelible ink on the lid. I blast the hamper with the garden hose inside and out and upside down. I let it bake in the sun. As a post-Depression baby, I've never considered dumping something still useful. But more, in a way I cannot grasp, disowning this homely relic feels dishonest, traitorous. Disowning it is turning my back on issues its presence demands be addressed: families need better choices for managing end-of-life care of their elders; elders need better choices for living out their lives with assistance and dignity.

These issues now are personal for me and many others. We've learned from experience what Dr. Joan Teno found in her study "Family Perspectives on End-of-Life Care at the Last Place of Care," published January 7, 2004, in the *Journal of the American Medical Association (JAMA):* The majority of Americans, 67.1 percent, die in hospitals or nursing homes where they receive their last care. Families of deceased loved ones in this group were most likely to report dissatisfaction with end-of-life care—symptom management, physician communication, lack of emotional support, and lack of respect for the dying family member. Home was the last place of care for 32.9 percent. For these dying patients who received home care from nursing services or hospice, family members were more likely to report satisfaction. A November 22, 2009, CBS *60 Minutes* program, "The High Cost of Dying," upped the percentage of Americans dying in hospitals or nursing homes to 75 percent.

Both the *JAMA* study and the CBS report show that home is the preferred, most comforting, and less painful place for end-of-life care—a realization not lost on two leaders in transforming the culture of nursing homes from the institutional model to that of home communities: Dr. Bill Thomas, internationally recognized geriatrician and founder of Eden Alternative and the Green House Project, and Steve Shields, president/CEO of Meadowlark Hills Continuing Care Retirement Community in Manhattan, Kansas. My sociable father would have loved these communities where he could share a small house with other elders, go to bed and get up when he pleased, choose his meals served in a pleasant dining room, pet a dog or cat, sit or pull weeds in a garden, joke with a regular team of caretakers who liked him and the elders they cared for, and retire to his own room with bath, furnished with his own belongings. It would have felt like home.

A study by the New York State Health Department of Chase Nursing Home, the first to convert to the Eden Alternative model under Dr. Thomas's leadership, found that infections decreased 50 percent, the daily drug costs for each resident fell 71 percent, and the turnover among the nurses' aides dropped 26 percent—proof that a change to home environment improves not only the spirit but also health and the bottom line.

With no children or siblings, I advise my extended family not just to follow my living will in my last days but also to consider what I would have done if I could have lived over my decade of caretaking.

In a replay of those years, I certainly would google Eden Alternative and Green House Project nursing homes. I'd make screening visits to those reasonably close to where I lived. If unavailable or unsuitable, I'd resume work and employ full-time caretakers for my father, even if that took all my salary. I would have felt fulfilled, and my father and I would have had more to share in each other's company.

I'd arrange hospice care sooner. I now know hospice services are available at nursing homes as well as private homes when death is probable within a six-month period. I'd gather information on the dying process early on from hospice and other sources. Especially illuminating was *Final Gifts,* a gift book I received too late: the day my father died. In it hospice nurse authors Maggie Callanan and Patricia Kelley discuss what dying persons often say or do in their final days and hours and how best to respond. Had I read the book, I would have known that when my father asked what I had heard from "Dad" (his father), his question was not just a symptom of dementia but a foreshadowing of imminent death.

In my father's more able nineties, I'd again engage graduate students in physical and occupational therapy to do exercises with him each day, take him to aquatic exercise classes at a nearby health center, and read his favorite magazines to him. He enjoyed the diversion and young people, and they enjoyed him.

I'd arrange again for my dad to attend the weekly programs and lunch at Shepherd's Center, an organization run for seniors by seniors with a variety of classes from philosophy to health updates, and arrange once more for a friend to accompany him to classes and lunch when balance became a challenge.

I'd again take my dad to church Sundays and on Fridays to meet with the Aging Bulls who visited him at home and later at the nursing home.

If I had one more conversation with my father, I'd say, "I'm sorry I didn't know more, sooner, Daddy. I wanted to make your last days as fine as all the years of good care you gave me. But let's remember the good times—the walks with the dog, the family reunions, the reading aloud. And I did give you one helluva hundredth birthday party—a Victorian-costumed soprano singing all of the songs you remembered from the turn of the last century that had tears running down your cheeks, a hall full of friends and family who came from all over the country to celebrate, followed by a big family dinner.

"'Learning by doing,' you'd quote John Dewey, and we struggled doing that. But Mother's perfect exit—dying in her sleep—didn't help either of us; one day she was gardening and the next day gone. So, I learned on you. Maybe as your only child, you learned on me. Let's forgive each other's bumbling errors. Instead, let's remember for eternity the winter after the tornado when you were ninety-one and I was fifty-six, and we worked together to plant fifty trees on your five acres, alternating the swing of our shovels so they never clicked, balancing the heavy burlap root balls between us and into place. You taught me how to brace a sapling, and when we retreated from the cold, pine-scented mist, I fixed us hot milk laced with cognac. The giant, perfect cone you gave me from the downed old sentinel pine sits on my mantel. I think of you whenever I look at it."

Phyllis Galley Westover*'s writing has appeared in magazines, newspapers, and anthologies. In 2003, she received* Boulevard Magazine*'s fiction award. In 2004 and 2009, essays of hers were finalists for the Iowa Award in Literary Nonfiction and the Salem College International Literary Awards. Previously, she taught English and directed adult degree programs at Oklahoma City University and Baker University. She holds an MA from San Francisco State University and a PhD from Union Institute and University.*

The General

LARRY D. CRIPE

A leukemia specialist, Larry D. Cripe wrestles with the request for aggressive treatment in a "hopeless" situation and his knowledge that sometimes "a chance is merely an unrealistic expectation driving the unwarranted."

After two years of battling adult acute leukemia, Mr. Doyle died in a spacious room on the Hematology-Oncology Unit of the newly built Indiana University Simon Cancer Center, in Indianapolis. I stood next to his bed, the sunlight streaming through the large picture window behind me, the soft wood surfaces and natural tones of the room rich and warm. I initially treated Mr. Doyle with eight months of intensive chemotherapy that required multiple hospitalizations. After an eleven-month remission the disease recurred, and I prescribed further chemotherapy. An allogeneic stem cell transplant in the second remission was complicated by recurrent vomiting, diarrhea, and episodes of severe abdominal pain due to graft versus host disease. The bone marrow donor's immune system cells were infiltrating Mr. Doyle's intestines. After the disease relapsed a second time, repeated attempts for a third remission, with more aggressive chemotherapy including experimental drugs, were unsuccessful. A final attempt at treating the disease led to the complications that caused his death. He had been unconscious for the final day and a half of his life as a result of shock from an overwhelming infection and the continuous intravenous infusion of morphine I prescribed. Mrs. Doyle was there. She had rarely been absent during the two years since he'd been diagnosed with acute lymphoblastic leukemia (ALL). A quiet, self-contained person who complemented her husband's gregariousness, she said, "I knew we'd end up here. But he wanted a chance. I'm not sure for myself, but I had to support his decision."

I was more ambivalent; I felt I had failed. I *knew* he would die. I *feared* he would die with more distress and sooner with further chemotherapy than with comfort care. But, of course, I only predicted he would die. There was a remote chance he might not. That was the chance Mr. Doyle wanted.

Death in the hospital is troubling for everyone involved—patients, health care professionals, and policy makers. Hospitals are foreign, nerve-wracking places people visit at their most vulnerable moments. Most people assume their health is assured and plan for the "what" of their future rather than the "if." Illness confounds that assuredness. At the same time the seriously ill person must deal with a bewildering array of consultations and procedures. Death in a hospital is contrary to the public's sense of a peaceful death. Surveys continue to demonstrate that most Americans would prefer to die at home surrounded by loved ones rather than in the sterile and impersonal environment of the hospital. And yet more than half of the people who die each year die in a hospital or health care facility. Thus death in the hospital, especially in the ICU, has become emblematic of the question both patients and physicians face countless times each day: is the technology a blessing or a curse? We appreciate the technological advances of modern medicine but intuitively fear what the medical anthropologist Sharon R. Kaufman, in her book, *And a Time to Die: How American Hospitals Shape the End of Life,* calls the zone of indistinction, a purgatory of sorts where people with only a remote likelihood of meaningful recovery linger, not quite dead and not quite alive. Kaufman illustrates how medical technology—CPR, mechanical ventilation, tube feedings—that simply "staves off death" without restoring health has shaped the way people die. But the technology is awesome, and new technologies will continue to appear. Their development is driven by a basic human inquisitiveness and, as such, is without an intrinsic morality. What alarms me is how ill prepared physicians are—and, as a result, patients and families are—to navigate the ambiguity surrounding reasonable expectations of medical technology. Patients with life-threatening or incurable illnesses suffer the consequences when these critical and often clarifying but difficult discussions about expectations near the end of life do not occur. In 1997, the Institute of Medicine report "Approaching Death: Improving Care at the End of Life" found that "too many people suffer needlessly at the end of life both from errors of omission—when caregivers fail to provide palliative and supportive care known to be effective—and from errors of commission—when caregivers do what is known to be ineffective and even harmful."

One potential way to improve care near the end of life is to consider the number of deaths in an individual hospital, or more important the rate of death there, as a measure of the quality of health care. The observed mortality rate, the percentage of patients who die in the hospital, is reported and can be used to compare the quality of health care provided in hospitals. In order to compare "quality of care" among hospitals that serve different populations of patients, organizations like the University Health Consortium calculate and report a risk-adjusted mortality rate. The calculation attempts to take into account differences in the risk of death between, say, younger people admitted for elective surgery and older adults with advanced-stage cancer and whether any given death was expected or unexpected. Death, in other words, is less expected in certain people who are hospitalized. The observed number of deaths is divided by the expected number to derive the risk-adjusted mortality ratio; a ratio of less than 1 is the goal. The difficulty with risk adjustment is estimating the effect of individual factors—age, prognosis in view of underlying conditions, other medical complications—on the likelihood of death. While it is possible to game the system by inflating the expected likelihood of death, I believe most hospitals and medical staffs, my own included, are genuinely trying to improve the care provided in ways that are meaningful to patients. One such effort is to review and discuss in committee each death. The goal is to identify errors.

Pat Kneebone, a nurse I've known since I started working at Indiana University Hospital fifteen years ago, reviewed the medical record of Mr. Doyle within a week of his death. An older woman with three decades of experience in caring for people with cancer at a research and teaching hospital, Pat knows the difference between good intentions and the havoc that can result from well-meaning but overly enthusiastic physicians. A short, substantial woman, Pat tends to peer over her glasses and speak in an urgent, compressed voice. "What," she might admonish the physician who prescribed overly aggressive care, "were you thinking? Or were you?" And yet Pat, respectful more than kind, and stern but not hard-hearted, is equally generous with her support.

After his leukemia relapsed the first time, I expected Mr. Doyle would die. He and his wife expected he would die. But he desperately wanted to live. I underestimated this desire, as well as his absolute confidence in me to provide him the opportunity to live longer. Exhausted from unrelenting diarrhea and the inability to eat, he was lying on the examination table in the outpatient clinic two weeks before he died, describing the horrendous pain he endured from the mouth sores induced by the drug he received in a phase I clinical trial for people with refractory ALL.

"I've learned a lesson," he said, his voice weak and strained. "I don't want to ever go through that again."

As the research nurse and I walked from his room, I said to her, "Well at least he has reached a place where we can care for him as he dies without further chemotherapy."

She looked at me as if I had not been in the room. "He will want more therapy," she replied. "He's learned he can survive. He doesn't want to go through that again. But he will if that's what it takes."

In her report, Pat noted that CPR was not performed and that Mr. Doyle had not spent any time in the medical ICU. A committee of my physician and nursing colleagues and data specialists reviewed the report she generated. They discussed the quality of the care I provided and whether additional review of Mr. Doyle's care was necessary. There were concerns about my final decision to prescribe chemotherapy. In Pat's review of Mr. Doyle's medical chart she found that I had conducted several care conferences with Mr. Doyle and his family. In my daily progress notes, I clearly summarized my opinion that further chemotherapy was almost certainly futile, that his quality of life might be better with palliative care, and that even his life expectancy might be longer if we avoided the risks of chemotherapy. And before agreeing to administer chemotherapy I insisted he accept a do-not-resuscitate status. I was willing to provide a chance, but I was not willing to pound on his chest or shove a tube down his throat if his heart stopped or he could no longer breathe, only to watch him die a slower but no less inevitable death hooked to machines. The disagreement within the committee was where I drew the line. To a few of my colleagues, prescribing chemotherapy that close to death was no less heinous. They felt I should have refused.

The research nurse was right. Mr. Doyle was hospitalized to treat the complications of the study drug. When he improved he insisted on further chemotherapy. Three days after the first dose I walked into his room and found him gasping in pain, his abdomen bloated from what I presumed was a perforation of his intestines.

"Enough," I said, "for God's sake, enough."

He nodded. We administered morphine.

Discouraged, as I watched him settle into the bed, I wondered if I had learned anything in twenty years of practicing medicine. I thought about Dr. Smith, an attending oncologist I knew during my internal medicine residency at Rush Presbyterian St. Luke's Medical Center in Chicago in the mid-1980s.

We called Dr. Smith "the General." In the hospital, we would brace ourselves when we heard the swish of his arms—swung with military precision against his starched white cotton laboratory coat with cloth buttons—as he walked down the hallway to find us after he had visited his patients. We accepted his dismissive questions, his impatient, growling responses to our questions, and the curses he liberally handed out for our errors, many of which seemed to us slight.

On outings to our favorite neighborhood tavern, we drunkenly mocked his authoritative stride—toes pointed slightly outward, heels crisply hitting the floor—as we marched around the table, knocking over a glass of beer or two. We would grab one another by the collar for some imagined error and mimic the prickly growl of his voice. "And exactly what medical school did you fail to graduate from?" We howled with delight when Dave—three years our senior and charged with organizing the outings to help us through the drudgery of the final months of our internship—portrayed the General obsessively buffing his brown wingtips late into the night while his wife begged him to rest. "Not now, confound it," Dave would mock protest. "There's still a spot; can't cure cancer with a spot on my shoe." But our parody was high praise; we were in awe of his dedication. He was one of the best. If we had cancer, we agreed, we would want the General as our doctor. With the General there was a fighting chance.

As I watched Mr. Doyle when I was getting ready to administer a larger dose of morphine, I thought about the last patient I saw with the General when I was a third-year internal medicine resident. I had elected to spend the final month of my residency seeing his patients with him to prepare for my fellowship in Hematology-Oncology at Duke University Cancer Center in Durham, North Carolina. It was a late Friday night. Because his outpatient clinic that day had extended into the early evening, he had asked me to go to the hospital, gather information on his hospitalized patients, and wait for him. When he met me on the first unit, the General was even terser than usual. The next to the last patient we saw was a father of two teenage boys, Mr. Johns, who had become wheelchair bound as the result of a brain tumor that had progressed despite chemotherapy; he had been admitted earlier that day when his speech abruptly became nonsensical.

"The neurology team saw Mr. Johns," I said as we reviewed the chart in the nursing station. "And they are certain this represents a new site of tumor involvement. The floor team is waiting for your plan."

The General responded to my implicit challenge by tapping me on the chest with a creased, glossy page he'd ripped from a medical journal. He smiled grimly, like a scholar who had searched a remote archive for a long-sought document. It was a letter to the editor of a cancer journal in which a doctor from Israel summarized his experience in treating a small number of people who had a variety of cancers that progressed despite standard therapy with unbelievably high doses of a drug, methotrexate, used commonly in the treatment of cancer.

"They survived," the General said, shaking his head in admiration as he dictated from the table in the letter the name of the drug and the dose for me to write into the orders for Mr. Johns. After that we spent five minutes with the patient telling him the plan was to treat him with very high doses of methotrexate so we could shrink his tumor. "We think," the General said, as if he had solicited my opinion, "this is your best chance."

After that the General's mood lightened considerably. As we walked to the other end of the medical center to see the final patient, I asked him about his decision to become a cancer specialist. As we stood in the glass-encased walkway between two buildings—a steady stream of headlights on the Eisenhower Expressway marking the commute to the suburbs visible over his shoulder—he spoke of his memories from a decade or so before of people with acute leukemia and how they were admitted to darkened hospital rooms so they and their family were not aware of the bruising and bleeding as life ended. It was a grim recital. But then he saw his first patient treated with a new drug. The month was rough, but that person walked out of the hospital. "It was amazing, absolutely fucking amazing. Suddenly we could offer people a fighting chance," he said. And his profanity seemed reverential in its appropriateness.

Now, twenty years later I was meeting Mr. Doyle for the first time. He was already bald from the first cycle of chemotherapy, known as induction therapy. He was a stout, talkative man with a protuberant stomach and a direct gaze. Most adults his age experience a complete remission (a condition in which the leukemia is undetectable and the normal bone marrow function is restored) after the initial cycle of chemotherapy. But his statistics were consistently negative: it was overwhelmingly likely he would die within the first year or so, of either relapse or complications from treatment. The challenge was to avoid the serious complications, including death, of the multiple cycles of chemotherapy we proposed to administer to try to prevent or delay relapse of the ALL. At the conclusion of our sobering conversation with him about the risks and potential benefits, Mr. Doyle told me he was the "go-to maintenance guy" at his factory: if there was a mechanical problem out of the ordinary, his opinion was sought. "That's what I expect from you," he said. "I want you to know I trust you'll figure this out and I'll be just fine. You are my go-to guy. You are my chance."

The first oncologist who met with the Doyles recommended they meet with me and receive care at the cancer center. Located on a sprawling urban and difficult-to-navigate campus, the cancer center was built connected with an older and less hospitable building. Mr. Doyle accepted the distant and expensive parking, the confusing hallways and floor plans, and my limited office hours because he believed in my expertise. My clinical practice, while dedicated to the care of adults with leukemia, was limited by my teaching, research, and administrative responsibilities. He trusted the combination of skills and duties would provide him a better chance.

I am not sure Mr. and Mrs. Doyle were ever unrealistic about the prognosis of older adults. He just couldn't imagine that was his prognosis. Physicians are trained to modify the future for the better. During our clinical rotations in medical school and residency, we learn the symptoms and objective findings that reflect the aberrant function of diseased molecules, cells, and organs. We strive to relieve the suffering of disease through well-applied diagnostics and therapeutics. People like Mr. Doyle trust our competence and our expertise in treating acute leukemia. The bedrock of that trust is an institutional assurance—visible in diplomas, certificates, and credentials—that we have worked and will work diligently to develop and maintain the skills necessary to diagnose, prescribe, and administer chemotherapy and then support people through the complications in order to provide, in a word, a chance.

But when is a chance merely an unrealistic expectation driving the unwarranted—and perhaps harmful—provision of medical technology? And therein lies the heart of the dilemma. As Professor Kaufman asks in *And a Time to Die:* how do we back away from the dominant—and I would argue distorting—belief in America that "death has entered the domain of choice, and we [can] think of death in terms of its control, quality and timeliness"? The first step, I believe, is to better understand what molds the expectations of physicians.

I've carried a photograph of a young woman named Miranda Thomas in my wallet since she died in 1999. She was nineteen; her grandmother mailed several photographs with a funeral card on which she had written, "I want to make sure you knew Miranda was far more than her illness." In it Miranda stands turned away from the camera, her left leg extended and her foot firmly planted perpendicular to her right foot. She glances crosswise over her left shoulder revealing an attractive face centered by a satisfied smile. Her left hand holds an unruly white pom-pom to the small of her back; her right hand holds a pom-pom next to her stomach. Her body coils like a spring. For a while I imagined her spinning like a top until she was a red blur with a white stripe in the middle. But she remains motionless, fixed on the dulled and chipped surface of the photograph.

Miranda's end started with a freshman orientation flag football game at Notre Dame, a bruised knee, and a mother's intuition that something was terribly wrong. So Miranda went to the student infirmary. Her blood test was abnormal, and she was referred to me for evaluation and treatment, as necessary. Miranda and her mother arrived well after nightfall because of a thick fog and freezing rain. I walked through the narrow, brightly lit anteroom and saw her sitting upright on the hospital bed, her legs crossed Indian-style and her hands clasped on her lap. Her mother was touching Miranda's wrist. A faint rain pinged against the large picture window opposite the bed, overlooking an enclosed courtyard. "The doctor thought I might have leukemia," Miranda said. I sat down. "I think so too," I replied.

Notre Dame was her dream, the first step away from life in a small town toward an international career. Starting college was so exciting, she said in a voice resonant with the rolling green stone-fenced pastures of Kentucky. She had already met so many interesting people. I immediately connected with Miranda. I too had used my education to take me away from La Porte, a small town with a shrinking industrial base in northwest Indiana. I still vividly remembered my excitement and sense of belonging when I walked onto the campus of the University of Chicago for the first time.

"Are there treatments?" she asked. "Yes," I said, "and the initial treatment requires several weeks in the hospital—chemotherapy to kill the leukemia cells, time for the bone marrow to recover, bruising and fatigue, transfusions, fevers, antibiotics—followed by repeated treatments to kill any remaining leukemia cells." Dumbfounded, Miranda asked, "What about college?" "Possible," I replied, "but we need to focus on the next few hours and days."

One hundred forty-three. That is the number of days Miranda, who had ALL, spent in the hospital between September and May. Her body's initial response to therapy was favorable. After her first period in the hospital she went home for what would be the longest time during her illness, twenty-three days. She received a second treatment. Then the leukemia recurred, first in her nervous system and eventually in her bone marrow. The last time I saw Miranda she had been hospitalized for seventy-four days in the bone marrow transplantation unit. She sat in a wheelchair waiting for her father to return. He had taken home a load of the things that had accumulated during her stay. Her mother sat on the edge of the unmade bed holding Miranda's teddy bear wrapped in a clear plastic bag to protect her from any infectious spores. Miranda's liver was failing, and two days before, the laboratory tests indicated the ALL was not in remission. Miranda was going home to die.

As I walked in a nurse was trying to put a shoe on Miranda's left foot. Miranda cried, "Ouch! You are hurting me." I saw the frustration in the face of the nurse—who knew better than anyone, other than her mother, what Miranda had endured—and I asked if I could try. I knelt before Miranda taking the shoe in my hand. She was hairless. Her skin was a mixture of a bright yellow and a dusky red with a white flakiness like an overly ripened apple in the frost. She was swollen, saturated with all the intravenous fluids she had received during her treatment. Methodically I stretched the shoe so it would fit over her taut foot without discomfort. As the shoe slipped on with only slight resistance, I looked up and said, "A glass slipper for my princess. I love you, Miranda Thomas."

I have come to believe, since that afternoon with Miranda, that what I do is similar to loving someone, especially as life is ending. There is a less guarded intimacy when I am present only as myself and not as a physician who can provide remedy or the means to restored health. As I have accepted this understanding, I have found myself able to share these loving feelings with more patients.

For a number of years I ended Miranda's story by saying I watched her father guide the wheelchair into the elevator, and in that moment, I felt affirmed in my decision to pursue a research career in leukemia. Surely the only rational response to a young woman dying of leukemia, I believed with decreasing certainty, was to develop better treatments. One of the greatest triumphs of contemporary medical science has been the ability to identify the molecular defects that account for leukemia. My tenacious laboratory colleagues have discovered and dissected the distorted molecules that initiate and perpetuate the disease. My clinical research colleagues and I test a greater range of drugs with greater promise since they were developed. Was there any reason to doubt, if we all doubled or tripled our efforts, that a cure was within reach?

However, I've come to realize, in the past year or so, that by telling Miranda I loved her I was, in a sense, asking for forgiveness. While treating her disease, I had lost sight of her. Miranda's life had been cruelly compressed: from normal to diseased, health to illness, college campus to hospital, wide horizons to limited goals, confidence to uncertainty, and a chance to no chance. I was not unaware of or insensitive to the collapse of her life. I did not know how to speak of it with her. So I recommended that Miranda try an allogeneic stem cell transplant (ASCT). More than recommending it, I encouraged her.

At that point in her care, it was clear the leukemia was not responsive to chemotherapy. ASCT is a technology that allows a patient to receive significantly higher doses of chemotherapy or radiation than we normally administer. Since the new marrow stem cells are infused after the chemotherapy is inactivated by the body, there is no concern of using doses that essentially destroy or ablate the recipient's marrow cells. In addition, the donor's marrow provides a new immune system for the recipient. The potential benefit is that the higher doses of chemotherapy and the new immune cells can collaborate and eradicate the leukemia cells that have survived despite the extensive treatments thus far. The potential risks of the chemotherapy and the new immune system are considerable. The recipient is without a viable immune system for a period of time and is at risk for unusual and difficult-to-treat infections. The new immune system also could essentially reject the vital organs of the recipient (called graft versus host disease). My stem cell transplant colleagues were not in favor of the transplant. The outcomes of ASCT are better if people are in a remission (Miranda was not), and we were using an unrelated donor (and at the time there was higher treatment-related mortality rate with unrelated donors). But I insisted. "It's her choice. She deserves a chance," I argued.

What I was really thinking as Miranda left the hospital was why had I recommended an ASCT? What had I done? It wasn't that I did not inform her of the risks of ASCT or the low likelihood of benefit. I informed her that either death from complications of ASCT or refractory ALL was the most likely outcome. What I wasn't able to say was that *I believed she would die regardless of what we did*. I was unable to tell her that the ability to perform an SCT was not a sufficient reason to perform an ASCT. I carry Miranda's photograph to remind me that the care of people who die will not improve unless physicians develop the willingness to speak about death and dying in a way that allows us to modify expectations and then care.

After prescribing chemotherapy (and developing new drugs) for a number of years—as I was trained to do, as I am expected to do—the central question for me as a physician, an educator, and a researcher has now become, how do we speak with the dying and their families in a way that is meaningful to the decisions we make near the end of life? My less charitable colleagues will say that, in framing the remainder of my life's work this way, I have lost my heart, which I suppose means, in one sense, I have lost faith that clinical expertise and technology are sufficient to *care* for the seriously ill. That is true, I have. But it feels more fundamental than an ambivalence about technology that overpromises and is overutilized. Ambivalence about technology has been with us a long time. In 1970 the Yale theologian Paul Ramsey asked in his book *The Patient as Person,* "Ought there to be any relief for the dying from a physician's search for exquisite triumphs over death?" To which he answered, the physician should consider the "dispensability of extraordinary life-sustaining treatments because he as a man acknowledges that there may be sufficient moral and human reasons for [the decision to allow life to end]." Professor Ramsey wrote his book in a much simpler time. The concept of brain death had only been recently promulgated by the Ad Hoc Committee of the Harvard Medical School to Examine the Definition of Brain Death. The matter of Karen Ann Quinlan and the right to die would reach the mainstream a few years later. Ms. Quinlan was a young woman in an irreversible coma after a drug overdose. After several months of physical decline while on a mechanical ventilator and nasogastric tube feedings, the family requested that the doctors withdraw care and allow her life to end naturally. However, the county prosecutors threatened legal action if treatments were withdrawn. The case was decided eventually on behalf of Ms. Quinlan and her family by the New Jersey Supreme Court. The court ruled that the physicians were not bound to use extraordinary means, in this instance, mechanical ventilation, if recovery was not possible and if the patient, or family on behalf of the patient, requested the withdrawal of such support. This case continues to highlight the ambivalence the public feels about the inappropriate use of technology and the potential for depriving a person of the right to a death with dignity and comfort.

In the final analysis, physicians are trained, first and foremost, to treat disease. We are trained to equate the treatment of disease with the potential to alleviate suffering. Thus, physicians' felt imperative to prescribe treatment is one valid and socially valued measure of our compassion. The shared expectation of remedy links physician with patient. There is, however, a more personally demanding measure of a physician's compassion: the capacity to remain present throughout the *lived experience of suffering* regardless of whether or not we can provide remedy.

My more generous colleagues will recognize that I am following my heart. And that is truer than having lost it. I am grateful to have spent a number of years seeking, with brilliant and dedicated colleagues, new remedies. But a more urgent question preoccupies my time: what will we do until the new remedies are discovered? I suspect Miranda Thomas would have chosen to proceed with the ASCT regardless of whether or not I shared my personal ambivalence. Certainly Mr. Doyle was well aware of my objections and my belief he would die with greater suffering with further chemotherapy. Both were delightful people who wanted a chance to live. And in neither case could I have ethically not revealed the options for further treatment.

My regrets are complementary and enduring. I was younger, more enthusiastic, and my behavior was in emulation of my teachers like the General when I advised Miranda to proceed with the ASCT. I was unprepared professionally and personally to accept her death. I was older, more judicious, and less willing to recommend an "all out assault" when I cared for Mr. Doyle. But he was unable, despite his trust in me, to accept the inevitability of his death, because Americans, while ambivalent about technology, cannot accept that there may be no remedy.

The Institute of Medicine report I quoted earlier went on to note that part of the problem with end-of-life care in America was that "the education and training of physicians and other health care professionals fails to provide them with the knowledge, skills, and attitudes to care well for the dying patient." What disturbs me is not the new technology or the inevitably steep and error-prone process of learning how and when to utilize the new technology to provide people the chances for longer lives. Rather, I am deeply troubled by how peripheral considerations of empathy, humility, compassion, respect, and integrity are to medical education and my daily work life. We will move away from the belief that the time of death is negotiable only if we—physicians, patients, and families—seek the shared values and language that celebrate the sanctity of life both in seeking to prolong it and in honoring its end with compassion and kindness. And that will first require an acceptance of the ambiguity and uncertainty that surround the end of life. The American public is conflicted; the countervailing concerns are that appropriate treatment will be withheld because of considerations such as cost and that treatment will be maintained to the detriment of personal choice and dignity. Physicians are trusted to do the right thing. What is missing is the dialogue with our patients and the public that will lead to a shared understanding of the right thing to do when there are no remedies, when the good fight fails.

Larry D. Cripe *is a leukemia specialist and essayist. In addition to essays in* JAMA *and other publications, he writes* Grace Notes, *radio essays read on Sound Medicine, WFYI, about end-of-life care. His research interests include studying physician-patient communication and medical decision making near the end of life.*

"The General" is a runner-up for the *Creative Nonfiction* Best Essay Award, chosen by the editors of *Creative Nonfiction.*

Yellow Taxi

EVE JOSEPH

Looking back over twenty years of hospice work, Eve Joseph reflects on the "invisible work" being done and the mysteries that occur at the end of life.

To work with the dying is to wade into mystery. In some situations professional training will be invaluable; in others, it will be of no use at all. On my first community visit as a hospice counselor, a naked woman stood on the dresser beside her bed and flung a perfume bottle at my head; she thought she was in the war and her arsenal consisted of little colored bottles of eau de toilette. She had captured the ridge and was there for the long haul. Two injections of Haldol by the nurse eventually cleared the woman's delusions, but what helped me to understand what the woman was seeing on that ridge and to talk her down into the safety of her bed—the bunker, we called it—were my mother's stories of the war.

It is a complicated thing to be employed to help people die. On the one hand, each situation, each person, is unique, and each death a profound experience; on the other, the job is like any other. You set your alarm to wake up and grab a coffee on your way to work. Traffic is bad, and you know the last parking spot is going to be gone. You vow again to leave earlier, but that never happens. As with any job, a certain set of skills is required; however, you never know exactly what it is you will need to be of some help.

A man dying of leukemia once asked me if I did anything useful. In his last months he had built a farmer's market on his land so that his wife and four sons would be able to support themselves after his death. Without thinking I answered that I baked loaves of bread. It was a lie, but it became a fortuitous lie. He told me to bring my loaves to the market and said his family would keep half the profit; the other half was mine. The first month after his death I decided I'd do what I told the man, and I made five hundred dollars selling banana, chocolate, blueberry, pumpkin, apple, and zucchini loaves. I followed recipes; I made them up. A few years later, when my marriage ended, I supported myself and my children with money from the loaves I sold at the man's market.

It's that way with the work of helping the dying; you start out with good intentions and sometimes end up in a bunker reeking of perfume.

The hospice where I worked in 1985 has been paved over and is now a parking lot. The chestnut trees that lined the street outside the patients' rooms are gone, along with the wild cherry trees that bloomed each February in a kind of mockery of winter. Bay Pavilion, as the old hospice was called, was a one-story horseshoe-shaped building built around a garden. These days they call hospice gardens "healing gardens." Back in 1985 the garden made no such claims; a gardener's garden, its raison d'être was to revel in its own beauty. For some patients it was the garden of their childhood; for others, it was the garden they wished they'd always had. This is not to say that Bay Pavilion was paradise but to muse over the idea it was only a step or two away from it.

In one of the rooms facing the courtyard, cherry blossoms blew in through an open window and fell onto a sleeping woman. I was in the room with her husband, whom I had met only moments before, when he had collapsed in my arms and said, "If there is a God and this is his plan, how can I ever believe in that God again; and if there is no God how can I live?" I was new to the work and had no answer for him. I hadn't even begun to formulate the questions. I remember looking at her pale skin and black hair and thinking she looked like Snow White in a Red Cross bed. Her window, like all the others on the unit, was kept slightly open in order for the spirit to leave.

Derived from the Latin *hospitium,* meaning both "host" and "guest," the word *hospice* represents an idea as well as a place. In Homeric times all strangers were regarded as guests; it was an obligation to be hospitable to strangers, an obligation imposed on civilized man by Zeus himself, one of whose many titles was *xeinios*, "protector of strangers." In the *Odyssey*, Alcinous, king of the Phaeacians, offers hospitality without knowing who Odysseus is: "Tell him, then, to rise and take a seat on a stool inlaid with silver and let the housekeeper give him some supper, of whatever there might be in the house."

The word *hospice* was used in the fourth century by monks who welcomed and provided sanctuary for pilgrims; it wasn't until the mid-1800s that it became exclusively associated with the care of the dying. The modern hospice, as we know it, did not come into being until 1967, when St. Christopher's Hospice was opened in London by Cicely Saunders, a young physician previously trained as a nurse and a social worker. The term *death with dignity* became a rallying cry for those working with the dying.

When I looked up the root of the word *hospitality*, I initially misread "friendliness to guests" as "friendliness to ghosts" and thought later that was not entirely inaccurate. It has been said by those who can see that the dead walk the corridors: mothers holding hands with daughters, grandfathers and grandmothers, husbands waiting for their wives, and others nobody knows, who are just there waiting.

One woman I worked with stared at the top left-hand corner of her room for days waiting for her late husband to come for her; others came, she told us, but she didn't know them and refused to go. On the morning of her death she said her husband had come. He'd tipped his hat in the slightly mocking way he'd always done in life, and she smiled. A wide, radiant smile.

A young man dying of AIDS asked me to be careful when I went to sit on a couch in his room; he didn't want me to sit on the old woman who had appeared three days ago with a bag of wool and needles. He asked me if I thought her arrival meant his death was near; I looked over my shoulder toward the empty couch and said my guess was that he had a bit of time, since she had brought her knitting.

I don't see spirits. But once, years ago, when I was eight months pregnant, I heard singing and drumming coming from the site of a Shaker church that had burned to the ground years before. My mother-in-law said spirits were singing to welcome the baby, but I was never sure what I'd heard or whether I had really heard anything at all.

Our first experiences with loss shape us in ways we don't understand at the time. When I was six, I roller-skated home like a bat out of hell from my friend's house with the still warm, limp body of a yellow budgie in my hand. I didn't know what death meant, but I knew it was big. My first funerals for animals were shaped not by belief in a send-off to the afterlife but out of love of ceremony—with the little graves, the procession, the tea parties on the lawn afterward.

When I was twelve, my older brother was killed in a car accident. It was 1965, the year Allen Ginsberg introduced the term *flower power,* and Malcolm X was shot dead inside Harlem's Audubon Ballroom, the year T. S. Eliot died, and Bob Dylan's "Like a Rolling Stone" was on its way to becoming a new anthem. In North America, at that time, death was regarded as a taboo subject. Most people died in hospitals, away from view. Grief was not openly discussed, and not a lot was known about what to do with a kid whose brother had suddenly died on the other side of the country.

In the late Middle Ages, no funeral procession was complete without a delegation of children from orphanages or foundling homes. In the 1870s, children played with death kits complete with coffins and mourning clothes. Up until the late nineteenth century the preparation of the bodies of the dead occurred mostly in people's homes. It wasn't until the 1920s that death moved to hospitals and funeral homes, and people began believing children needed protection from the reality of death.

I spent the days between the phone call and the funeral playing with plastic horses in the basement. The smell of lilies drifted down the stairs, and when I surfaced, the funeral was over and everyone had gone home. I watched my mother gather armfuls of lilies and throw them in the trashcan. The lilies would have been *Lilium longiflorum,* trumpet-shaped flowers native to the Ryukyu Islands of Japan, the lilies mentioned in the Bible as the white-robed apostles of hope found growing in the Garden of Gethsemane after Christ's crucifixion, lilies that were said to have sprung up where drops of blood fell.

•••

Thirty years later, I found a poem by a friend of my brother, in which I learned that his body had been shipped across Canada by train in a blue casket. Why that stays with me I can't fully explain. There is a story about a tribe of nomads crossing the Sahara Desert and pausing every few hours in order to let their spirits catch up with them. It seems right that it took my brother four days to arrive at the place he would be buried, right that he came across the country in a casket the color of the sky.

With death we see, as did C. S. Lewis, there are no lights on in the windows of the house, and we wonder if it was ever inhabited. I had no idea, when I studied social work and went to work for more than twenty years at a well-established hospice, that I was trying to sight grief through the scope of my past experience. I needed to find my way out of the basement.

The hospice that replaced the Bay Pavilion is located on the third and fourth floors of an old maternity hospital not far from downtown Victoria. In 1979, six years before I was hired as a counselor there, I gave birth to my first daughter in one of the rooms I later helped people die in.

There are seventeen beds on the unit, seven of them reserved for the imminently dying, nine allocated for patients with less than six months to live, and one for respite care that can be used by patients in the community for up to one week, a room I once heard a family member refer to as her "time-out" room. When you step out of the elevator onto the third floor you pass a vase filled with flowers to your left and a large hand-embroidered quilt on your right. The quilt contains the names of patients who have died; it is full, so new names are entered on a parchment scroll lying on the table beneath the quilt.

More than four hundred volunteers with various skills work at the hospice. Some sing, some play the piano in the family lounge, some know Reiki and therapeutic touch; many of them make tea and sit with the dying in their rooms. They come from all walks of life: they are doctors, teachers, filmmakers, waitresses, beauticians, dog trainers, painters and potters, CEOs, cops, and widows. Many, though not all, are retirees. There aren't many young volunteers; this is not their country yet.

On Sundays, Akako, a volunteer skilled in calligraphy, sits down at the table and carefully adds the names of patients who died that past week to the scroll. Some weeks there are three or four names; other weeks there are more. She remembers one week when it took her more than four hours to add twenty-three names to the list.

The nurses and doctors who do this work understand the language of pain. As the Bedouin must have for wind, the dying and those who care for them have many words for pain: *sharp, dull, aching, crushing, searing, tingling, red, white, hot, cold, malevolent, familiar, catlike, ghostlike, jabbing, cutting, burning, flickering, flashing, ravenous, gnawing, coiling.* (The Inuit, we are now told, have really only twelve words for snow.) For some it just hurts like hell; for others there are no words at all.

A language, says ethnobotanist Wade Davis, is not simply a set of grammatical rules or a vocabulary; it is a flash of the human spirit, a window of sorts into the cosmology of our individual lives. Many people, in their last days, speak of one thing in terms of another. Metaphor, the engine of poetry, is also the language of the dying. Those who work with the dying must learn to think like the poet who reaches for language the way a child reaches for the moon, believing it can be held in the hand like an orange at the same time it shines on in the night sky.

Without metaphor how could we comprehend the stars as small fires burning through the roof of the tent? Without metaphor how could we understand the man on his deathbed who tells you a yellow cab has pulled up outside his house, and even though the taxi has the wrong address, he says he'll go anyway? Or the woman who asks where she will live when they jackhammer her street? How could we understand the patient who repeatedly asks if her suitcase is packed and ready to go, the Buddhist who insists that the heads be chopped off all the flowers in her garden in case their beauty holds her back; how could we see what the woman crouched on her knees on her hospital bed sees when she smiles and tells the doctor she is peeking into heaven?

At birth, a newborn baby has approximately three hundred bones, while on average, an adult has two hundred and six. Our bones fuse as we grow; we are building our scaffolding without even knowing it. The twenty-four long, curved bones of our ribcage form a structure that shelters the heart, lungs, liver, and spleen. Like exotic birds we live within the safety of our bony cages.

One summer night a twenty-eight-year-old patient, with a rare form of bone cancer, asked to be wheeled outside in her hospital bed to sleep beneath the stars. In the days preceding her death, the bones of her ribcage were so brittle that one or two broke whenever she rolled over. I was horrified to learn that our bones could snap like dry twigs.

Pain speaks a number of languages. On one level it needs no translation; on another level it requires that we become translators and interpreters of another's pain if we are to be of any help. For her immediate physical pain, the young woman was on a morphine drip with breakthrough doses given subcutaneously through a butterfly in her upper arm. She was also seeing a counselor, Jo Dixon, who understood pain from a different perspective. Jo sat on the woman's bed every day and listened to her talk about what it was like to be trapped in her body. They talked about how each bone breaking was an opening, how the cage cracking was the only way she could fly free. The young woman used morphine to get on top of the pain and metaphor to try to understand it.

The metaphoric language of the dying is the language of the boatman. *Metaphor,* derived from the same word in Greek, in which it means "to transfer" or "to carry across," is the language of transition: a bit like the false work of the whole dying process, it holds us up until the crossing is strong enough to get us to the other side. In Athens, delivery trucks careen around the streets with METAPHOR written on their sides. Pedestrians, I've heard, use their own metaphors when jumping out of the way. Aristotle believed the use of metaphor was a sign of genius: the dying as geniuses. On some level we know we will all be there one day, climbing into the yellow cab idling at the front door.

In my experience, very few people are aware of hospices until they need them. The actual work that goes on is invisible; we keep death as far away from us as we can. Hospices are part of a health system, and hospice workers part of an overriding bureaucracy. Traditionally, healers often lived on the outskirts of the village; shamans, prophets, tricksters, magicians, holy men, eccentrics, crazy men and women had a specific role to play as mediators between the living and the dead. There were times, over the years, when I thought that's what those of us working with the dying needed: huts on the edge of the city, places where people like Jo would be revered and feared, and, instead of biweekly pay checks, people would approach with stories, scraps of memory, a goat, a bag of potatoes, a basket of eggs, a chicken.

I was wrong about the trees. Today, driving past the parking lot the original Bay Pavilion has become, I see one oak still standing, the same tree Joseph Garcin's room overlooked. Metaphor didn't interest Joseph: "One leaf falling," he said, "can occupy me all day." But metaphor still concerns me—in his last week Joseph couldn't understand why it was taking him so long to die. Every night he knocked at death's door, asking to be let in.

Each of us brings our own beliefs to the work—beliefs based on our history with death, our culture, religion or lack of, beliefs based on mythology and psychology and on our motives and expectations. We come to our beliefs one death at a time. On New Year's Day, the Japanese believe, the dead arrive on the back of a horse, and, when the holiday is over, they return to their world in small wood and paper boats bearing a lighted candle. In Africa, a widow might run a zigzag course through the woods after her husband's burial so that his ghost will not follow and haunt her. Spain, says García Lorca, is a country open to death. Everywhere else, death is an end. "Death comes and they draw the curtains. In Spain they open them." Many Spaniards, he writes, live indoors until the day they die and are taken out into the sunlight.

What beliefs compel the living to carry the dead out into the sun? A mother whose premature baby spent her short life in a hospital asked only that her daughter be allowed to die outside. The doctor agreed to take her off life support and bag her, giving her oxygen by hand, until she was out of the hospital. A strange cortege of nurses, family, and friends walked single file behind the doctor through the corridors, out the back door, and across the parking lot to a nearby grassy hill. The baby's grandfather took up his drum and sang a farewell song to her. She breathed on her own for a good five minutes; when she took her last breath, a single clap of thunder reverberated across the sky. The grandfather believed the clap of thunder meant the Creator had opened the heavens, swooped down, picked the baby up in his arms, and booted it right on back to heaven.

A few years ago I read a story by the poet P. K. Page about an ornithologist who raised song birds in isolation in order to understand how they learned to sing. On their own, the birds cobbled together a kind of song, not species perfect, but a song nonetheless. When they were introduced to the songs of other birds, not of their own species, he discovered they chose the notes and cadences that completed their own species song.

In my work with the dying I was drawn instinctively to certain rituals and practices. I know very little of my Jewish ancestry, since my lineage is on my father's side, and Jewish identity is passed through matrilineal descent. From Baghdad and Russia to Calcutta and Shanghai and on to Israel, my ancestors studied Kabbalah and steeped themselves in Jewish and Arabic philosophy; they were Levys and Cohens and had names like Seemah, Mozelle, Solomon, and Dafna. Still, I do not qualify as a Jew. On the other hand, my marriage to a Coast Salish man made me legally an Indian under section 12(1)(b) of the Indian Act. I am at home in the longhouse and a stranger in the synagogue.

I drew on native beliefs and rituals about death and dying in my work. It made sense to light a candle in order to hold the spirit in the last days and hours; it made sense that someone should sit with the body from the time of death until burial or cremation so that the spirit would not feel frightened or abandoned; it seemed right to pick up a handful of dirt and throw it onto the coffin before the plot was filled in, a last handshake, as the Coast Salish people call it.

What I didn't know and was stunned to find out one afternoon, reading *Kaddish* by Leon Wieseltier in the sun in my backyard, was that the native rituals that had resonated with me were also the rituals and beliefs of Jewish culture. From lighting candles and sitting with the body to covering mirrors and throwing dirt into the grave—I had unwittingly been learning my own species song, wading knee-deep, waist-deep, over-my-head-deep into mystery.

In addition to bringing our beliefs to the work, we also bring what we do not yet know about ourselves. We don't know our tolerance or our saturation point.

We don't know what enough will look like. A nurse I knew, who burned out after eighteen years on the job, calculated she had helped over fifteen hundred people die. She left hospice and went to work in labor and delivery, where she vowed to deliver fifteen hundred babies before retiring.

My memories of life are stronger than those of death in the room I gave birth in. I remember lying beside a long window through which the sun was streaming in and looking over at my brand new baby daughter lying in her bassinet. I remember the sensation of falling in love: the quick jerk of it, the way one sometimes finds oneself falling backward into sleep and flailing to keep from disappearing into the void.

I believe it would be a fine thing to leave the world in a small wood and paper boat holding a lighted candle.

In my mother's last year she was so weak she was unable to leave her house; in her last months she was confined to her bedroom. Later when I saw her in the hospital morgue, she was lying on a steel gurney in a half-zipped body bag. Her face was uncovered, and her hands, with their magenta nails, were resting on her chest. I asked the undertaker, when he arrived, to leave her face uncovered—which he did, although reluctantly, as it was against protocol. When we took her outside to the waiting van to take her body to the funeral home, rain fell on her cold face. The rain fell on her without knowing she was dead; it fell on her as it fell on earth. It fell on her the way it fell on Holly Golightly and Cat in *Breakfast at Tiffany's*, and it fell on her the way it had fallen on the attic roof when I was a girl and everywhere water was running, and my mother and I were dry in our adjoining beds and full of sleep.

We labor to be born and we labor to die. The obvious analogy is the clichéd one: we come from the unknown and depart for the unknown; however, the similarities are striking in other ways. Breath is crucial to both kinds of labor. Prenatal classes focus on breath and pain; the progression in Lamaze classes is from deep to shallow breathing. The dying, too, move from regular deep breaths to rapid mouth breathing. At the end, the dying often look like fish out of water, their mouths opening and closing in a kind of reflex. One could almost mistake these last breaths for silent kisses.

Babies arrive on their own time; there is an estimated due date, but it is the baby who releases a signal and triggers labor. Much like the white rabbit in *Alice in Wonderland,* the dying, too, are often preoccupied with time. *I'm late, I'm late for a very important date; no time to say hello, good-bye. I'm late, I'm late, I'm late.* Sometimes they wait for someone to arrive from out of town; sometimes they die when people have stepped out of the room to have a smoke.

You can't help but wonder. When I worked on the crisis team in the community, I went with a nurse to the home of a woman who seemed unable to die; a bee buzzed insistently against the inside of a sliding glass door until someone finally slid it open and let the bee out. The dying woman took her last breath when the door was opened and was gone before it closed again. To find a honey tree, says Annie Dillard, paraphrasing Thoreau, you must first catch a bee when its legs are heavy with pollen and it is ready for home. Release it and watch where it goes and follow it for as long as you can see it; wait until another bee comes, catch it, release it and watch. Keep doing that, and sure enough it will lead you home. Bee to bee leading us home. How does the spirit leave? We don't know, but every window on the hospice unit is open, just a crack, just in case.

In 1969, with her book *On Death and Dying,* Elisabeth Kübler-Ross brought the subject of death out of the privacy of medical schools and delivered it to the streets. She gave the layperson a language and a framework to understand the process of grief. Her five stages of grief provided new ways to think and speak about loss and helped give a sense of movement to the dying process. Her model is largely responsible for the ubiquitous idea of the "good death," the idea that there is a best way to approach the end of life, that we will reach *acceptance* before our last breath. A central concept of a good death is one that allows a person to die on his or her own terms, relatively pain free, with dignity. As if we have control. I was regularly asked, by family members, to describe the dying process. I would tell them about how people often lapse into a coma in the days preceding death and how breath moves from the deep and regular to the shallow and intermittent. I would explain apnea and how many people hold their breath for long periods of time, up to three minutes sometimes, and how all others in the room also hold their breath until the gasping breath breaks the silence in the room.

I would explain that people rarely die in the space between breaths, that they return to the body as if they have been on a practice run. I would go over the possibility that phlegm would build up, resulting in what is known as a "death rattle," a term that invokes a kind of dread, a term that conjures up scenes like the one Dostoevsky described in *Crime and Punishment:* "She sank more and more into uneasy delirium. At times she shuddered, turned her eyes from side to side, recognized everyone for a minute, but at once sank into delirium again. Her breathing was hoarse and difficult; there was a sort of rattle in her throat." I would talk about how the hands and feet get cold as blood leaves the extremities and pools around the heart and lungs in a last attempt to protect the vital organs and how those hands and feet turn blue shortly before death. And I would talk about how breath leaves the body, how it moves from the chest to the throat to little fish breaths at the end.

For a long time this work was for me a calling: not religious, not selfless. I left hospice three years ago after nearly twenty years. I can't say that I've ever come up with an adequate answer for the questions about God and fairness from the man whose wife lay dying as the cherry blossoms drifted in through the open window. The closest I've come is my own realization of what hospice work asks of us: that we enter the darkness without a map of the way home, that we accompany people as far as we can. "Closure," says a friend of mine, "is a pile of crap." We go on with the dead inside us. My brother, the woman whose bones broke like twigs, the boy dying of AIDS. My mother. The innumerable others.

Eve Joseph *grew up in North Vancouver. Her first book of poetry,* The Startled Heart, *was published by Oolichan Press in 2004 and nominated for the Dorothy Livesay Award. Her second book,* The Secret Signature of Things, *came out with Brick Books in the spring of 2010. She recently received the 2010 P. K. Page Founder's Award for poetry and was short-listed for the 2009 CBC Literary Awards in the creative nonfiction category.*

"Yellow Taxi" is a runner-up for the *Creative Nonfiction* Best Essay Award, chosen by the editors of *Creative Nonfiction.*

Wake-Up Call

CATHERINE A. MUSEMECHE

When surgeon Catherine A. Musemeche's mother's aneurysm ruptures, Musemeche goes from being a physician to being a worried daughter, and must balance her professional medical knowledge with faith in other doctors and her human capacity for hope.

I can hear something beeping downstairs. Is it the pager, the cell phone, a smoke alarm running low on power? It's five in the morning; why would anyone be calling me so early? I wasn't on call last night, but maybe somebody has paged me by mistake.

I get up, go to the bathroom, and start down the stairs. Next to the patio door, I see my tennis shoes, caked with dried grass from a round of golf yesterday. I open the door and look out at Puget Sound and the light, early-morning mist. I knock the shoes together and watch the grass drift down to the street below. Whatever's making the noise is still chirping like a dying bird. It could only be the pager, running out of juice. A thought flashes in my mind, jolting me to my senses: *Mom.* Something is terribly wrong.

Five years earlier, my mother called me at work.

"My doctor says I have an aneurysm," she said.

"What kind of aneurysm?" I asked.

"In my aorta," she said. "He says it starts above my kidneys and goes into my chest."

I drove to my hometown of Orange, Texas, and looked at the CT scans with her and the surgeon who had made the diagnosis. My mother had an aneurysm ight, not big enough to operate on yet, but big enough to worry about just ne same. Orange had sprung up on the Texas-Louisiana border during World War II as a petrochemical hub that supplied the defense industry. For several decades, however, it had been in decline. Hotels were converted to assisted living facilities. Most of downtown was boarded up or bulldozed, and the next generations were migrating to urban centers to find jobs and better schools. There was a small community hospital in town, but it was not equipped to handle the kind of operation my mother would need. The next step was for her to see a vascular surgeon in a city nearby, just in case there was an emergency.

"What happened?" I had asked her over the phone later.

"He wanted to operate right away," she said. "But not before he told me everything that could go wrong after the operation. I could wind up on dialysis, have a stroke, or wake up paralyzed. Oh, and I could bleed to death on the table."

"What did you tell him?" I asked.

"I told him I would think it over," she said.

Eventually she got an appointment with an aneurysm specialist in Houston. He told her nothing needed to be done right away. They would monitor the size with an ultrasound every six months. This was something she could live with. No cutting. No complications. No drastic decisions to be made. It was an approach that allowed her to return to life as she knew it with no compromise.

I knew about aneurysms, of course. Every surgeon does. When I was a general surgery resident, I had assisted on the repair of several ruptured "triple A's"—abdominal aortic aneurysms. All three patients had been transferred by Life Flight helicopter and taken directly to the operating room. There we had unzipped their trunks from breastbone to pelvis and scooped out blood with quart-sized stainless steel buckets.

In every case, it was the same drill: eventually we would get the blood out, move the intestine out of the way, and find the aorta blown out like a rusted wall in a sewer main. Years of unchecked blood pressure and dietary excess had caused this life-threatening collusion of erosion and blockage. Now, all that was left was a thinned-out sleeve of crusted calcifications and cholesterol sludge, thick like paste wax. The aorta, the main thoroughfare of the vascular tree, was damaged beyond repair. It would have to be replaced with a woven Dacron tube, if somewhere in the debris we could find a rim of tissue sturdy enough to sew it to. If we weren't that lucky, we would have to open the chest and attach the tube closer to the heart. While we fought the technical side of this nightmare, the anesthesiologist was holding down the physiologic front with vast quantities of blood products and medications to prop up the blood pressure. It was always a chaotic race to the finish. The sooner the repair was done, the sooner we could unclamp the aorta and reestablish blood flow to the lower half of the body.

My three patients survived, but not without extended stays in the ICU, failed kidneys, dead and damaged colons, and countless other near-death ordeals. It was months before any of them left the hospital.

Over time, every untreated aneurysm enlarges, and when it passes the three-inch mark, the risk of rupture increases exponentially. At the time of diagnosis, my mother's aneurysm was about two inches in diameter. If she lived long enough, it would surely grow large enough to raise the risk of rupture to the danger level, but no one could predict when. It was like living in the shadow of Mount Saint Helens. Everyone knows that someday it almost certainly will erupt again, but no one knows when or what the consequences will be.

Having the diagnosis didn't change my mother. She carried on with her routine. She was a whirlwind in the kitchen, cooking and cleaning. She chased dogs and grandchildren around the yard. She dug up trees and pulled weeds. She kept living.

And before we knew it, five years of normal, everyday life had passed. Around that time she decided she didn't need to go back to Houston anymore. Whether it was out of a sense that she had come out ahead by avoiding surgery or whether she was, by then, fully insulated by denial, I didn't know.

She never brought up the aneurysm, and if I did, I was met by a short "I'm fine."

Subject closed.

I skip through a string of missed calls on my cell phone and hit redial when I come to my sister's number. She's in the car driving through the endless sprawl of Houston toward Orange, a hundred miles away. Between sobs she tells me the news. The aneurysm is leaking. They are making arrangements to fly my mother to Houston.

"Which way do I go?" she asks.

I know she is asking something more than which direction to go. What do you do when the life of the most important person in the world is seeping away, drop by drop, and you can't do a thing to stop it?

My sister is an ICU nurse. She and I both know that for some patients in this situation, the bleeding is a steady trickle. For others, the weakened wall gives way like a levy in a flood, spilling a person's entire blood volume into the abdominal cavity within minutes. And we wonder: Will our mother even live to get loaded onto the helicopter? If she does, will she bleed out somewhere over the Houston Ship Channel? Will she make it to Houston only to die on the table?

Minutes later the world's slowest cab driver is trying to find his way to the Seattle-Tacoma airport. As we putter down the highway through the vestiges of fog and a steady rain, I tell him which way to go and that I've got to catch a plane, but still he is driving too slowly. If I have to, I will throw him out of the car and drive myself. Doctor mode is completely out the window by now. A feeling of absolute desperation like I have never known before has come over me. My mother is dying, and I must get home.

I am the last person on the plane, crammed into a middle seat. I sit between strangers, unable to stop crying. I wish I could explain, but, of course, that would be impossible. I can't speak, much less tell them how my mother comforted me when I couldn't pass swimming lessons and my sister went ahead without me, about all the late nights she spent sewing costumes for my ballet recitals. I can't tell them how she patiently taught me to read and write and drove me to the library every day or how she fed me her fried chicken and cantaloupe when I came home from college. I could never tell them what they would need to know to understand where I am going on this trip.

I wonder if this is what profound grief feels like, a kind of grief I have never known. I've avoided it up to now, but I have seen it before, in the eyes of my patients' families. I have been on the other side, silent and remorseful, helpless to intervene. I'm not ready to join the club of those who have lost someone who cannot be replaced, someone who means the world. I feel like I'm being pulled down a long dark tunnel to a place I don't want to go. Two things are quite clear to me: I can't stop it, and I don't get a choice. I hate this feeling.

The flight attendant starts handing me things: a cereal bowl, a banana, a box of cornflakes. I don't want any of it. I can't eat or read or listen to music. I can only do this one thing. I can only think about my mother. If I try to do anything else, I think I will lose my last remaining connection to her. If I concentrate hard enough, maybe I can keep her alive.

Did she make it to Houston? Is she in the operating room now? I think of each step that must be done right for her to make it. First of all, there must be an operating room set up with the proper equipment. There must be O negative blood in the refrigerator, fresh frozen plasma and platelets. A vascular surgeon must be gowned, gloved, and ready to open the moment she rolls through the door. The anesthesiologist must be fast enough to keep up with a torrential amount of blood loss.

I want to tell the surgeons what they already know. The aorta is the main blood vessel in the body. For goodness sake, please pay attention. Keep the outflow to the kidneys intact. Don't knock off her intestine. Make sure her blood pressure is high enough so she doesn't have a stroke on the table. There are numerous opportunities for error, and I think of all of them.

If she is going to survive, someone like me, or better, has to step up and orchestrate a miracle. She is flying, and I am flying. By the time I land it could all be over. Is she still alive, even now? Not knowing is an unbearable state. I am barely breathing when I walk off the plane and turn on my cell phone.

I take a cab straight to the hospital. My family is gathered in a private waiting room—my father, my brothers and sisters. By now I know my mother has made it out of surgery and is in the ICU. They are relieved, almost joyful, but I'm not. Nothing that has happened so far changes the fact that a ruptured aneurysm carries a mortality rate of 70–90 percent. The odds are still against us.

I know the surgeon has given promising news, but I also know how doctors talk to families who are in shock. They try to give some good news even in the bleakest of scenarios. They try to offer some hope. I'm sure he told them the operation was a success. After all, they did manage to get the bleeding under control and sew the graft in place without losing her. The real definition of success, however, depends on how—and whether—she comes through the next few days. I have seen what survival looks like in this situation. If she makes it, she will never be the same.

I find my sister back in my mother's room, taking care of her in the same ICU where she normally works. She looks at me like we share a secret. We knew this day was coming, but we didn't know it would look like this. My mother has a foot-long incision running from her chest to her abdomen. Tubes drain blood from her chest and abdomen. Bags of blood hang from both sides of the bed and drip into large tubes snaking into her neck and groin. A ventilator breathes for her. Intravenous medications control her heart rate and blood pressure. She'll probably need dialysis in a day or two. Finally, I am looking it in the face—the picture I have been dreading for years. There is no escaping the reality now. My mother is in critical condition, possibly near death. She has to pull out of a deep hole if she is ever going to leave here.

Later that night, after the rest of my family has drifted away, my sister is still there, working alongside the other nurses. I stand in the doorway watching her run from one end of the room to the other, taking down IV bags, hanging new ones, printing out lab results, checking my mother's pulses. She doesn't know how to stop.

Finally, I walk up to her and I take her by the shoulders.

"You have to go home," I tell her. "I'll stay."

Tears well up in her eyes. She's no longer a nurse. She's just another drained and helpless family member, like me.

My mother is in and out of consciousness for hours. Sometimes she wakes up and makes hand motions. I'm not sure what she wants. I moisten her lips with a wet towel, put eye drops in her eyes, and rub lotion on her hands. These could be the last hours I spend with her. Whatever happens, I will remember them the rest of my life.

I wonder if she knows what time of day it is now. Does she know I'm spending the night? If she does, she surely knows she's in deep trouble. Does my presence comfort her or scare her out of her wits?

When she goes back to sleep, I pull the reclining chair up next to her bed and turn it around so I am facing the monitors. I can't help thinking of the other times in my life I have spent the night in this same hospital, taking care of some of the sickest people I can remember.

I remember an elderly woman with failing kidneys who developed uncontrollable bleeding from her gastrointestinal tract. The chief resident and I were trying to stabilize her so we could take her to the operating room. She had been sick a long time, and it was difficult to find a vein. We stuck her everywhere, trying to get another line in so we could administer blood products and medications. We stuck her in the groin, the chest, all up and down her arms and legs. Occasionally she would withdraw, moaning. The next thing I knew, she coded, and we started what was to be the first of many rounds of CPR. After the second or third round I was sensing the hopelessness of the situation. By that time the woman was comatose.

"How long are we going to keep doing this?" I asked the chief resident.

"As long as she keeps coming back we're going to keep going," he said. "I'm going to get some sleep for a couple of hours. Let me know if anything changes."

I stayed at the woman's bedside until morning, occasionally sitting down in a rocking chair for brief periods when she stabilized. But then her heart would start to slow, and I would jump up again and start CPR. The air was saturated with the stench of blood mixed with feces as the bleeding continued. I had to transfuse her to keep up with what we were losing, but that only made her electrolytes worse, and then her heart would start to slow again. It was becoming obvious how this was going to end. She was never going to be ready for the operating room.

Her death, hours later, was the conclusion to one of the worst nights of my life. I had participated in a full-blown flail—a sequence of medical maneuvers that couldn't possibly be successful but are performed against all better judgment. I felt terrible about it—for the patient, who deserved better, and for those of us who participated. Whatever comes next for my mother, I hope she is not flogged this way with painful procedures that cannot save her.

I stare up at the green, red, and yellow tracings on the monitors above my mother's bed. Doctors, nurses, and respiratory therapists come and go. I get up, reach under her blankets, and check the pulses in her legs and the output from the chest tubes. I suction her mouth and give her a sip of water. Eventually, I lie back, tuck the pillow behind my head, and pull the sheet over me. I am not the least bit tired. An endless stream of patients is marching through my thoughts, a parade of those who could not be saved. Every single one of them was just as bad off as my mother is now.

I have seen it over and over. There is a limit to what we can do to help people who make it to the ICU at this stage of life. She is getting the best of care with one-on-one nursing. Well-trained doctors are measuring, calculating, and performing tests. We want to believe she is safe here, but I know better. There is a final common pathway for older patients like my mother. She was in shock for hours and spent even more hours in a huge life-saving operation. Her organs have been severely taxed and are now susceptible to failure. They could go one by one or they might all crash at the same time. She would never survive it.

I want to believe the doctors will do what is best for her, but I know even that isn't always guaranteed. Sometimes their judgment is clouded by ego or the inability to face the possibility of failure. I remember taking care of an elderly man with extensive vascular disease. The blockages in his arteries were threatening the viability of his leg and causing him severe pain. The only way the leg could be saved was with a bypass operation. He was eighty years old, anemic, and a Jehovah's Witness. His religion strictly prohibited a blood transfusion. His blood count was already low, and he was going to lose more blood. He and his family were facing a difficult choice. Did they risk an operation to save the leg? It might not be successful. He might lose the leg no matter what we did, and of course there was going to be more blood loss if he had the bypass. They needed reliable information so they could make as close to an informed decision as was possible. The attending surgeon met with them. He reassured them and told them everything would be fine. The man might need to be in the ICU a few days, but he should pull through. They should at least give the bypass a try.

As the resident it was my job to assist. There was more scarring than expected from a previous operation. Working our way through the dense tissue took time and created more bleeding. I started counting the blood-stained sponges in the bucket at my feet. There were too many. We were losing too much blood. I asked if we should change our strategy. Maybe we wouldn't complete the operation. Maybe he would lose the leg, but at least our patient wouldn't die a cold, lonely death on the table.

The surgeon, however, saw the situation differently. He was confident we could safely complete the bypass. But as the hours ticked by the sponges kept dropping into the pail. The patient's blood pressure started to drop. The EKG showed signs of cardiac ischemia. There weren't enough red blood cells to carry oxygen to the heart. The anesthesiologist started to fidget. He opened up the intravenous fluids and told the surgeon to hurry up.

When we finally finished, our patient was barely alive. His blood pressure was dangerously low and his heart was racing, pumping his few remaining red blood cells as fast as it could go. We ran as we wheeled him back to the ICU. When the stat labs came back, he had the lowest blood count I had ever seen in a living person, a hemoglobin incompatible with life. He was comatose. His heart muscle was dying, and he was going to die unless we acted quickly. But we couldn't. The family was not going to consent to a transfusion. They were firm in this decision, but it was clear they felt betrayed. Death was always a risk, but they never expected it would come to this, their loved one bleeding to death in a poorly planned operation that took much too long.

The next thing I know the night nurse is turning on the lights. It's 6 A.M., and she has brought a pan of soapy water to my mother's bedside. Visiting hours are over for now, and I have to leave. I am heavy with exhaustion as I walk out and head for the elevator.

I don't know how long my mother has or where this will end. There were times last night when I was almost able to act like a normal family member. I want her to recover, and I cling to every sign that she might. She has woken up. She has tried to write messages on a clipboard. She has used hand signals and sipped water. She is very much alive at this moment, and she still has a chance. But I am not just her daughter. I am also a surgeon, armed with too much medical knowledge. It gets in the way of my ability to hope.

I replay the previous five years, from the moment of my mother's diagnosis to the present. I second guess myself, wondering if she should have had the operation sooner. There might have been some way to avoid where we are now.

But where would we be instead?

Like everyone else in this situation, I have had to learn the difficult truth. We don't get to script these endings. We make the best decisions we can with whatever information we have, but, in the end, death chooses its own time and circumstance, as it has done with my mother. It leaves us with questions, doubts, and what ifs. All we can do is hang on for the wild and blistering ride and learn to live with the questions.

***Catherine A. Musemeche** is a pediatric surgeon and an attorney and lives in Austin, Texas. She divides her time between writing, teaching, and practicing medicine. Although she has authored numerous scientific publications, this is her first published creative nonfiction essay.*

Simple Gifts

BEECHER GROGAN

For Beecher Grogan, the relationship between the living and the dying is a complex interplay of intense emotion. The dying need to know the living will be all right, and the living need to come to terms with letting a loved one go.

For my twelve-year-old daughter, death was a welcome friend. She cried out for it and embraced it when it came to her. The most selfless gesture I have made in my life was giving her my blessing to go in peace. It went against every fiber in my being to do so, but she desperately needed to know I would be all right, that I would somehow continue living and breathing without my heart.

Her death has taught me many things, but the most powerful is that although Lucy was born *to* me, she was not *of* me and did not belong to me. She existed in another place before we met, identified me as a channel and a partner, and came *to* me, then *through* me. Her death was a birth of another sort. There was the same intense and searing physical pain—though this time, she was the one required to bear it. And just as she did at her birth, Lucy at her death made a passage from a place of familiarity to another place, strange and unknown. For me it was a surreal experience. On the one hand I was witnessing a tragic and incomprehensible event, and on the other, I seemed to be floating above it, detached and in awe of the power of death.

Lucy was an active and healthy eight-year-old girl until the summer of 2002, when she began to have unusual and seemingly unrelated symptoms, including a stiff neck, pain in her left leg, a case of strep throat that was resistant to treatment, and an upset stomach. When she appeared pale one morning, we called our pediatrician's office in West Newbury, Massachusetts, for a same-day appointment. She was seen by our nurse practitioner, who had known Lucy since she was two years old. This consistency of care was critical in securing an early and accurate diagnosis. The practitioner seemed concerned and asked me to take Lucy to the local hospital right away for blood work. That evening at 9:30 I received a call from Lucy's pediatrician. He was reluctant to tell me what was wrong until they had more tests done, but when I pressed him for more information he took a deep breath and said, "We think she may have leukemia."

Those six words were the opening scene to a horror film in which we lived for four years. Lucy was diagnosed a few days later at a Boston hospital with acute myeloid leukemia, a rare form of blood cancer more often seen in adults. Her chances of survival were the same as a coin toss—she had a fifty-fifty chance of surviving five years, with a 50 percent chance of the cancer relapsing. Her best option for treatment was a bone marrow transplant from a sibling donor, but her four-year-old sister was not a match, so instead she went through six rounds of highly toxic chemotherapy over an eleven-month period.

Lucy experienced eighteen months in remission after her treatment was completed, during which she suffered from depression and intense survivor guilt (fifteen of her closest hospital friends had died). In early January 2005, after new snow, I took Lucy and her little sister, Jane, out to the orchard near our home, to do some sledding between the rows of peach trees. I was three months pregnant at the time and decided to wait for the kids at the bottom of the hill. Lucy normally had more energy than could be contained in one body, but that day, she climbed the hill once, slid down, and then sat quietly with me on her sled, saying she was too tired to climb the hill again. It was too cold to be sitting still in the windy field, so we went back to the house. I feared her cancer was back—and in our hearts, I think we both knew it was. I took her in for blood work, and we were right. One little cancerous white blood cell had escaped the six blasts of toxic chemotherapy and lived to multiply profusely. Over time, they crowded out the red blood cells and caused her exhaustion. The monster was back.

This time Lucy's only option was to have a bone marrow transplant from an unrelated donor, a risky and often very painful ordeal. Lucy had another round of chemo and was brought into remission. She was then prepped for her transplant with high doses of chemo and radiation to kill all of her own bone marrow, then received her bone marrow transplant in March 2006.

What followed were sixteen months of unyielding physical and emotional torture. Lucy developed chronic graft versus host disease (GVHD), which occurs in 10 percent of transplant patients. We had been warned of this and were told if it occurred, Lucy would wish she had died. With GVHD, the new immune system (the graft) does not recognize the cells of the sick patient (the host) and continually attacks the host's organs. A little bit of GVHD is a good thing—it proves that the new immune system is working—and happens up to 80 percent of the time in bone marrow transplant patients. In Lucy's chronic situation, the GVHD started with her skin but then continued to attack every organ in her body.

By July 2006, Lucy was transferred to a children's hospital in Boston. The GVHD was attacking Lucy's liver and no longer responded to the usual treatment of high-dose steroids. She spent six weeks in the hospital, and despite her oncologist's best efforts and consultations with experts around the country, Lucy's condition continued to deteriorate. Her doctors were still hopeful and continued trying more and more aggressive treatments while Lucy grew more and more distant. On July 21, my sister came to be with Lucy for the day so that I could meet the local vet at our home in Salisbury, Massachusetts, to take care of routine shots for our dog, cats, and horses. Lucy called while we were working with Lucy's horse, and I didn't answer the phone. When the vet left I went into the house to clean up so I could go to the hospital. I listened to my voicemail and heard a tone in Lucy's voice I had never heard before. She did not mince words. She said, "Mom. I'm done."

I got into the car and raced down the highway toward Boston, calling to let her know I was on my way. Lucy didn't want to talk, so I spoke briefly with my sister and told her I was coming as fast as I could. Lucy's message scared me. Halfway down to Boston, the heavens opened, and it rained in sheets for the rest of the ride. Despite my panic, I felt an intense and fierce concentration take over. I was determined to get there safely, despite the poor visibility and enormous puddles flooding the sides of the highway. Traffic was backed up, and I was in the middle of Tobin Bridge when a massive lightning storm came up. I started to pray. Lucy needed me desperately, and I couldn't get to my girl. It was a simple prayer, "Please, God. Please, God. Please, God . . . ," over and over.

The moment I walked into the room, drenched and shaken by the storm outside—literally, at that moment—she sat up in bed and started vomiting blood. She'd waited for me to come to take over from my little sister, her aunt, and then she went. It took two and a half hours and was traumatizing to all those present.

When death—suddenly and with very little warning—entered Lucy's hospital room that stormy, electrified July evening, the doctors and nurses who fight death every day didn't recognize it at first. Because it was early evening, the attending had gone home for the day, and we landed in the hands of a young and inexperienced resident who was terrified and overwhelmed by the situation. Lucy was in such severe pain that he ordered X-rays at her bedside. I remember pleading quietly with the radiologist, "Please, please, be gentle with her."

Lucy was furious and glared at me in disbelief when she recognized that the purpose of the sudden chaos was to keep her alive. She knew she was dying, and she was disappointed the adults in the room could not accept and support her wish to be done with her struggle. She tore at the feeding tube that snaked along her cheek and into her nose—taped generously with pale pink adhesive. She clawed at the tape and bandages that protected the IV in her wrist. At first the nurse tried to restrain her, to keep the IV and feeding tube protected. I understood that I had to support Lucy in her rage and asked the nurse to allow Lucy to remove the tube and the IV. We recognized that she was casting aside, in one heroic last stand, all the evidence of her illness. If she could have reached it, she would have torn out her central line, a plastic double lumen line inserted surgically into the major artery that goes into the heart. It, or one of its many cousins, dangled for years from Lucy's chest and provided consistent access to blood products. It was the point of entry for most of the medicines and treatments, including her bone marrow transplant. Later, after Lucy's death, I told the nurses how important it was to remove Lucy's central line while she lay in the morgue. She didn't want any trace of her illness to be cremated with her.

She had lost so much of herself, and she resented and despised all the plastic bits and pieces that are the badges of cancer patients around the world.

As Lucy began to die, she entered into a state of panic. She and I had been pleading with the resident to give her more pain medication, but he refused, because it would compromise her breathing. Her pain was so acute, and her need to die was so immediate that she literally begged her doctor to kill her.

The pale-faced young resident was stricken when she looked at him and screamed, "Kill me—kill me, now. Help me die!"

He replied quietly, "I am doing everything I can to help you, Lucy."

What he didn't understand was that their two ideas of "help" were at opposite ends of the spectrum. He was trying to help Lucy live while she was asking him to help her die. I asked him to kneel down beside her and explain to her why he couldn't facilitate her death. He knelt down, and with his head near hers, he looked into her eyes and explained that he was not allowed to help her die. We then asked him to leave, and Lucy turned to me to ask me to help where the doctor had failed. "Mama, help me."

I hovered over Lucy and whispered to her, encouraging her to relax and assuring her I was there to help her. We were experiencing the most intensely private and personal moment of our lives together in a fish bowl. The doctors had left us alone, and one of our favorite nurses had taken over. She came and went silently—there when we needed her and in the background when we didn't. Years later, during a visit to the hospital and to the room where Lucy had died—room 750—I learned that this nurse had bodily blocked the door when the resident and another doctor had tried to come in to persuade me to allow them to take Lucy to the ICU to be intubated. I was told that she had said, "This woman has just made the most difficult decision of her life. Leave them alone."

While this was going on outside her room, I explained to Lucy that her body and her mind had become distant from each other because of the years of cancer treatment. I assured her that her body knew how to die, and if it was time for her to go, she didn't need anyone's help. I encouraged her to relax and breathe deeply so that her mind and body could connect. I told her she could tell her body, which had been fighting valiantly for so long to live, that it was all right to let go. I talked quietly about letting go of living and being open to dying. I wasn't able to hold her because she was in such extreme pain, but I was close enough for her to feel the heat from my body and hear the love and calm in my voice.

Very soon after, Lucy had a seizure and lost consciousness. When she seized, her teeth clenched down on the hard plastic suction tube we were using to suction blood from her mouth. Without thinking, I reached into her mouth with my thumb and finger and tried to pry the tube from her teeth, because I was afraid she'd choke on the plastic if it broke off in her mouth. Lucy was actively dying, and I was trying to prevent her from choking. Lucy's father, whom I had been calling repeatedly and had been unable to reach, arrived at this moment. Lucy had asked to be baptized a few days before, so in her last moments we called a minister friend, and she guided Lucy's dad through the baptism over the phone. Lucy was baptized by her own father, with bottled water from her bedside. I have always been thankful that he did not have to witness the full trauma of Lucy's last hours and that my daughter Jane was visiting friends in Maine during this last struggle. Although Jane regrets not having the chance to say goodbye to her sister, I am relieved that she won't have to live with the recurring images and sounds of Lucy's excruciating death experience.

A few days before her death, Lucy turned her face to the wall and her back to the world. She shut me out, which she had never done throughout the four years of cancer treatment. It was so unlike her, and I knew that something was terribly wrong.

In my heart, I knew what the trouble was, but it was the one thing I did not ever want to know, agree to, or acknowledge. The day before Lucy died I asked a hospital employee, a family liaison, to help me talk to Lucy about feeling "done." I needed someone to approach the topic so Lucy wouldn't have to wrestle with these feelings by herself. We started the conversation using words like *feeling done,* and Lucy started to pay attention. This dull, listless child, once a radiant girl—exuberant and fairly bursting with life—sparked and turned to me. "You're talking about dying, right?" When I answered, "Yes," she sat bolt upright and said, "Good, because I can't live like this another week."

Then she brought her face close to mine, looked deep into my eyes, and said, "Mama, I can't live like this another *day*."

I said, " Okay. I know. It's all right."

Lucy had never cried in front of a doctor or nurse. Her stoicism amazed me. Now, she asked the family liaison to leave and started to weep. I hugged her and then held up two fingers, intertwined. "Lucy," I said, "we have always been like this."

She looked at me with sadness, then said in a voice full of tears, "But I don't want to be like this," and she flung her arms open wide with her hands as far apart as they could go.

I had given this subject four tormented years of thought and had my answer ready. What began as my stubborn mantra of "Dying is NOT an option," slowly and with much effort had become acceptance of the possibility that Lucy could very well die and that I had better learn to accept that her survival was not in the realm of my control. It took an enormous amount of opening up and letting go to learn to live with this powerlessness, but in the end I believe this acceptance that I was not in charge helped me be a better mother to Lucy when she needed to go.

"Lucy, I always thought that if I died before you I would wrap myself around you like a shawl and I would be with you always. If you die before me, I think you'll sit right here, on my right shoulder, and we will always be together. Nothing can separate the two of us," I told her that night.

This child, with a heart so pure and good, confessed her secret to me. "The only reason I am still alive is that I didn't want to let you down."

I realized then that my daughter, who was suffering with constant, indescribable pain was only holding on, against all odds, out of the sheer force of her indomitable will, for fear of disappointing her mother.

I remember telling her, "Sweetie, you could never let me down. Dying isn't letting me down. Freeing yourself from this nightmare isn't letting me down. I can't ask you to live for me. If you are done and if you need to go, I will be all right." The fact is, I wasn't all right. I am still not all right. While we spoke that day, I wanted to comfort her by letting her speak freely about very difficult feelings. I resisted the urge to tell her she would be all right and that her fighting spirit would be restored. I believed I still had at least three months to help her recover and begin to heal. I'd seen this child approach death three times over the years. Each time, she had mystified her doctors by turning abruptly on her heel at the last minute and returning to us. But the next evening, true to her word, she died. She was stable, and then suddenly she wasn't.

Later, when I needed to know why her death was so excruciating, the chief of pediatric oncology at a major Boston hospital told me he believes deaths that occur suddenly are always very painful. He believes when the spirit is torn suddenly from the body, it causes great pain. He told me that during his thirty-year career in pediatric oncology he had seen it over and over again. When a life ebbs away, it is peaceful and painless. But deaths like Lucy's are always intensely painful.

Three years after my daughter's death, I began working with a woman healer who has helped me view Lucy's death from different angles— allowing me to interpret its meaning differently. I had been struggling to absorb the reality of Lucy's death and was caught in despair that was frightening in its grip and intensity. I was not suicidal, but I wished many times a day—for a very long time—that I could just be dead. It felt absurd that I was expected to go on living without Lucy. I felt as if I weighed one thousand pounds. I moved slowly and in a fog. My former passion for life and enthusiasm were gone, and it took everything I had to function just well enough to care for my other two children, who were one and eight at the time of Lucy's death.

Looking back, I struggle with every decision I made that night. Lucy had demanded that I fill out a do-not-resuscitate form, which she'd learned about during those other close brushes with death over the years. She was adamant about it, and I honored her wish, but later it tormented me. I went back to the hospital a few weeks later and spoke to her attending physician. I asked if we could have prolonged her life if we had moved her to the ICU and put her on life support. His answer was very clear: "We would have prolonged her death, not her life." He assured me there was nothing anyone could have done to save Lucy's life that night. In fact, no one knew exactly *why* she had died.

Through the conversations and healing work I did with the shaman, I began to view Lucy's illness and death as part of a broader picture—part of a spiritual, iterative process—and I was better able to absorb and encompass the loss of her, shifting slowly from despondency to a sense of gratitude and exhilaration that she had lived at all, that she had chosen me as her mother, that she'd shared her knowledge about the power of living life with love and had given my spirit the information and the nudge it needed to fulfill its purpose. She was a selfless, generous child who derived joy from giving to others. I imagine her joy now, as she watches me summon and embrace the courage to return to my life.

In the four years of Lucy's struggle with cancer, navigating our way through the world of life-threatening illness, I learned so much. There was constant fear and anxiety but some beauty, too—beauty in being forced to live in a moment-to-moment appreciation of the wonder and the gift of our children. Beauty in the connection and the love between our children and the families who lived there in the trenches together. Beauty in the grace with which our children bore suffering and tried to protect us from the darkest places. After the death of a child, some turn away and never look back. Some raise money or awareness and fight to cure the disease. Some find ways to help those currently suffering from cancer. Some need to return to that world and work there, because the wisdom was so hard-won that it must find an outlet to be put to good use.

I am in that last category. I paid dearly for the lessons I have learned and now must make something beautiful emerge from my daughter's experience. She was the "Queen of the Silver Lining" and often found it in her illness. To a dying friend—a sister in spirit and someone she looked up to, Lucy had said, "Emily, if I had to choose between never having cancer and not knowing you or having cancer and having you in my life, I would choose to have cancer."

And this beautiful friend, eighteen-year-old Emily, when all hope for a cure was gone and she was days away from her own death said, "I'm not afraid of dying. What frightens me is that I don't know how I am going to help Lucy when I'm gone."

Later that same evening I had to give Emily permission to die when her parents couldn't. Dying children need to know their parents will be all right when they go. They hold on for us far beyond their endurance, when they are desperate to be done with their struggle. Many parents understandably cannot give this blessing. Many parents throughout the cancer treatment can't acknowledge to themselves that their child might die. Oncology wards are full of superstition. Magical thinking prevails, and children sense they are not allowed to voice their own fears or concerns, knowing how upset their parents get by any expression of doubt or negativity.

But it's *not* negative; it's realistic to have these fears, and I think the children on these units need to be allowed, even encouraged, to talk about death and dying. What is it? Where do you go? What does it mean? Why did they get cancer? Was it because they stole a butterfly-shaped hair clip in second grade? Will they die, or will they survive? Will they ever feel normal again? Will they ever fit in?

In the four years of Lucy's illness, at two major Boston hospitals we never saw a support group for the children. There was one for parents that met weekly, and there was a monthly one for the parents who had lost their children, but no support group *for* the children. There are social workers to talk with the children, but the children were never given a forum of their own where they could speak freely about their hopes and fears. And the social workers are employed by and, therefore, are loyal to the hospital. We found that we had far better support and understanding from mental health professionals who were *not* employed by the hospital. Although I believe the social workers meant well, it was our experience that they weren't able to be strong advocates for the ill children when problems or disagreements with doctors or hospital policies arose, which they often did.

Before Lucy died, we established a nonprofit organization in her honor called Lucy's Love Bus, whose mission is to ease the suffering of pediatric cancer patients by providing free integrative therapies such as massage, acupuncture, and therapeutic horseback riding for children with cancer and children coping with the late effects of cancer treatment. We strive to educate the medical community regarding the benefits of integrative therapies that reduce stress, manage pain, and improve the overall well-being of sick children and their families. Lucy received integrative therapy treatments such as acupuncture, massage, and Reiki during her illness, and it was her dream to provide these services to children with cancer. Very near the time of her death, she dictated a letter to her primary oncologist that now inspires the work we are doing through her nonprofit.

Dear Dr. Steadman,

When you look at the sick children follow them to the place they can speak to you in. Notice their bodies are two things, love and illness, and help them remember the love and not the sickness. The Healing is [in] knowing who you were, not what you might be. I love you like a father. I wanted you to be the one who healed my body and my body trusted you, and I want you—you have to promise me now—that you will make yourself know, you did heal me.

We are honored by you.
L.G.

Through the volunteer work I do at Lucy's Love Bus, I help sick children remember who they were before they were sick and help them connect with the spirit within them that is still flourishing. I strive to help oncologists understand the emotional and spiritual needs of the children whose bodies they are treating. I help families who are facing a child's impending death support their child in the passage from this life to the next. I try to help families who have lost their children find new hope.

I noticed immediately after Lucy's death that people could not comprehend how a long drawn-out fight against cancer could end in a death that was so *sudden.* What people failed to realize is that until the moment Lucy drew her last breath—even a few minutes beyond that point—we all hoped she would live. Anyone who knew Lucy—the absolute spark and spunk of her—could not believe she would not prevail.

When I was living in the moment-to-moment fear of my child's death, an experience our cancer community called "living grief," I could scarcely allow myself to ponder the question of Lucy's survival. The slightest, fleeting moment of doubt caused me intense feelings of guilt, and I feared the mere thought of Lucy's death could somehow make it happen.

This is torturous, because parents of a sick child need to be able to express these fears without feeling they are somehow failing their child. The outside world wants us to bear our lot bravely, with constant and vigilant stoicism, and they want us to make it easy for everyone else by consistently showing optimism and faith. This creates a sad and lonely isolation and alienation for many parents when what they really need is permission to voice their deepest darkest fear—that their baby might die, and there's not a thing they can do about it.

The morning after Lucy died, I sat in her room at the hospital with the resident from the night before. We sat next to each other on the hospital bed—shoulder to shoulder—and he wept. I was numb, and he was raw. Lucy's death was his first, and he felt the loss keenly. I remember trying to comfort him and was touched by his sorrow. I asked that he never forget Lucy and the lesson he learned from her the night before: When a child says she is dying, it is best to listen. If not with your scientific mind, then with your warm and beating heart.

Beecher Grogan *is the volunteer director of a nonprofit organization founded in 2006 by her daughter, Lucy Grogan. Lucy's Love Bus delivers comfort to children with cancer through free integrative therapies such as acupuncture, massage, yoga, meditation, and therapeutic horseback riding. Grogan is committed to healing the medical community and strives to educate physicians regarding the benefits of integrative therapies that help reduce stress, manage pain, and improve the overall well-being of sick children.*

Living and Dying Well

THERESE ZINK

There are aspects of healing and death we can control and those we cannot. After a workshop hosted by Elisabeth Kübler-Ross, Therese Zink realizes she has less control over her patients and events than she assumed.

Crunch. Her ribs cracked as I thrust my palms down on her birdlike chest. *Crunch, press, press,* try to restart her heart. She was eighty-five years old, for heaven's sake. Her skin was like tissue paper stretched over bones. She looked so frail in her hospital bed, the antiseptic smell swirling around us. It seemed cruel, inhumane. But we didn't have a code status, so my resident directed me to start CPR. And I broke her ribs. Torture, that is what it was, torture—for her and me. I did not want to do CPR; couldn't we just let her die peacefully? This was not the way to end a long life. But what could we do with a little old lady "found down"—collapsed on her back porch and discovered by a neighbor—with no identified family? It just wasn't right. But we kept at it until my resident called the code. Jane Hamilton was officially dead.

Dying is part of doctoring. As a young doctor completing a family medicine residency at the county hospital in St. Paul, Minnesota, I encountered patients like Jane and agonized about the experiences. It was the mid-1980s, and policies about dying and resuscitation were still being established. Even with the technological capabilities in medicine at that time, I needed to understand more than I'd learned in medical school about the dying process. Although we have come a long way, medical training still focuses on how to save lives, and physicians struggle with knowing how to help patients have a peaceful death. Both

DNR orders and advanced directives are commonplace, but unfortunately many physicians don't make full use of them.

Dr. Elisabeth Kübler-Ross's groundbreaking book, *On Death and Dying,* first published in 1969, synthesized the experience of two hundred terminally ill patients at the University of Chicago. Although her work was considered "soft science" because she only did interviews, she initiated a national discussion about a respectful end to life. Physicians began to talk with their patients who had terminal illnesses, like cancer, about whether or not they wanted CPR at the end of their lives. Since being established and distributed throughout the United States in the 1960s, CPR had become the standard of care to perform if a patient's heart stopped beating. But sometimes this seemed to prolong a patient's agony, especially in someone with an illness like cancer. About the same time, the hospice movement, which started in the United Kingdom, reached the United States. After the success of her book, Kübler-Ross started her own healing center and conducted workshops for both health professionals and patients around the world.

Following the death of Jane Hamilton, on the advice of a colleague and mentor, I signed up for Kübler-Ross's week-long workshop on death and dying. After a busy day in clinic, I caught an evening flight and arrived in Arizona. The workshop was held at a chemical dependency treatment complex on the outskirts of Tucson, where the residents of the center shared their ranch-style dining and conference rooms with the workshop attendees. As I waited for the front desk attendant to locate a bed for me, I shed the layers of clothing required in Minnesota's frigid temperatures—down jacket, woolen scarf, and gloves—and breathed in sage and creosote, fragrances so different from those of home.

Inside my cottage seven roommates slept in single beds; the open bed in the center of the room left for me (I learned later that three other women had come and gone from that bed before I finally claimed it at midnight). I was so tired, having spent most of the prior night admitting patients to the hospital in Minnesota, and now the full force of my exhaustion hit me. I was relieved to leave my residency and all my patient duties thirteen hundred miles away. I unpacked my suitcase and slipped into my flannel nightgown. The room felt cramped. Someone snored. Another roommate mumbled in her sleep. Near the bathroom lay a woman, bald, with the faint sour scent of sickness, probably some type of cancer. I was surprised to see someone so ill but would learn later Kübler-Ross encouraged patients and health professionals to attend the same workshops. Soon, I too snuggled under my covers and fell asleep.

The words *I can't breathe* jolted me awake. I sat up, still in doctor mode, now always in doctor mode. The clock flashed 1 A.M. I heard shouts coming from the beds near the bathroom. Someone had turned on the bathroom light. I jumped out of bed, the floor cold on my bare feet.

"I can't breathe," the bald woman panted. She had the chipmunk cheeks often caused by the medication prednisone. Propped up against pillows, she gasped for air, her hands thrashing. Her face was red like a radish with a fine sheen of sweat. "Help me, help me . . . ," she choked.

I stared at her from my position at the foot of her bed. I did not know her, did not know her medical history, but I guessed chemotherapy had caused her baldness. A ziplock bag filled with pill bottles sat on her bedside table. A folded wheelchair leaned against the wall. The woman who had been in the next bed spoke with her and tried to calm her.

I needed to do something; after all I was a doctor. I stumbled to her side and blurted, "How can I help? I'm a doctor." Her arm was clammy and sticky, like a fish.

But the bald woman was not consoled. "I can't breathe. I can't breathe. Help me. Help . . ."

My red flannel provided no protection from her panic.

My other roommates were now out of their beds, all the lights in the room turned on. We crowded around the bed like bees hovering around a hive.

"Does she have oxygen?" I asked.

"There's a physician somewhere at the retreat center," another said. "He knows something about her. I'll find him." She threw on her coat, slipped into clogs, and sprinted out the door.

The bald woman continued to thrash and cry, her face now purple. I offered water, rummaged through her pills. Damn, I thought I'd left these situations back in Minnesota. I had come to the workshop for some self-care and reflection, and now only hours after my arrival I was called into action. I resented it and at the same time felt helpless, no tools, no information.

Gasp. Pant. Thrash. Sheets twisted and mashed.

The bungalow's door swung open, and the roommate returned with a man dressed in jeans and a flannel shirt cradling an oxygen tank in his arms like an infant. He took charge. "Her name is Chloe. She has metastatic breast cancer," he said. "I've called the medics." He set the tank next to the bed and slipped a plastic mask over her face.

I stuttered that I was a doctor and could help. I had to say it twice. When he finally heard me, he smiled and directed me to wipe her forehead with a cold cloth.

I could do that; I hurried to the sink in the bathroom and returned with a cold washcloth.

Two medics burst through the door and immediately went to work. Dressed in navy blue uniforms, one carried a cardiac monitor, the other a case of medications and supplies. I squeezed against the wall to make room for them. One checked for a pulse, then wrapped the blood pressure cuff around Chloe's arm. The other unbuttoned her nightshirt, stuck pads on her chest and clipped wires to the cardiac monitor.

I felt exposed—exposed for my ineptness, exposed in my nightgown.

All eyes were watching the dark monitor that suddenly jumped to life with a beeping green fluorescent line. First, peaks of sinus tachycardia invaded the screen, a normal heart rhythm but too fast. An occasional wide squiggle indicated that something worse was looming. The tonguelike waves of ventricular tachycardia marched across, then within minutes converted to the irregular hills of ventricular fibrillation—not a good sign. Finally, flat line.

Gasp. Grunt. Chloe's body rattled the bed. The smell of a fart. Silence.

"Death has come," the doctor said and bowed his head. The medics collected their equipment and left. The doctor shook out the sheet and folded it smoothly under Chloe's chin. He said he'd send someone to collect her body. The door clicked shut behind him.

Silence. I put down the wet washcloth and looked at my roommates who kept vigil around the bed. We looked as if we'd attended a pajama party and a prank had left us all tongue-tied.

Within ten minutes the door snapped open. A salt-and-pepper-haired woman entered the room and introduced herself as Phyllis, one of the facilitators for the workshop. She smelled of patchouli and orchestrated the bathing of Chloe's body, explaining that it was a ritual that Kübler-Ross encouraged to create closure for those present at a death, a way to show respect for the deceased. She talked about Chloe's death as no coincidence but an example of *synchronicity,* when the inner and outer events in life coincide. "Your workshop has started early," she said matter-of-factly. "This week you'll figure out why you were in this room tonight." She handed out towels.

With Chloe's death my workshop began. I'd come to Arizona to learn about dying but also to have some time to myself. I did not expect to be called into action in the middle of the night before the workshop started. The burden of being a caretaker with all my current inadequacies was laid before me.

The workshop lasted for a week and included didactic information about the dying process and end-of-life care, as well as lectures from both Kübler-Ross and the physician who had attended Chloe's death. Some sessions were experiential, with opportunities to examine some of our own personal challenges, our "stuff," as they called it. Afternoons were dedicated to "mat work" where a small group worked with a therapist.

Phyllis facilitated my group. One woman banged out her anger at her absent father with a rubber mallet. Another sobbed into a pillow about the death of her child from leukemia. The rest of the group knelt or sat at the edge of the mat lending support. Sometimes it was simply witnessing "the worker's" pain; other times it was giving a hug or asking probing questions as the worker shared.

At the time this style of therapy was controversial, but Kübler-Ross believed patients often sorted through life's unfinished threads and traumas, "the stuff" of their lives, during the dying process. By helping them understand the realities of their illness and what could and could not be done to cure them, they were able to do a better job of planning how to use their final days. Working through the issues of their lives—examining old resentments and healing severed relationships—made for a more peaceful death. The experiential part of the workshop, the mat work, focused on the living. Kübler-Ross emphasized that we did not need to wait until we were dying to deal with the thorns and resentments and disappointments we all carry with us. We should feel the urgency of living now, set our priorities, be honest about what is important, and move through our grudges, so that we can get on with living life fully in the present.

The mat work was hard for me. I was used to ignoring my feelings and soldiering on. My issues were centered around self-esteem. I often felt inadequate. I could never do anything well enough or completely enough, and I was depleted. This was not my first emergency, my first ill patient, or the first death I had witnessed, but somehow I felt responsible. As I shared these reflections with Phyllis during my time on the mat she asked me, "Why are you being so hard on yourself? You knew nothing about Chloe. You were not responsible for her." My expectations for myself were grandiose. I assumed I had much more control over patients and events than I did. I had unrealistic expectations for myself. In Arizona, I began to recognize my limitations; there was only so much I could and should do. I returned home to my work better able to move ahead in spite of my self-doubts, to see my role as a facilitator, to realize there were aspects of healing and death I could control and those over which I had no control. I became a better listener.

Several months after the conference, I cared for Bill. A sixty-year-old gay man and a longtime smoker, he was dying of lung cancer. His wry sense of humor and gravelly laugh made him one of my favorites. After discharging him from the hospital, I kept in contact with him as a friend.

One wintry afternoon I visited him at home in St. Paul. A neighbor had shoveled the sidewalk to his bungalow, piling the foot of snow along the edge of the path. The chemotherapy was not benefiting him much, not slowing the cancer, just making him nauseous. He was deciding what to do. A rotund man, he filled the metal kitchen chair. As we sat at the Formica table, he told me about his conversation with his tumor.

"She's hot pink, very pretty. It's a she of course, but she smells." He chuckled. "I'm trying to build a wall around her, but she keeps jumping over."

"What is she telling you?" I asked.

"She says it's my time, time to quit fighting."

Bill enrolled in hospice, and I visited him at home on several other occasions. We chatted or sat quietly, and I stroked the back of his thick dry hand when he was too tired to talk. He died within the month.

With Bill I began to understand the privilege I had as a doctor, to bear witness to life, the resourcefulness and the foolishness, the unexpected ways of coming to terms with the events over which we have no control.

Robert was a middle-aged mentally handicapped man brought to the hospital from the group home where he lived when he became critically ill. He was assigned to my team toward the end of my residency. Large, pale, and doughy, he had the acrid smell of illness. Blood tests and X-rays confirmed a diagnosis of sepsis—infection in his blood. We started him on antibiotics and admitted him to intensive care. After several weeks in the hospital he stopped eating and was losing weight. The infectious disease consultant posed the question: Should we insert a feeding tube so he could better fight the infection that racked his body?

With no close family, only an estranged sister, the state appointed a guardian to act as his power-of-attorney. The guardian, someone in a law office who had never met Robert, agreed to the feeding tube. But as his physician, I wondered if this was the right thing to do. Robert lay in his hospital bed, his eyes closed, uncommunicative. Anti-depressants made no difference. The feeding tube would keep him from starving to death, but what kind of existence were we preserving? How much would he suffer? Could he even understand the pain for the gain?

I called his group home to get a sense of Robert. I'd met him only as a sick patient unable to communicate, and I wondered what was his life like before. I learned that he loved to sit at the table with his housemates and plunge into a plate of spaghetti. "Spaghetti's his favorite; he wears it after a meal." Then there was watching television with his housemates, especially Monday night football.

None of that was possible now. Staff would turn him every two hours in the nursing home. He had no visits from family or friends. It seemed more humane to allow him to die, without the tube. We'd keep him pain free, and nature could take its course. The guardian disagreed, so we took his case to the hospital ethics committee.

I don't recall the outcome, but I do remember the fervor with which I made my point: This was not about curing. This was about death with dignity. Robert would suffer if we used the feeding tube, and it would most likely not save him anyway. As a healer I could not torture my patient.

Rita lay on freshly stretched sheets in her private nursing home room. The hum of her humidified oxygen was punctuated by the hiss of her continuous positive airway pressure (CPAP) machine, which pumped air through the tracheotomy tube in her neck. Her husband asked that a classical music station play during the day. Outside her window he had hung bird feeders, filling them weekly. Rita never opened her eyes and did not vocalize, but she was responsive to stimuli, like a pinch on the arm. The nurses turned her every two hours, bathed her daily, changed her diaper, fed her through a feeding tube, and suctioned her saliva. Her husband was convinced a cure still loomed, that some miraculous intervention would restore Rita to who she was before her stroke ten years earlier. He asked that we put her on vitamins, and he looked into treatment possibilities at the university. Every week on nursing home rounds he had a new request. The nurses reported these to me dutifully but rolled their eyes.

Rita was a full code; her husband wanted her to go to the hospital, which was thirty minutes away, when her pneumonia did not respond to antibiotics administered through her feeding tube. "Give her that intravenous stuff," he said.

I mentioned my concern about her potential distress in strange surroundings if we moved her to the hospital.

But he was convinced she would recover, and he became angry if anyone questioned him. Silently, I cringed at the thought of performing CPR and pressing on her sallow chest.

It was ironic that with the assistance of technology, Rita outlived her husband. After his death, their children changed Rita's code status. She died in her sleep within the month.

I met Ethel twenty years after my experiences at the Kübler-Ross workshop. I had matured as a healer. She was well into her seventies, with a full head of gray hair, the skin of her face and neck wrinkled like an accordion above her plump frame. She smelled of lilac soap. As a result of the bone cancer she'd survived twenty years earlier, her left hip and leg were missing. She came to see me for abdominal pain one spring day; the lilacs outside were in bloom. After a CT scan, I diagnosed a tumor in her liver, probably cancer. We had a family conference in the office with two of her children to discuss how aggressive to be. "We can send you to a specialist to find out exactly what this is. That probably means doing a biopsy, which would require some sedative," I told them.

She winced. "But do I need to know?" she asked holding her hand over the right side of her abdomen, the location of her liver.

"Mom, it might be nice to know," the daughter interjected.

"How would they do the biopsy?" the son asked.

I explained that the doctor would give her something to relax her, numb the skin over the area, insert a needle into her liver guided by the fluoroscope machine, take a little sample of the tissue, and send it to the lab to see what it was. There would be the risks of bleeding and infection. If it was cancer, then she could talk with the oncologist about treatment. That would mean chemotherapy, radiation, or surgery.

Ethel nodded and moved her hand from the right side to her left pelvis, where her leg had been removed two decades earlier. She slowly rubbed the area. "You know, I've been through this once before."

"We don't have to do anything," I reassured her, saying we could prescribe medicine to control her pain. We could consult hospice.

"Oh, I'm not ready for hospice," Ethel said. Over the years, Ethel had done some volunteer work for hospice, so she understood what they offered. She said she needed some time to "put her ducks in order."

"Mom, are you sure you are okay with not knowing?" her daughter asked again.

Ethel set her jaw and said, "I don't need to know."

So I typed a prescription for pain medicine into the computer and invited Ethel to call me when she needed more. A month later, after she had arranged her will and the plans for her disabled daughter, we enrolled her in hospice. She died several weeks after that, surrounded by her family. Ethel had a clear mind; she knew what she wanted and how she wanted to wrap up her life. Her children respected her wishes, and so did I.

We physicians must do a better job of helping patients die a good death and of modeling to our students how we switch from curing to facilitating a good death. There are important ways to assist patients and families at this point: managing pain, helping the patient and family understand that death is near, giving them choices about how they want to spend the final days. There are gifts that come at this time for all involved. Our Hippocratic Oath observes, "I will remember that there is art to medicine as well as science, and that warmth, sympathy and understanding may outweigh the surgeon's knife or the chemist's drug." Being asked to assist at life's critical junctures was why I became a doctor. These glimpses into the universal human struggle and the concrete ways people deal with profound experiences rekindle my awe.

***Therese Zink** is a family physician and professor at the University of Minnesota. She sees patients in a small town in Minnesota, teaches, and does research. Her stories have been published in both medical and literary journals. She edited the anthology:* The Country Doctor Revisited: A 21st Century Reader, *a collection of stories, poems and essays about rural health care today (Kent State, 2010).*

A Better Place

VALERIE SEILING JACOBS

Lawyer Valerie Seiling Jacobs learns the hard way about negotiating the health care system as she tries to arrange the best care for her widowed, elderly father.

I stood in the doorway and stared. My seventy-nine-year-old father lay on the bed in a sleeveless undershirt, his thin, long feet protruding from wrinkled pajama bottoms. It was only five days since my last visit, but the decline was plain.

Scanning the room, I took in the pale furniture, purchased when my parents were newlyweds, and the faded curtains, hung by my mother in happier times—my eyes landing on the rolling metal walker parked next to the nightstand. An open package of saltines filled the tiny wire basket at the handlebars.

Was that all he'd eaten?

I tiptoed closer, near enough to take in the sour smell of a man too weak to shower and spied the two flesh-colored adhesive patches just below his collarbone. A stranger might have mistaken them for Band-Aids, but I knew better. They were *transdermal patches,* ingenious little delivery vehicles for fentanyl, a substance eighty times more powerful than morphine. The drug of choice for patients with advanced prostate cancer.

I knew all about those patches. With my mother gone—dead for almost a decade—and my sister so far away, getting Dad to his doctors had fallen to me. Not that he wanted my assistance or anyone else's. He issued a flat-out *no* at the suggestion he move in with my husband and me in Connecticut. ("You can have your own bathroom," I promised, "and spend more time with your grandkids.") But nothing could pry him from his tiny house on Staten Island.

And he was determined to remain independent. He fired the aide after only one visit. "I don't need help," he'd said, waving a bony hand at me, as if he could shoo me, and maybe the cancer, away. Never mind that it had taken a month to find someone who was: (a) licensed, (b) willing to trek to that outer borough, and (c) fit enough to hike the mile, all uphill, from the nearest bus stop.

But lately, Dad could barely walk. I'd been sneaking out of my office early every few days and driving the fifty miles to check on him, racing from the pharmacy to the supermarket to stock his medicine cabinet and freezer. I knew the exact date that his Foley, the catheter they'd inserted, had to be changed, and the precise number of milligrams in each of those little patches.

Now, apparently, they weren't enough. The pain seemed to be galloping ahead of the drugs. And I was pretty sure he was running a fever. He'd called at dawn to say his legs hurt so much he couldn't get out of bed. For the first time, he'd sounded frightened.

I leaned over the bed and spoke softly, reluctant to disturb him. "I need to take you to the hospital, Dad."

"No," he said, opening his eyes. With one hand, he clutched the front of his undershirt.

I paused, searching for the right words, studying his prone figure. He'd never been robust. "Skinny," my mother used to say, with more than a hint of envy. Now he was skeletal.

"We have to go to the hospital," I repeated, trying to keep my voice calm, my tone neutral, the way I would when my children were small, when I would pull a thermometer from a hot little mouth and try to hide my panic. "I already called the doctor. He said to take you in."

My father turned his head toward me, his blue eyes moving a split second behind the rest of his face—as though someone had mistakenly set them at a slower speed. "Have him come here," he said.

"You know they don't make house calls." I shook my head and smiled as if he'd made a joke. But my mind was racing. What if he wouldn't go voluntarily?

"Call him back and ask," he said. "He'll do it for me."

How could I tell him that I *had* asked? Begged, actually—and that the doctor had refused. He wouldn't even come to the phone. "There's nothing more we can do for him," his nurse had said after leaving me on hold for fifteen minutes. I'd wanted to scream: my father had been under this urologist's care for close to ten years. Was he really going to abandon him now?

Or was it revenge?

He knew I was a lawyer. And I'd asked a lot of pointed questions. ("Do you always wait so long to intervene?") It wouldn't have surprised me if he considered me a potential plaintiff. Plus, there was that little skirmish over the biopsy. "What do mean you can't schedule it for *three* weeks," I'd said, my voice rising—frantic at the thought of waiting so long. But even when the delay turned out to be justified (the specialist who performed the procedure traveled to Staten Island only twice a month), I didn't apologize. I think I was too stunned. Flabbergasted, actually. How could a place with almost half a million people—a borough of New York City, no less—*not* have someone who did this full time?

"The doctor's going to meet us there," I said, the heat creeping up my face.

My father stared at me, unblinking.

"He probably just needs to run a few tests," I continued, aware that I was talking too fast. "You know how they are." I let my voice trail off, half expecting him to agree.

He disliked doctors. He thought they relied too much on medication. "They hand this stuff out like it's candy," he would say to my mother, holding up one of her prescription bottles and rattling it for emphasis. And he blamed the medical profession for her death, conveniently forgetting that liver cancer had an especially poor prognosis.

But he didn't chime in with his usual criticism.

"You know how this works, Dad," I said, switching to my rational lawyer voice, the one I reserved for difficult negotiations. "First, they have to figure out what's wrong—*then* they can fix it." I ran a hand along the edge of the mattress. "I'm sure you'll be back home in no time."

I wasn't playing fair. I knew how much he wanted to stay at home—in his beloved house—the one he and my mother had built on that hill. It had taken fourteen years, with both of them working and my father grabbing as much overtime as he could, to realize the dream. But they had succeeded: the living room had floor-to-ceiling windows and a spectacular ocean view. Since my mother's death, I'd often found him sitting in front of those windows, bathed in sunlight—and memories.

"So what do you say, Dad? Can we get going?"

He closed his eyes and nodded.

Much later, of course, I would wonder whether things would have turned out better if I'd told the truth, if I'd admitted that I'd seen the last bone scan, that I knew, or at least was reasonably sure, why his legs hurt so much. In the heat of the crisis, however, deliberate ignorance, telling him what I thought he wanted to hear, seemed the safer course.

"Do you think you can sit up?" I asked.

He paused, as if trying to decide or perhaps summon the strength to speak. "No," he said without opening his eyes.

What must it be like to surrender your dignity? To allow your grown daughter to dress you? To lie there, a catheter snaking from your briefs, a bag of urine strapped to your leg, while your daughter pulls on your pants? And how much more terrible for a modest man? A private man who never failed to draw the shades, who except for Christmas morning, dressed for breakfast.

Or did the pain make him oblivious?

I tied his shoes and tried not to think about it.

He weighed so little, and yet it took all my strength to get him standing. Once upright, he dangled from my arms, his feet barely brushing the floor, his head drooping as though someone had forgotten to attach a string.

I grabbed the walker, and he managed to hold on to the handlebars while I supported him from behind.

"My wallet," he said, nodding toward the nightstand, his voice barely a whisper.

I should have remembered: he always had to have cash in his pocket—a carryover, I suspect, from his Depression-era childhood and years of penury. And he prided himself on always paying his way, sometimes tipping even when it was against the rules. Not so much from a need to impress, I think, as from lack of confidence. Because he could never quite believe that anyone would be nice to him without money changing hands.

With one arm, I reached for the worn billfold and slipped it into my purse.

He groaned as we shuffled down the hall and made our way from the house. I lifted him into the backseat and then ran around to the other side to buckle his shoulder belt. As I leaned over his limp form, I could see the redwood exterior of the house—his house—through the car window. I remembered how he and my mother had handpicked the boards at the lumberyard and how proud they were of the modern design. "The only California ranch on Staten Island," my father always said.

A knot of panic gripped me. What if he never comes home? Wouldn't he want a last look?

I peeked at his face, but his eyes were shut, his lips twisted against the pain. *Open your eyes,* I had the urge to cry out. *You might not get another chance.* But something stopped me.

"Hang in there, Dad," I said, rubbing his arm. "We'll be there soon."

We arrived at the ER, and I ran ahead to nab a wheelchair. As the automatic doors swung open, I rushed straight into an icy blast of air-conditioning. Ahead lay the receptionist's cubicle and to the left, the waiting room. The décor (plastic-molded chairs, fluorescent lights, and a blaring television) did not surprise me. But the crowd did. It was not yet noon, and already it was standing room only. A hundred people filled the space, their voices, many in languages I could not understand, raised in angry chatter. One elderly man paced with a wailing infant while a bald woman (his daughter? the baby's mother?) sat slumped in a chair.

I stood and stared. Was it always like this?

Much later, I would discover that the answer was *yes,* that the ER had been designed to accommodate fewer than a third of the patients it actually served, population growth having exceeded even the most bullish estimates, and that fiscal problems at other facilities on the island, including the government's decision to shutter the only public hospital, had aggravated the situation. And much later, after it was too late to help my father, the hospital would finally find the funds to expand the ER—enlarging the waiting room and adding fifty-six new treatment stations.

But that day, I knew none of those statistics. The only thing I knew was that my dad was in too much pain to tolerate this kind of wait—with or without a wheelchair.

"We need a stretcher," I said to the receptionist.

For hours, my father lay on a gurney in the dark hallway where the orderly had parked him: around the corner from the nurses' station, wedged between a service elevator and an overflowing trash bin. A large red sign mounted not two feet from his head warned of the biohazard risk.

My protests (about the location, about the delay, about the lack of privacy) had done nothing but generate hostility. ("If you don't like it, you can sit out there," the supervisor had said, pointing to the waiting room.)

Four times I'd cornered the head nurse, pleading for attention, only to be told there were more pressing cases: a toddler with asthma, a stabbing victim, a man with chest pain. Another entire shift had come and gone, the guard ordering me out while the patients were handed off like chattel. ("Don't leave me," my father begged.)

By the time a doctor, a young woman in her late twenties, finally showed up, I'd been standing next to Dad's stretcher for almost ten hours.

"What seems to be the problem?" she asked. She glanced at the bag of urine that now hung from a hook on the side of the gurney, then turned toward me, her back to my father.

I took in her name, embroidered in fancy script on her crisp white coat, as well as the photo ID clipped to her pocket. An *intern,* I realized, remembering with a start that it was August: the second-to-worst month to be in a hospital, if you believed the data.

One study put the risk of dying in a hospital during July, when the interns arrived, at 4 percent higher than the average mortality rate. An "accelerated death" they called it—the kind of mistake that might get discussed at a morbidity and mortality conference, but absent a lawsuit would never become public. The unavoidable price of teaching programs, according to some.

I cleared my throat and launched into my father's medical history: his previous heart attack, early-stage Parkinson's, and, of course, the cancer. I spoke clearly, careful to use precise, clinical terms. Words like *cardiac cath, febrile,* and *metastases.* Words a doctor might use. Words that warned her to pay attention—and to take me seriously.

Reaching for the index card in my purse, I rattled off the names of his medications. When I looked up, she was checking her pager. I had the urge to snap my fingers in front of her nose but settled for a long stare.

She noticed and slipped the pager back in her pocket. "How old is he?" she asked, barely concealing her irritation.

"Seventy-nine," I said, and the look of disgust that flashed across her face made me think of something else I'd heard: the nickname residents had for old people, for patients who required tons of paperwork and tests but were unlikely to get better. "GOMERS," they called them—short for *Get Out of My Emergency Room*.

"I don't have a bed available right now," she said.

"Well, we'll just wait here until you find one," I said, reaching for my father's hand.

It was 1 A.M. before they moved him upstairs. I followed in a separate elevator ("Patients only," the orderly had said when I tried to tag along), and by the time I found his room, he was settled in, propped up on pillows in the semi-darkness.

I stepped closer and pulled the curtain, blocking the view but not the sound of his snoring roommate. Leaning over, I whispered that I had to go. His eyes were closed—they'd given him a shot—and I wasn't sure he'd heard. "I just need to change my clothes," I continued, reluctant to leave.

"Go home to your family," he said, without opening his eyes.

His words took me by surprise, and I was tempted to blurt: *You're my family too.* But I didn't trust my voice. With the rails up, and his thin arms protruding from the hospital gown, he looked so vulnerable. "I'll be back as soon as I can," I said, kissing his cheek. A second later he was asleep, and I left to make the long drive back to Connecticut.

When I returned in the morning, two women stood at his bedside. Each wore a flowered smock and a frown.

"You have to," the taller of the two was saying to him as I stepped through the door.

"It's the law," the other added, nodding with the kind of certainty reserved for bureaucrats.

"What's the law?" I said.

The women looked up, startled. My father turned toward me, struggling to lift his head to see over the rail. But he was too weak, and I saw how shrunken and helpless he was—and that he was crying.

I froze. I couldn't believe it. He hated when anyone got emotional. "Everybody needs to calm down," he would say at the first sign of tears, holding one hand up like a traffic cop. The only other time I'd seen him cry was when my mother died.

"What's the matter?" I said, rushing to his side, my heart thudding in my chest.

He raised a shaky hand and covered his eyes, but the tears continued to slide down his unshaven cheeks.

"What's going on?" I said, turning to the women.

"We can't be responsible," the tall one said, gesturing with her chin toward my father's other hand, which lay on top of the cotton blanket.

I followed her gaze and saw that he still held the crumpled twenty-dollar bill I'd tucked into his hand the night before.

"They won't let me keep my money," he said, his lips quivering.

Of course, I gave them hell and, of course, they backed down. But in the end, it was nothing more than a speed bump.

Three days later, the hospital declared that, medically speaking, there was nothing else to be done. ("Where do you want him moved?" the social worker asked me, as if he were not lying right there in front of her.) And since he couldn't walk, and because he still refused to come live with me, the only alternative was a nursing home.

Granted, I found him a private room, and it was in Connecticut—so at least he'd be closer. And since he'd been in the hospital for more than three days (a "qualifying stay" in Medicare jargon) *and* needed rehab, the government probably would pick up part of the tab—at least for the first few months. ("One of the lucky ones," the social worker said, glancing at her clipboard.) But still, he wound up in diapers, looked after by overworked nurses who thought nothing of discussing his bowel movements in front of me.

"I want to go home," he kept saying. "My insurance will pay."

At first, I was dismissive: I knew that neither Medicare nor his supplemental policy covered the kind of home care he needed. But he was so insistent that I dug through his files and discovered he was right. Four years earlier he'd purchased another policy—and yes, it included home care. The problem was, it had a one-hundred-day deductible. My father (or maybe Medicare) would have to shell out almost twenty-five thousand dollars before the insurance company would pay a nickel.

Apparently, this was not uncommon. In fact, I learned that many policies were specifically structured to take advantage of government money. "We like to dovetail with other funding sources," the insurance agent explained in classic doublespeak. (No wonder Medicare is going broke, I thought.)

Never mind that 71 percent of men admitted to nursing homes don't last three months—or that 80 percent don't last six months. And never mind that he was already sick when he bought the policy. But what good would it do to tell him that he'd been paying seven thousand dollars a year for a policy he would likely never collect on?

And besides, money wasn't the only obstacle. The logistics were equally problematic: even if they paid, I would still have to find an aide (or aides, since he needed round-the-clock care) who could meet the insurance company's licensure requirements and who would be willing to trek to his house—a neat trick, as I had discovered before. Plus, who would coordinate his care? He couldn't get out of bed. Who would open the front door to let them in? And what if they didn't show up? I lived fifty miles away.

"Look at the bright side," I said to him, forcing a smile. "You need to use up your hundred days no matter what—and maybe Medicare will pay for it. In the meantime, let's just concentrate on getting you stronger."

But anyone could see he wasn't getting stronger. In fact, the pain was getting worse.

"He needs to see the doctor," I finally said to the nurse.

"Who's his doctor?" she said.

"Excuse me?" I said.

She explained—and I stood there dumbfounded. It hadn't occurred to me that I would have to arrange for doctors. I had just assumed that the medical director at the nursing home would care for him.

By the time I found a local MD willing to take him on as a new patient and booked an ambulette to transport him, another week had gone by and the pain was out of control again.

"He needs to be admitted," the doctor said.

My father spent the next two months being shuttled back and forth between the hospital and nursing home—the same plight that hundreds of thousands of other Medicare beneficiaries endure each year. ("Shall we hold his room?" the nursing home administrator asked each time, dutifully reminding me that Medicare would not pay for two places—if they paid at all.)

I think everyone knew (except him, perhaps) that he was dying. The cancer had spread to his pelvis, legs, and spine. But no one ever spoke of that. Not one person ever mentioned hospice or palliative care. Instead, they talked in terms of "tumor response rates" and offered him the latest in chemo and radiation—things Medicare would pay for. Medicine that masqueraded as hope.

Meanwhile, my father talked about getting better—of going home.

"Soon," I would say, stroking his cheek, complicit in the charade.

But things came to a head when I arrived at the nursing home one day and found him clinging to the bed rail with both hands, writhing in pain—refusing to let anyone touch him.

"He needs more medication," I said, turning to face the nurse. The doctors had already upped the fentanyl and prescribed an additional narcotic. But for the past few days he'd been having trouble swallowing the pills.

"He needs to be *changed*," the nurse said, wrinkling her nose, "before he gets another bedsore."

I looked at her and remembered that she'd been on duty when they'd discovered the first one. I'd walked in that day to find her with a ruler, measuring a small ulcer on his buttocks while the nursing supervisor—also in latex gloves—recorded the data in a special log.

I glanced at my father—he was curled in a fetal position, still gripping the rail—and then back at her. "Can I see you outside?" I said, nodding toward the door.

She peeled off her gloves with a loud snap and tossed them in the trash. I followed her as she strode from the room. In the hall, she stopped and turned to face me.

"He needs more medication," I repeated. "Maybe a morphine drip, or one of those machines where he can press the button himself."

She was shaking her head before I finished speaking. "We don't have those."

"Well, can't you order one?"

"You don't understand," she said. "We're not licensed for that." She turned on her heel and walked away.

It took a second for her words to register. How could a nursing home *not* be licensed to administer intravenous painkillers? What did they do when patients couldn't swallow anymore?

I pushed open the door to my father's room, still dazed. As I neared the bed he opened his eyes.

"Please get me out of here," he said, starting to cry.

It took me two days to find a hospice bed. Not that I ever used that word in front of him. I just didn't have the heart. To have used the *H* word would have been to admit defeat and, more important, to abandon hope. Because even if he knew he was dying—and how could he not have known by then?—he simply was not ready to acknowledge he would never go home again.

"I found you a nicer place," I said.

"You're a good daughter," he said, squeezing my hand.

By the time they came to move him a day later, he was barely conscious.

An aide at the home tried to pull me aside: "Are you sure you want to do this?" she asked. "He doesn't have much time."

"That's *why* I'm doing it," I said, brushing past her to greet the woman from hospice who stood outside my father's door.

The woman wore street clothes—a wool blazer and pants—and a lanyard with a large photo ID around her neck. She introduced herself, and we shook hands. As she reached to open the door, the lanyard swung toward me and I noticed the word *Hospice* displayed in bold letters.

"Do you have to wear that?" I asked, nodding at the badge.

She paused and looked down at her chest and then back at me, puzzled.

"It's just that I haven't told him where he's going," I said, my words trailing off.

A look of comprehension spread across her face, followed almost immediately by a frown. I could see the wheels turning as she weighed her options. Could she lose her job over this?

I stood and waited—and then watched as she slowly flipped the badge over, so that only the plain white backing was visible.

"Shall we go in?" she said, taking my arm.

We moved my father that afternoon. As they loaded him onto the gurney he stirred, and I leaned over to whisper that we were taking him to a different place.

"Let's do it," he mumbled—the last words he ever spoke.

He died peacefully the next day in a sunny room—with me at his side and tended to by people who cared only for his comfort. People who understood that sometimes dignity is more important than the rules. And though he never regained consciousness, I think he knew he had finally reached a better place.

Valerie Seiling Jacobs *is the author of "Packing for the Ineffable," which was published in the* New York Times, *and "The Million Dollar View," which was performed live at the Westport Arts Center and later broadcast on public radio. Before turning to writing full time, she practiced law for more than twenty years. She teaches at the Westport Writers' Workshop and currently holds a fellowship at Columbia University, where she is working on an MFA.*

Waiting (to Go Home)

HOWARD MANSFIELD

"You can't deny the Godot-like absurdities of the nursing home. It's a vast diorama of waiting," writes Howard Mansfield. "You walk through lives, walk down the hall past centuries of experience, left unspoken."

The woman in the wheelchair has been left in the hall next to the busy nurses' station. She's slumped forward, wearing a bright red sweater, a merry color that throws her sorrow into deep contrast. Her skin is smooth, youthful for someone in her eighties. There is a pile of mashed up tissues in front of her; it's a clock marking her day, tissue by tissue.

"My family doesn't know I'm here," she pleads.

"They know," the nurse reassures her.

"My family doesn't know I'm here," she repeats. "Call them."

"They know."

"My family doesn't know I'm here."

"They know."

"Call them."

I walk by her on the way to visit my mother. I will walk past the woman in the hall many more times. Her dialogue with the nurse is unchanging.

We are in the cafeteria for French Fry Friday. Four or five tables of old and older people are waiting for their french fries—old-fashioned, crinkle cut, and glistening with oil.

Today is: *Thursday,* it says in blue script on the fill-in-the-blank white board.

The date is: *February 14*

The weather is: *Sunny and Cold*

The next holiday is: *Valentine's Day*

Today is actually Friday. Valentine's Day is over. The sign in the nursing home's cafeteria addresses the residents as if they are in preschool.

At my mother's table there are only two other residents. They are beyond conversation. Sinatra plays on a cheap portable stereo. Songs of love forever and forever, love when you're seventeen, devotion night and day. The music is loud. No one is listening. Or maybe no one is hearing. Directly across from us a woman with waxy smooth skin leans back in her wheelchair, head thrown toward the ceiling, mouth open, asleep. At the head of the table a bald guy droops to one side, the eye closest to us opening and closing, looking toward us, and closing again. The eye is like a deep-sea creature peering out from a cave. And then there's my mother. It's a shock to see her. She looks so old. This is what everyone thinks when, after a month or two, they visit their parents, relatives, neighbors, and friends in a nursing home. *These people* look so old.

In that moment we are saying they are old and we are not. We don't intend it this way, but we feel them pulling us over the edge into old age and death, so we pull back. They're leaving us; they've left. We have come to say: you haven't left us. We sit around, but as time congeals, the small talk gets smaller until it vanishes, confirming that they have indeed left.

Out in the hall I hear a family talking as they walk by. "She's eighty-two. She was a vibrant woman—up to now. Did you see her?" A voice replies, "She'll bounce back." He might as well have said, "She'll beat this rap. We'll get her out of this joint. She's not eighty-two—not really."

Hours pass. Then more hours pass. Nothing happens. Nothing. My wife and I sit and look at my mother as Sinatra sings, the same songs repeating. *Night and day . . .* My mother is deaf, so conversation is constrained to a game of Western Union—a few words telegraphed repeatedly. *Night and day . . .*

Each time I visit I'm hit with the enforced lethargy of the nursing home. Sea View, this place is called. There's no sea, no view—no surprise. It's a three-story brick bunker with foul, murky fluorescent light. Row after row of wall lights segment the narrow halls into one dun, dusky, frame after another. Everything has a tannish hue.

I see a woman at the hall's end, collapsing into herself the way the aged do when they're wheelchair bound, taking on the shape of a soft, deflating ball. She pulls herself forward with her feet, walking her chair along, slowly, frame by frame.

Wheelchair-bound patients are lined up to the right and left, parked like cars, bumper to bumper along the wall. The patients—inmates? wards?—sit there waiting to go to lunch. No one talks. No one moves. A few sit with their heads fallen down. One or two stare right at you, but it seems they see nothing. No expression registers, no smile, no eye movement. Just a hundred-yard stare. They are like marionettes on a shelf. They seem to be partly filleted.

The bulletin boards add to the cheer: *10:30 Word games. 11:30 Bingo. Enjoy your day!* Next to this are a dozen coloring pages by the residents. Two scenes have been colored in—one of dolphins arcing out of the water and the other showing two kittens sitting under a rainbow.

"It's like a return to elementary school," my wife says.

But now they really have you, I think. You're weakened. You need them to walk, to shave, to go to the bathroom.

The rooms leak TV noise. In some, families visit with the TV on. The TV is the painkiller in the IV drip—it's the hearth, it's outside, it's familiar. It's the tock-tock beat of life going on.

After just a short visit, the nursing home sticks to you. One is on the nursing home's time, in a spaceship, adrift. Here time stops. Here you wait and wait.

I'm just visiting. What would it be like if I had to live here today? Kristen Murphy, a healthy thirty-eight-year-old, wanted to find out. As part of her medical education, Murphy lived in a nursing home for ten days. She was assigned a condition—a mild stroke, difficulty swallowing, and chronic lung disease—and she was treated like any other resident. Murphy was confined to her wheelchair, hoisted out of bed with a lift, subjected to regular checks for bed sores, given pureed foods, and had to be helped in the bathroom. When she got her wheelchair stuck in a corner and couldn't move, she cried. "All I wanted to do was shut my door and stay in here," she told the *New York Times*. But she knew she had to get out.

She went to bingo, hung out by the nurses' station with other residents, and made some friends. "At times I felt really lonely and got depressed," Murphy said. "Sometimes it was an emotional roller coaster, up and down, up and down." Many residents cry, she learned. They miss their family, their old life. They cry because they won't be going home.

You forfeit your privacy in a nursing home.

One room, one scene: Two doors are open—the room's door, which is always open anyway, and the bathroom door. A nurse in the hall is almost laughing: "What do you want me to do with him?" she says to another nurse. A sudden view: a man in the bathroom, standing up, no pants, facing the wall. His ass is pink. The view, the waiting helplessness of the man, is like those photos of the prisoners at Abu Ghraib.

In the hall by the entrance, a fragile couple sit in their wheelchairs facing each other with an arm extended, fingertips touching, heads bowed, unmoving. The final bow of a *pas de deux*. You walk through lives, walk down the hall past centuries of experience, left unspoken.

We are meeting my mother for lunch. My dad stakes out a table in a small room with five or six tables and a few patients—one man with a pink face that looks as if it's been sandblasted. He has a long regular face, a banker's or an insurance broker's face; he must have been handsome in his day. Another man has bloodlike stains down his front. He speaks like a zombie, slow and guttural: *Take . . . me . . . out . . . of . . . here*. The words are forced up with great effort from the depths, each word breaking on the surface like a bubble. He thinks I work here. I shake my head "no." He looks at me with rage. Finally a nurse comes by, and he repeats his slurred request. She takes him out, saying, "Did you have chocolate today?" That's what's on his shirt.

Another inmate tells us that everyone has assigned seats in this room. We have already claimed a table—set out roses in a Styrofoam cup "vase," a deli lunch, and my dad's hat, jacket, and cane. We move. The nursing home is high school with dementia.

A dozen times I pass the door marked SOILED UTILITY. A key hangs from a cord taped to the door. The key is in the lock. Have they had thefts of soiled utility? If people are stealing dirty sheets, then we have a big problem. A sign on the door says: leave this key in the lock. So: why have the lock and the key? There is probably a skein of regulations, memos, and meetings behind that sign. We are in the grip of institutional craziness—not the "crazies" who are "institutionalized," but rather the craziness of our institutions.

At lunch my mother wants a fork. She's eating food we've brought her; she hasn't picked up her lunch tray. I can't get a fork, I'm told. But I can get her entire tray. It's a system.

You can't deny the Godot-like absurdities of the nursing home. It's a vast diorama of waiting.

In the dayroom two men are talking about the Marx Brothers.

"He could really play the harp," the first says of Harpo.

"He couldn't talk," says the second man.

"He *could* talk."

"He *couldn't* talk."

They stumble along over this until the first man finally explains that Harpo could talk but didn't as part of his act. Then he says, "There were five Marx Brothers." He starts to name them—Groucho, Harpo, Chico . . . and after a while he comes up with Zeppo. But the fifth? They start the list over and are stumped.

I'm sitting across the room with my dad. He's in this nursing home—a different one from my mother's—after a bad fall for a few weeks of physical therapy. We're paying his bills. The two men are still trying to name the fifth Marx Brother. I call over, "Gummo."

"Dumbo?"

"Gummo."

"Dumbo?"

"Gummo. He dropped out early."

"Gummo? *I* don't remember him," and he waves his hand to the side—the classic New York gesture: eh, take it away. Having an answer has disappointed them. I feel like I have taken a bone from a dog. Who knows how long they could have pursued the mystery of the forgotten Marx Brother? They have all day, and the next.

They shift in their chairs, are quiet, and then find something to complain about. This warms them right up again.

Our late years are the story of the dwelling we take for granted, the body—leaving. We are doubly dispossessed, losing our homes and our bodies. Late in life, with our abilities eroding and many of our friends dead, we are forced on an arduous journey. No one wants to go to a nursing home. "People go to a hospital to get fixed up and then return home. But people generally go to a nursing home fully expecting to get worse and die," says a former nursing home worker, Thomas Edward Gass, in *Nobody's Home.* I read his book when I was thinking about the qualities of home. The mystery that holds my attention is that some houses have life—are home, are dwellings—and others don't. *Dwelling* is an old-fashioned word we've misplaced. When we live heart and soul, we dwell. When we belong to a place, we dwell. A true home shelters the soul.

Gass started out as a nurse's aide and worked his way up to be the director of social services at a nursing home in the Midwest. On his first day he "gagged at the pungent aroma of fresh diarrhea." The director of nursing had tried to discourage him from applying for the job. Gass bravely and with an amazing grace faced the stench and doddering of nursing-home life. His job became a pilgrimage. He loved the residents and learned to accept the "cascade of lives in free fall." The body breaking down, functions ceasing, language shredded into "word salad," personality devolving into complaint, compliance, or stiff-backed pride in a soft body, and shit shit shit—hard, soft, loose, liquid. The stink of it. Cleaning it up. On his way home at the end of the day, still wearing his scrubs, people would ask him if he was a doctor. "No, I'm a butt-wipe in a nursing home," he would answer. And he'd remind himself of the Buddhist monasteries in Tibet and Nepal "headed by lamas who reserve the dirtiest toilets for themselves to clean."

"In the beginning I saw these people as human aliens, a sweet harmless subspecies. But now I feel their sad seeds sprouting within me. I know that I am becoming one of these odd beings I lift and roll and wipe every day," Gass writes. "We are all infirm. We all have cancer and dementia, and we are all dying," he says. "We all start out the same and we end up the same." Nearly half of those of us who will live to age eighty-five may end up here, he notes. Gass spent years in Catholic seminary and in Buddhist meditation. He has the poise and the spiritual depth to face decay and not despair of it. "The nature of things dictates that we must leave those dear to us. Everything born contains its own cessation," he quotes the Buddha on his deathbed.

He is attuned to the suffering around him, and comforts the residents—touching them, looking them right in the eye—even as he realizes he doesn't have the time to "help even a quarter of the folks who plead for it. . . . Our residents have nothing to do but focus on their pain. At times our halls become a veritable sea of moaning, crying, begging, and whimpering. It is simply not possible to alleviate the waves of pain, anger, anxiety, boredom, despair, and loneliness."

A nursing home is a laboratory for cultivating suffering. "The great pain, the gut-wrenching void of nursing-home life has little to do with old age or infection or dementia. The dominant reality in our nursing home is ubiquitous separation," he writes. "Everyone here is torn away from home and families." They have surrendered "all pride and privacy. In the end, they're left possessing nothing but their thoughts."

Of one patient he says, we treat his body and crush his spirit. Health is defined as a lack of illness. But good health, Gass says, is joy. Recall those times when you felt great—you'd fallen in love, gotten a good job, won a race, he says. That's more than not being sick, "but since we can't measure wholeness, boundless expansion, peak experiences, or contentment, we simply act as though they don't exist."

Reading *Nobody's Home* makes you feel like an old tree—new skin around a dead core. You feel the death inside of you. And you fear in the end you will become your own worst self—your petty fears, complaints, arguments. A petty ball of fear in the dying fortress of the body. After all you've done, suffered, achieved, you end up with strangers wiping your ass, cleaning your body, forcing mush into you, telling you what to do and when to do it. It's a horrific double prison: a dying body in a cinderblock nursing home, cut off from the life you've made—or at least, the best part of it—and living as a symptom of the worst of it, as if you had become all scar tissue, all injury.

But Gass has compassion. It's his hard-worn laurel. He quotes the Vietnamese Buddhist monk Thich Nhat Hahn. Life is flowers and garbage. Hold reverence for garbage; transform it into compost. A gardener can see compost in flowers and flowers in the compost. Buddhas and the enlightened suffer too, says Nhat Hahn, but they know how to transform their suffering into joy. They are good gardeners.

"Fighting life's displeasures only solidifies our suffering. It's like wanting to have a magnet with only the positive pole," says Gass. "Only through a fearless comprehension of our own mortality can we achieve a clear view of reality. In the profound realization that we cannot hold on to health, nor to possession, nor to relationships, comes spiritual maturity."

The body isn't leaving us. This *is* the body.

The saddest place at Sea View is the third floor. Here the self is broken; time is broken. Here they put those with dementia. My mother and many others have landed here for a few months because their floor is closed during a renovation.

The ward hits you with the smell of shit and piss—the odors rising and falling as you pass the twisted, crazy, and sometimes moaning patients. Their moaning hits you full on, too, mixing with the shit and piss. One woman cries out, "Oh! Oh! They're coming for me!" And another woman answers with a parrotlike shriek. Call and response, back and forth. The Preacher, as he's known, leads his private service: "Sing with me, Jesus!" He's a tall man, withdrawn into his world. He looks within and booms out in a beautiful bass voice, "Sing with me, Jesus!" over and over, the needle stuck on an old record. The oldtime-oldtime-oldtime religion.

A man endlessly shakes maracas: *Cha-ka-ka. Cha-ka-ka.* Another woman says, "Telmpt" or something, and says it again and again. She doesn't know why no one can understand her. You can see that in her eyes. Nearby a woman lying on her side in a chair plays with the same piece of string over and over. Once the Preacher quiets down, a woman with long gray hair cries out, "My teeth! My teeth!"

This is the day on the third floor: *Oh! Oh! They're coming for me! Sing with me, Jesus! Telmpt. Telmpt. Sing with me, Jesus! Cha-ka-ka. Cha-ka-ka. Telmpt. Telmpt. My teeth! My teeth! Sing with me, Jesus! Sing with me, Jesus!*

The better-off just sit in their wheelchairs. Just sit. Some look as if they have been scoured by high-velocity winds you can't see or are frozen in some silent moan. They have thin, pale, purple-gray skin.

On this day a circle of wheelchairs is pushed up to a large screen TV, like cars at the drive-in. They are watching *West Side Story*. It's instantly identifiable. The colors are smudged on this TV, like thick makeup. Tony and the Puerto Ricans look like Valley Girls just out of the tanning booths. In this room the movie seems to be pitched at an impossible heart rate—blood couldn't possibly move that fast; life couldn't be that dramatic.

I have also been in hospitals a lot lately, visiting family. My mother has had two close calls with death, and my father has fallen twice, breaking bones. Hospitals are another rung on the ladder of dispossession. We are unsheltered here, as we wait with our illness and worries. In the waiting rooms and hallways we are dwelling in anxiety.

The fluorescent light, the antiseptic smell pushes at us, pushes us farther from home, upends the hearth. We curl tighter into ourselves. We walk and sit in a nimbus of worry. We've left the earth—we feel ourselves and our loved ones exiting. Good-bye to all that. The doctors and nurses, the white coats and forms and hard edges, the noise of televisions and coded announcements, all of it pushes us on. Hospitals are supposed to be an Olympus of technology and knowledge, but they are partly vast bumbling Victorian institution, partly twenty-first century, and partly River Styx. What parts? The ratio is constantly changing. This throws us again and again.

Hospitals are the machine arrayed against us. Hospitals deny all qualities that can't be quantified. In the body's darkest hour, the body is cut off from home, from the stories that bind us to a place on earth. Body and place are orphaned by the modern hospital. The body needs place—calls out for it. "We might say, in sum, that body and place are *congruent counterparts*. Each needs the other. Each suits the other. Put otherwise, *place is where the body is*. It is certainly *nowhere else*," writes philosopher Edward S. Casey. We are most ourselves, most "ecstatic" when in place, says Casey.

And in the hospital? We are our symptoms, our illness, our insurance forms.

We won't die, dust to dust, ashes to ashes, but rather we will just be drained away—our fluids, our life, love, and memories, all draining out different tubes, all monitored by green flashing lights, by the machine's stock market report of our mortality, by the nurses stopping by to check on our signs, some with evident care, others as if we were a pot roast and they were running late.

The hospital is industrial; it's a disassembly line. We come in whole and hurting, and we leave, if we are fortunate, less whole and hurting—but hoping we'll heal. We must leave to heal; we must go home.

Hospitals abduct us from the earth. They insert us into a medical machine. We are like the "Borg" in *Star Trek*, a human being overtaken by the machine. We are tied to hoses, prodded, monitored, injected. In the hospital we leave the earth. Those stories of alien abductions sound to me like surgery and postop recovery.

What would I do for the ill in hospitals, nursing homes, and hospices? I'd give them the sun, moon, and stars. I'd give them daylight and trees and flowers. I'd give them the sound and view of running water. I would open all the paths to peace, to the childhood memories of roaming, to the person's love of the earth. We will still die, but at least we will die on earth.

The woman in the hall by the nurses' station is still there when I leave after a long day. Her pile of mangled tissues is higher. The nurse she is talking to is shuffling through trays in a cabinet.

"I am so tired of staying here. I wish I could go home," the woman says. Her sentences are thick, sorrowful. They have a weight you can't ignore.

"I know, hon," says the nurse. She says this with her head in the cabinet. She grabs something and dashes off.

The woman in the hall wants to go home—to her place, her routine, her cat, Oprah at four, her friends over to play cards. But no one goes home from here. Maybe they go on to another nursing home; likely they go to the hospital, fail, weaken, and die.

Home is no more. The home she first knew, the home of her crib, of mom and dad, brothers, sisters, dogs and cats. The home she ran to at twilight from play. The home after school, after dates, first jobs, first year away, wedding, first child. That home—whether it was ideal or a tyrant's kingdom—is gone. The home of her first apartment, of the first place she lived when married. Gone.

You could write your autobiography by listing all the doors you've opened, said the philosopher-poet of dwelling, Gaston Bachelard, in *The Poetics of Space*. Once you've arrived in the nursing home, there are no more doors to open.

Every visitor walks out slowly. Everyone leaves burdened. Some of the older men look as if they've been hit by a car. Everyone is weighed down.

Howard Mansfield *is the author of six books about preservation and history, including* The Bones of the Earth; In the Memory House; *and* The Same Ax, Twice. *His latest book is* Turn and Jump: How Time and Place Fell Apart *(Down East, 2010).*

Mr. Stone

DIANA FLESCHER

Intern Diana Flescher finds herself caught in the middle—between a bumbling medical student and a patient with chronic lung disease fighting the lung specialist's insistence that the patient be intubated and hooked to a respirator.

I met Mr. Stone during my second swing through the internal medicine ward. He was admitted in the late evening, like most emergency room patients. It was the witching hour in this Boston hospital, when the admitting office has closed, the clerks in their dark blue suits with carefully knotted scarves having slid the glass windows shut and tucked their multiple-line phones under designer plastic covers. It was the hour when the piped-in music was silenced, the volunteers in their pink jackets banished, the candy and magazine carts stowed away. When the operator announced in her stilted, gracious (but firm) manner that visiting hours were now OVER, the lights in the hallway were dimmed, and the hospital, like some glass and formica Jekyll and Hyde, took on its true form, soiled with blood and urine and stool. Teams of code personnel raced down darkened corridors, and elderly patients, the "sundowners," lost without the orientation of daylight, wandered and babbled and shrieked, "Somebody help me!" over and over, until the nurses came with their sedative needles and their spotless restraining Posey vests and tied them to their beds.

In these hours the other interns and I scrambled to stay ahead of the "hits," patients who arrived as from a military front, disgorged upstairs in wheelchairs or on stretchers from the bowels of the emergency room, where other interns stonewalled valiantly, trying to weed out the "crocks" from the "sickies."

The important thing was not to fall behind. I learned to run from one admission to another, getting a bare-bones history, the list of meds, just enough information to be able to write orders and get the IV started, buying time, buying time. Start with the sickest first; there's nothing like having a patient "crump," or go down the tubes, before you've worked him up. Get respiratory up on the asthmatic, slap some nitroglycerin cream on the chest pain in the ICU. Make sure the acute abdomen still has bowel sounds. When was the last time that bleeder in 408 had his CBC drawn?

Then, after all the dikes are plugged, it is time to go back around all over again, to ask about the past surgery, the previous heart attack, and does he smoke, and could you be pregnant, and . . . oh shit, I didn't know this guy's an alkie; he's going to DT on me tonight for sure.

Now it is so late at night that I wake the last few patients, shaking their shoulders gently, to finish my physical exam, so I can present their cases at morning rounds without lying. (Do you mean to say, doctor, that you did not SEE the double hernias on this patient, or that you simply did not LOOK?)

And inevitably, just as it seems that I might catch an hour or two of restless sleep in the on-call room before morning rounds, the nurse pages me to report on the patient who has fallen out of bed or the man who hasn't urinated in twelve hours or the woman who has pulled out her absolutely-impossible-to-reinsert IV and is wandering the halls in the throes of paranoia—and don't forget, she is allergic to all sedatives.

For us interns, the workday never ended. There was no night-shift staff that would come in, bright-eyed and cheerful, to relieve the day shift. I gazed resentfully at the nurses, who gaily tossed on their coats and went home to spouses and children. We were left behind, left to work on and on through the night until daybreak came and the hospital awoke. Well-rested, neatly dressed staff arrived, but we would have to start the morning rituals all over again, the blood drawing, the endless rounds, the pointed questions from the attendings in their starched white coats. There were lab results to review, X-rays to read, disasters to avert: increase the potassium, decrease the potassium, regulate the insulin, work up the anemia. By the end of the second day, the fatigue made the ring of a telephone sound like a harsh jangle. It was only in the late afternoon that we were finally set free and allowed to stumble out of the hospital, blinking in the sunlight.

And so it was that I met Mr. Stone amidst the chaos of a bad on-call night, one of ten admissions I had been hit with. I saw right away that he rated as one of my sickies. He sat on the edge of his bed, his body thin and breathless from chronic lung disease, and he leaned forward, his hands on his knees, his elbows splayed out, his lips pursed as if to suck the oxygen more powerfully from the atmosphere around him. When I entered, he glanced up briefly and smiled, his blue eyes flashing, then resumed his work of breathing. He couldn't have been more than forty. His wife was quietly hanging his clothes in the closet, so I presumed she had seen him this breathless before. In between breaths, Mr. Stone nodded, yes, this wasn't the worst. But it was, he panted, sure going on a long time. Getting pretty tired out.

I listened to his chest, almost silent despite the desperate pull of his muscles, and then, patting his shoulder gently and giving a small smile to his wife, I left to write his admission orders.

At the nurses' station, I found my medical student, Bernie, poring over Mr. Stone's old charts in a state of excitement. I hated Bernie. He was a caricature of the nerdy medical student: pimple-faced, greasy-haired, with a propensity toward ridiculous ties and an unsurpassed ability to spill whatever he had in his hand on his already graying lab coat. He was useless to me; worse, he was forever getting in my way, bending my ear with improbable diagnoses, and when I tried to send him to get pizza, he said he was allergic to tomato sauce.

Bernie also had a fault that, under the laws of residency, was the kiss of death: he got flustered during morning rounds, stuttering and turning red and otherwise revealing the chinks in his armor through which the attendings could gleefully pierce him. Confusing two similar-sounding terms one morning, Bernie was reduced to rubble by the chief of medicine, who contemptuously asked, in a slow, deliberate, clipped British accent, if Bernie thought that since they sounded the same, perhaps *urEmia*, *anEmia,* and *meningococcEmia* were the same diseases?

So Bernie's face, shining with discovery, annoyed me, and I listened impatiently when he announced that Mr. Stone was suffering from a genetic disease: alpha-1 anti-trypsin deficiency.

"Not just regular old asthma!" he exclaimed.

I searched my memory. This meant that his blood did not produce the enzyme that protected the elastic scaffolding of his lungs, and his alveoli, the little sacs of air that delivered oxygen to his bloodstream, were collapsing like so many burst balloons. Mr. Stone's disease would inexorably suffocate him, and not even the best lung specialist or the most advanced drugs would be able to save him.

His stubby finger on the page of the opened textbook, Bernie looked at me eagerly.

"Bernie." I glared at him. "Have you written his orders yet?"

"No, I, uh, I just got his old charts, and I, uh . . . ," he stammered, and I rose to the hunt, tasting blood.

"You are reviewing his old charts, and Mr. Stone is crumping in there," I said severely. Bernie looked alarmed and shriveled up a little. Turning away, I reached over with a little resigned sigh and stamped an order sheet with Mr. Stone's plastic hospital card. I scribbled down his diagnosis, condition, diet, activity, and lab work. I paused and looked over.

"What do I want to give him, Bernie?" I shot the question irritably.

"Um, aminophylline?"

"That will help him sometime tomorrow, Bernie; meantime he'll go out on you."

"Well, uh, probably some antibiotics?"

"His airways, Bernie! We have to try to open his airways, remember?"

"Well, I know you called respiratory." Bernie was sweating now, and he kept flicking the end of his ballpoint pen nervously.

"Oh, never MIND." I turned and began writing. Bernie was hopeless. He leaned over to peer at the order sheet. "Steroids, Bernie. He needs steroids."

"Sure . . . sure! I was just going to say that." Bernie took out his dog-eared copy of the Washington medical manual hastily and thumbed through the section on asthma.

"The dose is . . ."

"I know the dose, Bernie, thank you very much." I finished the order sheet, handed it to the ward clerk, and left Bernie in a dismal heap at the desk.

A half hour later, I came back to listen to Mr. Stone's lungs again. He had improved slightly. Now at least I could hear some wheezes. He wasn't so tight, but I was still unhappy with his exam. His muscles were working visibly, and despite his smile, I could see he was tiring out. Upon my questioning him, Mr. Stone shook his head. No, he had never had to be intubated and placed on a respirator. He shot a glance at his wife, who sat in the armchair near him. Her lips tightened.

As I knotted his hospital gown and picked up my clipboard, I asked her if they had any children. Yes, she nodded, a son and a daughter, both in their teens. I chirped politely in response, and she looked up at me.

"They both carry the gene," she said, then paused. "I've told them they should choose appropriate careers."

I looked at her face and thought, my God, what career is appropriate to dying? But I simply nodded, twisting the bell of my stethoscope back and forth.

Mr. Stone's condition worsened despite the steroids and the intravenous medicines, despite the physical therapists who came to pound the mucus out of his lungs, despite the respiratory techs who came armed with aerosolized treatments and masks that delivered moist oxygen, despite the elegantly dressed pulmonary specialist, who laid his stethoscope on Mr. Stone's chest and then pursed his lips, glancing over at me.

I moved Mr. Stone to the ICU, but all I could do was have him watched hour after hour as his breathing worsened. Finally I had to approach him with the question.

"No!" he said fiercely, between breaths. "No tube!"

I tried to explain that his lungs needed to rest. But all the while I was hoping he would keep refusing. I knew, and I suspected he knew, that once he went on the machine, he would never come off.

I went out to talk to his wife. She was sitting alone in the ICU waiting room on a mauve faux leather armchair. The walls were tastefully adorned with impressionist prints. A magazine lay open on her lap, but she was not reading it, just staring ahead absently. When I told her, she leaned back heavily in the chair and closed her eyes. She had a faded prettiness about her; the lines around her lips were etched by worry, but her hair was carefully combed and her figure slender and graceful. I thought they must have been a handsome couple before Mr. Stone's illness. I saw tears gather at the corners of her eyes, and then she opened them and gazed at me.

"I don't know what to do," she said. "Tell me what to do."

I looked at her in confusion.

"Maybe you should speak to the lung specialist," I said weakly, hating myself for my cowardice.

"All right," she said quietly.

The specialist advised intubation and a respirator, as I knew he would.

"Just think," he said, drawing me aside. "We advise against intubation, and then after he dies, some relative in Texas decides we didn't do all we could, and we have a malpractice suit on our hands."

I nodded gravely.

The specialist persuaded Mr. Stone to agree to the tube, painting a cautiously optimistic picture of the length of time he would have to be hooked up to the respirator. Then he went home and left me to do the intubation. I went about laying out the nasal spray, the laryngoscope, the endotracheal tube, ruminating to myself all the while:

Without the tube he would die, no question about that.

So what, was it better to be dependent for the rest of his short life on this machine?

He just might get off. Nothing is certain in medicine.

Then again, he'll probably be right back on in a matter of days or weeks.

On the other hand, it's so much easier to feel that we've done everything we can.

I wheeled the Bird, as we called the ventilator, over to his bedside.

Easier for us, that is . . .

I calmly explained the procedure to Mr. Stone. Bernie hung over my shoulder, his hot breath at my neck. I had forbidden him to help me, knowing his propensity toward clumsiness. I was sure he would knock over the tray and contaminate the sterile instruments. I elbowed him away slightly. After numbing Mr. Stone's nasal passage with cocaine spray, I slipped the thin, stiff tube up through his nostril, cupping my hand behind his head to stop his instinctive thrust backward, and tears jerked out of his eyes.

"Okay, okay, Mr. Stone," I said urgently in his ear. His hand clenched my elbow. "That's the worst, breathe normally, in and out."

He relaxed slightly, and keeping my ear at the other end of the tube to time his breathing, I slipped the tube down between his vocal cords when he inhaled. The respiratory therapist moved in quickly to inflate the cuff that would hold the tube in place, while I checked the tube's position with my stethoscope on Mr. Stone's chest. Had I put the tube too far down, inflating only one lung? I felt a little surge of satisfaction when I heard the breaths equally on both sides. Per protocol, I told Bernie to order a chest X-ray to make sure and watched the tech hook up the Bird, swiveling the dials, adjusting the respiratory rate. Mr. Stone lay with his eyes closed. As the machine took over the work of his breathing, his muscles relaxed, and he seemed finally able to rest. I took hold of his hand.

"Everything okay now, Mr. Stone? Getting enough oxygen?"

Mr. Stone, unable to speak through the tube, gave the thumbs-up sign. I drifted out of the ICU. Maybe it was the right thing to do after all, I thought, look how comfortable he is. I'll bet we can wean him off as soon as he's rested a bit.

But we couldn't. Day after day we measured his weaning parameters, to see how well his lungs could pull on their own, and every day we turned down the ventilator a little bit, only to have him become restless and agitated as his oxygen levels fell. The respiratory tech would hand me the latest set of arterial blood gas readings, and I would stare at them unseeing, knowing already what the results would be. I wrote orders: more steroids, more intravenous medications, more monitoring lines. The nurses stood endlessly at his side, passing slender tubes down his endotracheal tube and suctioning up mucus, until he gagged.

"Sorry, Mr. Stone. Just one more time," they would say, as he coughed and strained against the tube.

After two weeks the pulmonary specialist decided it would not be possible to wean Mr. Stone at this point in time off the machine, and he was moved to a private room out on the floor, since after all, his condition was stable. Mr. Stone's wife was overjoyed, viewing this as a sign of progress. Being in the ICU is unnerving for both patients and families, with the windowless walls, the harsh fluorescent lighting, the incessant beeping, the frantic commotion of the staff caring for patients *in extremis*. The evening-shift nurses try to create a semblance of night, dimming the lights and admonishing the residents to speak quietly, but in reality, it is difficult to run a cardiac arrest code in hushed tones. After a while, not a few patients become confused and agitated, exhibiting what is termed "ICU psychosis."

Mr. Stone had become Bernie's regular patient, and he would sit and write long notes in the chart every day, until I finally told him with irritation that if he didn't have anything new to add, he should keep his note confined to that day's physical exam, so I wouldn't have to plow through paragraphs of Bernie's illegible scrawls.

I was surprised to find that Bernie and Mr. Stone seemed to have developed a close relationship. Many times when I needed Bernie, I found him sitting by Mr. Stone's bed, talking to him and reading in return the notes Mr. Stone had written in a shaky, spidery handwriting.

A few days later, Bernie hovered over me as I was writing in a chart, and I finally turned to him and sighed.

"What, Bernie?"

He flushed.

"Well, I wanted to talk to you about Mr. Stone. He's not doing too well."

I reached for his chart with concern.

"What? Weren't his last blood gases good?" I began thumbing through the lab results.

"Yes . . . well, no, I mean, it isn't that," Bernie mumbled, then paused. I looked up at him.

"He's very angry."

I sat very still.

"What is he angry about?"

"He wants to get off the ventilator."

I turned back to my writing, keeping my eyes on the page in front of me.

"I'll go talk to him."

Mr. Stone's eyes flashed at me in fury as I walked in. With a reassuring smile, I strode to his bedside.

"Mr. Stone? What's the problem?"

He scratched out his response with a shaky hand.

"Get me off this thing."

"We're trying, Mr. Stone, you must be patient. Your lungs aren't quite ready yet . . ."

He grabbed the pad back from my hand and wrote again.

"They'll never be ready."

"Oh, now, Mr. Stone . . ." I patted his hand encouragingly. He gazed up at me, his eyes full of dull rage, like the eyes of a wild animal, its leg caught in a trap. My hand reached up automatically to his IV pole, as I pretended to check his line. My beeper went off. I hurried out, promising to return.

I didn't, though. I suppose I got busy; I had a lot of admissions that night. At ten o'clock, I was finishing with a central IV line on one of my new patients. Bernie was flushed with pleasure, as I had allowed him to help me, and things had gone surprisingly smoothly. I had noticed that his almost exclusive care of Mr. Stone had given him some confidence, and I had willingly given him the reins. We were walking back toward the nurses' station when my beeper went off. A panicky voice crackled, "Call 492 stat, 492 stat." I ran to the station and dialed.

"I'll be right there." I took off at a run, Bernie panting behind me.

"What is it?" he cried.

We reached Mr. Stone's room. He lay on the floor, breathless and blue, staring at me with dull defiance and pushing away the two nurses who were desperately trying to get him back on the bed. He had pulled out the endotracheal tube and had ripped out his intravenous line as well, so that the medications lay puddling uselessly on the floor.

"Wait!" I said and crouched down beside Mr. Stone. With his last remaining strength, he pushed the pad off his lap toward me. On it he had scrawled, "No Tube." I glanced over at Bernie, who stood frozen in the corner.

The lung specialist pushed his way hurriedly in. He had been paged from the ICU, where he had been consulting on a patient. He was visibly upset.

"What are you waiting for?" he demanded. "Can't you see he needs immediate reintubation?"

"He doesn't want to be on the ventilator," I answered dully.

"This man is ill and incapable of making any decision of that kind. If you won't intubate him immediately, I will do so myself." He turned to the staff. "Nurse! Bring me the intubation kit."

I stood by silently, watching as he took off his jacket and carefully rolled up his sleeves. Mr. Stone had become semiconscious, and the nurses lifted him back up on the bed. He offered no resistance as the specialist slipped the tube deftly back into place. Soon the rhythmic whoosh of the bellows of the Bird took up their monotonous syncopation, delivering life ceaselessly to Mr. Stone. The lung specialist picked up his coat and walked out. I followed him to the nurses' station. Bernie was nowhere to be seen.

The specialist turned to me and, in a not unkind tone, said, "You shouldn't let emotions cloud your judgment. In my opinion, this is a clear case of ICU psychosis. Mr. Stone simply spent altogether too much time in the unit. Ask the staff psychiatrist to evaluate him. Please make sure his steroids are restarted as soon as possible. I'll round on him first thing tomorrow morning."

He shrugged on his jacket and adjusted his tie. "Oh, and be sure to restrain his hands so he doesn't try this again. Good night."

•••

I found Bernie sitting next to the potted plant in the darkened waiting room of the ICU. I saw he'd been crying. He looked up at me.

"He didn't want it. He didn't want to be tubed. Why did you let them tube him?" he almost sobbed. I sat down in the chair next to him.

"Bernie . . ." I paused, unable to go on. I rested my head wearily on the back of the chair, feeling a sudden fatigue wash over me. My legs ached, and I noticed my sleeve was wet from Mr. Stone's leaking IV tube.

We sat together silently in the dark. Outside the waiting room, the nocturnal sounds of the hospital rose and fell.

My pager went off, the shrill beep piercing the darkness. I peered down at the number, then looked over at Bernie, slumped dejectedly in his chair.

I put my hand on his shoulder and shook it gently.

"Come on. We have some orders to write."

Diana Flescher *is a native New Yorker currently living in Israel. A specialist in internal medicine and women's health, she directs a private consultation practice and a nonprofit center for women in Jerusalem. She works to promote women's health issues at the policy level and teaches gender medicine to students and physicians.*

"Mr. Stone" is the winner of the *Creative Nonfiction* Best Essay Award,
chosen by the Jewish Healthcare Foundation.

Rules

MARIA MEINDL

Writer Maria Meindl learns some surprising things about her mother's Jewish legacy when she has to place her in a nursing home.

On our final visit to Dr. Goldman, she picked up one of my mother's hands and held it in both of her own. My mother's hands were brown and speckled, with long, thin fingers and hyperextended thumbs.

"Remarkable," Dr. Goldman said. "I wish I had a camera." She delicately turned my mother's hand this way and that, and my mother responded to her touch as if a lover had taken her hand or her own mother had risen from the dead to comfort her. She gazed up from her wheelchair at Dr. Goldman's face.

By "remarkable," Dr. Goldman meant the extent to which my mother's nails had clubbed. Over her years of illness, her fingernails had become rounded, as if a ball were growing under each of them. Recently, they had begun to grow closer and closer to the ends of her fingers. Now, they curled right over the tips. This was, said Dr. Goldman, a sign of advanced lung disease, but my mother did not seem to register her words, only the attention being given to her. I might have found what the doctor was saying clinical, unfeeling, but we'd been visiting her for more than a decade now, and I wasn't fooled by her gruffness. I think she was just looking for an excuse to hold my mother's hand.

My mother spent fourteen years on her deathbed. Not literally—she wasn't always lying down for one thing—but she was terribly sick and somehow managed to keep getting sicker. And sicker. The clinical name for her condition is systemic lupus erythematosus. It's a kind of bodily police state, in which cells that are meant to protect the system go on a rampage, attacking healthy tissue. To me, the description could have stopped at "disease." Dis-ease. That word described my mother's state, most of the time. Her joints were affected, her organs were affected, and so were her brain and central nervous system. It was hard to believe a person could have so much wrong with her and yet stay alive.

There were emergencies, many of them. Those were the days of deep cuts to public spending in Ontario. Many of Toronto's teaching hospitals were scattered among insurance companies and investment firms in the city's pristine business corridor. From the street, I could still believe I was living in "Toronto the Good," the safe and prosperous city where I grew up. Step through a door marked EMERGENCY, and I found chaos. It seemed no one was being looked after anymore. Bleeding, coughing, weeping patients were lined up on gurneys in the hallways. With the shortage of nursing home beds, overburdened caregivers had developed the strategy of leaving their dementia-afflicted parents in emergency for the night, just so they could get some sleep. Sometimes, it would take all night to find my mother a bed. When she finally was admitted, it was often to a place that did not have her history on file. One of the city's earnest young medical residents would sit by her bedside to ask a series of questions she had answered a hundred times before.

At a certain point, she refused to give any more information. On a good day she'd say something like "Well, my eyes work pretty well." And on a bad day: "I'm sick; can't you figure that out with all your goddamned degrees?" A few times a year, an earnest doctor would take me aside for a discussion of what to do in case my mother's heart stopped. Once, she seemed to be completely unconscious, and the doctor spoke to me about it right in the room, standing at the foot of her bed.

"I notice that your mother has not signed a do-not-resuscitate order," he said, "Would you like to—"

"You're going to have to speak to *her,*" I said, and my mother's eyes fluttered open.

The doctor began, "We're wondering—um—whether you would like us to take heroic measures if your heart stops, not that we're expecting . . . But in your present condition . . ."

And my mother interrupted: "Of course I do."

"Of course you . . . ?"

". . . want heroic measures."

"Well, you know, it would involve a pretty aggressive impact to your chest. There might be broken ribs, and the chances of us actually *starting* your heart again . . ."

"You heard me," she said and closed her eyes.

I learned to act calm in the face of all this. Steely, even, but it didn't go very deep. At night, I would start up, gasping for breath, with a blind compulsion to get to her—right away—in case . . . *In case what?* I asked myself. *Do you think you can keep her alive?* It wasn't that I thought I could prevent my mother from dying. It was that I felt I needed to be there when it happened. I didn't understand why I had this feeling, and I tried to reason myself out of it. *She might live a long time,* I told myself. *You can't let it run your life.* Friends said, "The important thing is to do what you can for her when she's living, and after all, most people die alone . . ."

Reasoning didn't help. Nor did it help that some of the time I wished she would die, if only to end the ongoing emergency in which we both lived. The threat that my mother might die alone kept me tethered to her for fourteen years, sent me rushing for the telephone no matter what I was doing, pushed me out of bed and into countless cold cabs to countless emergency rooms in the middle of the night. And those times when I deliberately went out of town or deliberately did not answer the phone, my choice was just that: deliberate. Rebel against or accede to it, the possibility that my mother might die alone dominated my life.

And there was a last-chance quality to every interaction with her. If I were impatient, distracted, or less than warm, I would be haunted by it until the next time I saw her. Truthfully, none of this started with her illness. There was always a quality of blind, breathless panic in my mother, as if she were being pursued by a menacing force. It was there beneath all her competence and decisiveness when she still was well—if you could ever have called her "well." I wondered how someone who lived so close to death, for so long, could still fear it. Eventually, I realized she was afraid not of death but of something else, something that I could never identify and that she herself was too frightened to name.

This threat had to do with religion, with anything ritualistic or solemn. My mother was a Sephardic Jew from England. Her family had stopped attending services around the time she was born, in 1930. Maybe they feared the anti-Semitism rife throughout Europe at the time. I like to think it was because my grandmother, Jemima, found the Sephardic community too conservative. (Before she married, Jemima had held a job and campaigned for women's suffrage.) Whatever the reason, the family did their best to assimilate. My grandfather, Aaron, became known as Harry. Daily, he stood at the mirror and tried in vain to slick down the shock of kinky hair that betrayed his North African heritage. My mother was given the name of Hetty, an anglicized version of Eti or Esther. But the rituals and customs lingered around the edges of the household and were performed furtively and without explanation. There were no celebrations—no Purim, no Shabbat, no bar mitzvahs (at least not for the younger children in the family)—only sudden, capricious changes in their diet and daily routines. The house would become suddenly quiet for a day or two—too quiet for the comfort of children—and then all would return to normal again. Every spring, a box of matzo would appear on the table, and my grandmother would eat from it for a week, brooking the teasing of her children in resolute silence.

My mother did not even hear the word *Jew* until she was evacuated during the war. Taken from her family at the age of nine, she was sent to a coastal town where she was to be billeted with a local family. Except that no household would give shelter to "a little Jew," a child with olive skin, an aquiline nose, and tight black curls. She ended up with a Salvation Army family, who prayed over her daily and made her stand in an oversized bonnet on a street corner, singing hymns.

My mother did not stay long on the coast. She suffered from what she called "nerves" and was sent back to London just in time for the worst of the bombing. At war's end her father, Harry, suddenly died, and their home was transformed by mourning rituals she did not understand: mirrors were draped in black, and groups of relatives she had never met trooped through the house to chant strange prayers and take over the management of the kitchen. My stricken grandmother rent her clothes and cast herself to the floor. "She died a little bit every day," my mother used to say of Jemima. It was nearly two decades later that Jemima actually dropped dead from a massive stroke. My mother was in Canada by this time, and the news came in the form of a telegram to Toronto: "Mother dead." I heard many times about the traumatic way my mother received that announcement, but there was a piece missing from the story. Years later I did the math. My mother had recently given birth to me when she heard the news of her mother's death.

My mother dwelled on being Jewish, even as she disavowed it. Trying to make her way in show business in the 1950s, she had surgery to remove the bump on the bridge of her nose. She married a man of Scottish descent whose family had been in Canada for five generations. Her mother-in-law did not even try to conceal her anti-Semitism, and she was not unusual for her time. Yet the "secret" of my mother's background was one of the first things anyone would know about her. "I'm an old Jew," she'd say. It was one of the self-mocking descriptions that formed her persona. Also included were her dark complexion ("a touch o' the tarbrush"), her "fat face," and her "nerves." My mother had the instincts of a clown. She said these things lightly and with perfect timing. Still, her remarks all added up to the same sobering message. My mother felt there was something wrong with her. Being Jewish was at the root of it.

My mother summed up her objections to Judaism in four words: "Too Many Fucking Rules." Myself, I was in it for the rules. Judaism appealed to me for the same reason my mother balked at it. She had always seemed completely consumed with grief over her parents' deaths, a grief unbounded and without any shape. As my mother's illness descended, it became clear that I would become intimate with all the grief and fear that haunted her. And I knew I would spend a lot of time thinking about death. It was more than I could handle on my own, and it seemed the situation would go on indefinitely. What

I needed were formulas, traditions, rituals; I needed someone to tell me what to do. Judaism provided this for me.

Feeling like an impostor, with my half-WASP background, I began attending Jewish services once a year for high holidays, observing other traditions with a group of friends. Not that I found any answers in mourning a death that went on for fourteen years. *She died a little bit every day.* No one seemed to have rules for that. Yet Judaism did offer something: the celebration of life's imperfection, the sense of what Susan Sontag once called "moral seriousness." Morally serious was a description of my life at that time. Every day I wrestled with enormous questions. How much could I give my mother without harming myself? How could I say no to her needs and still look at myself in the mirror every day? *If not now, when?*

Being Jewish did not provide just spiritual support. The practical help started with my mother's first hospitalization, back in the late 1980s. She was placed in intensive care for congestive heart failure. My father had long ago remarried. She had no family in Canada, only my sister and me, both in our twenties. We were all overwhelmed with making sense of her illness, wondering how she was going to get the care she needed through her inevitable decline. As soon as we mentioned we were Jewish, a social worker magically appeared at the end of my mother's hospital bed. In the years that followed, she got help in her home, subsidized housing fell into place when she needed it, and finally, one of the best nursing homes in the country had a place for her, costing no more than a regular government pension. No, we didn't have to belong to any particular congregation. My mother was Jewish; that was all it took.

I wished my mother were religious, because it would have made her easier to deal with, but still, I admired her for her iconoclasm. Iconoclasm *was* her religion, and she held to it vehemently, rejecting anything that might resemble a crutch. She had a hard lot in life, and she wasn't going to say or do anything to sugar-coat that reality. It wasn't that she didn't have faith. She refused to speak about it, though, or even give it any form, as if this would diminish it in some way. Her friend once told me she often asked herself how my mother managed to keep going without faith, when she was suffering so much. Then she realized that my mother expressed her faith by staying alive, day after day. Life was, to her, a challenge, and it was her job to face up to it.

The nursing home was in a part of town my mother contemptuously called "the country." It was Way up North: half an hour on the bus. My rides to see my mother began in the Annex, the cosmopolitan downtown neighborhood where I grew up. The bus then climbed a steep hill through a district of low-rise, aging apartment buildings and culminated in an area where streets curved away from the bus route, affording glimpses of substantial family homes in yellow brick. There were no movie theaters around the nursing home, no cafés you could walk to, only strip malls, garages, and the odd tenebrous kosher restaurant. Here, my mother spent the last two years of her life surrounded by the very people she had tried so hard to dissociate herself from: Jews. Anxious, angry, curious, hungry, flirting, arguing, dancing, *kvetching,* laughing, singing, weeping Jews. People like herself, in other words. She took guests on a tour of the home's valuable art collection as if she were Peggy Guggenheim, made a dinner of chopped liver and fresh bread every Friday night, and complained that I had moved her out to the country to live with crazy people in ridiculous hats.

Week after week I used to walk around the halls beside my mother while she rode her newly acquired scooter. This was her prized possession, a red scooter that had the brand name of "Jazzy." The social worker and physiotherapist had worked for hours, filling out forms and making phone calls to get funding for it. They also ordered an old-fashioned car horn with a rubber bladder she could squeeze to produce a rude sounding "toot" as she came around corners.

My mother had always worried that pushing her old manual wheelchair was hurting my hands. She was right. After visiting her I'd have pains like electric shocks running up my arms. Still, every time she pointed out that my hands looked red and swollen I changed the subject. Just because it hurt my hands to push the wheelchair didn't mean I could stop.

With the Jazzy, my mother was in charge of her own locomotion again, and, to her delight, I could walk beside rather than behind her. She was a dangerous driver. Disoriented, weak, she was constantly dropping off to sleep with her hand on the controls. She would slam into furniture and walls and the glass sides of the elevator. She would even run into the other people making their way along the halls with their walkers and wheelchairs and canes. Everyone did their faltering best to get out of the way when they saw her coming.

She was always on the verge of having the scooter confiscated. Yet the glances I shared with the physiotherapist over the crown of her graying head held the terrible knowledge that to take away this scooter would be a hurt beyond bearing. Another loss in an endless sequence of losses. But it didn't matter if the hurt was unbearable. One day, she would lose the scooter anyway.

I encouraged her to wait for my visits before taking a "walk." I would lean over and steer the scooter for her, using the lever on the armrest. She would rest her hand on my hand. Two ladies who always sat in the lounge would incline their heads toward each other as we passed: "The Daughter," one would whisper in a thick eastern European accent, and the other would nod with approval. "Very nice."

Early one morning, my mother's doctor called to tell me she wasn't well and that it was different this time. I'd better come right away. And so began a week when I sat by her bed, occasionally wetting her lips, covering or uncovering her when she seemed to need it. Whenever I was sitting in the room alone, certain images clamored persistently in my mind. I was mentally rehearsing what I would do if I had to lift her dead body from the bed and take it somewhere. A ghost body rose from my own and arranged itself around her. I slipped one of her arms over my shoulder, one of my arms under her knees. *What do I do? With her body?* The weight of my impending responsibility struck me in a way it never had in all the years I had spent expecting her to die. At some point over the next twenty-four, forty-eight, seventy-two hours, I was going to have a body to deal with. *There are people who do this,* I thought, *people whose job it is to know what to do,* but still I couldn't get rid of the feeling that I was going to have to carry her body, clean it, dispose of it in some way, and I didn't know how.

An atavistic fear? Some primal vestige of the days when family members prepared their elders' bodies for burial, when there was no designated other to do it? No, I had a practical problem to deal with. And, I realized, I had to deal with it right away. My mother had asked to be cremated, and she was Jewish, living in a Jewish nursing home. Jews aren't supposed to be cremated. Strange little dramas surged in my imagination. I'd have to fight with someone who was trying to take her body away:

No, you can't take her and bury her. She wants to be cremated.

"Well, in that case . . . get her out of here."

I would haul the limp body through the atrium of the nursing home in the middle of the day. *Those two again!* People would scurry out of our way.

"Can I speak to you for a minute?" I asked the doctor.

"Sure."

"I'm wondering, if—it happens, this week . . . "

"Well, you don't have to think about that yet."

"For how long? I mean, how long *don't* I have to think about it?"

"Well, not long. But you don't have to think about it yet."

"But how long is yet?"

"We can't really say."

I shook my head. Shook away all this evasiveness. I had to know. "Well, when," I said. "When. What do I do with her . . . with *it*? I mean: when my mother dies, what do I do with her body?"

"Oh." The doctor became solicitous, as if explaining the facts of life. "Well, you call a funeral home and you say, 'My mother has just died.' You might want to do some research on funeral homes this week. It's best to actually *choose* your funeral home, before somebody dies. There's the Basic Hebrew Burial across the street . . ."

"She wants to be cremated."

The doctor took a long breath. "There are many families," she said, "who make the decision to go against their parents' wishes. After all, it's you who'll be living on afterward. I'm not in a position to pressure you into anything, but you don't have to—you don't have to do what your mother says."

I had spent two years taking this doctor's advice and urging my mother to take it when she wasn't willing. But now, it was my mother and me against the doctor. When it came to what to do with her body, I knew I had to let my mother make her own rules. And so, when I wasn't at my mother's bedside, I gathered information on the telephone. In the end, it turned out to be very simple. There was a large, well-established Jewish funeral home that would pick up her body and hold the funeral, then transfer her somewhere else for the cremation. Apparently, it happens all the time. As the week wore on, friends gathered. My sister called often from her home in Europe. I dug through my mother's boxes of papers and found her will, her birth certificate, passport, papers for immigration, citizenship, divorce.

The drone of oxygen machines filled the room as I approached my mother's inert form on the bed. I saw no breathing. I touched my mother's hand and found it still warm. "I'm here," I said. She was turned away from me, toward the window, her eyes down, lips pulled away from her teeth, hands clenched inward. Her hands were spirals, seashells: fingers enclosing thumb, following the line of her nails, which curled around the ends of her fingers as if to walk away on their own. For once she did not respond.

I was not sure yet whether the moment of death was approaching or whether it had passed. *Were you there?* was the question I heard most often afterward. *Were you there?* (Now, everyone finally admitted it was important.) No, I was not. This week, it had become clear, would be the end, the real end, yet the night before, I had kissed my mother on the forehead at 11 P.M. and gone home to bed.

Tentatively, I passed my hand over my mother's eyes and cobbled together my best approximation of a Hebrew prayer. *She'd better be dead,* I thought, not even daring to imagine the stinging mockery that would come my way if she'd heard me. At last a nurse arrived. "Is my mother dead?" I asked her, and she said, "yes," as if she'd rather spare me the news. I asked her to turn off the oxygen machines.

"You might want to open a window," she said.

"You mean . . . for the smell?"

"No—no, it's just . . . You might want a window open."

I took her advice.

For the next few hours, I stayed in the room with my mother's body, waiting for her death to become official. First, the doctor had to sign a death certificate; then, the funeral directors had to take her body away. I paced the room and hummed to myself, trying to feel something spiritual or profound. I felt only blank. One moment after another slipped by as I sat with this lifeless body. In the last fourteen years I had come to believe I would never stop looking after my mother, and so it seemed that these particular, predawn hours would never end. Or they might not, in fact, be happening at all.

I began to feel an ache deep in my belly, in my womb. Here it was, exposed at last: the mystery of our connection. My mother was my child as much as I was hers. I had spent the last fourteen years protecting my mother, doing what she could not do, and now, dead, she could do nothing at all. Now I felt I must be the movement, the speech, the sentience she did not have. I was responsible. I must, at all costs, look after this body. I ranged around the room like a tiger in its cage.

In these empty gray hours I felt the first shreds of separation from my mother. The difference between us was manifest. I was alive; she was dead. At the same time, all boundaries between us seemed to disappear. The presence of death opened a kind of wormhole in which my experience was indistinguishable from hers, and this moment was merged with the moment, forty-three years before, when my mother learned of her own mother's death. That death was sudden and unexpected, an ocean away. I knew this morning, with a force that almost knocked me backward, how alone my mother must have felt when she got the news. She had no mother to show her child to. No mother to make me—or herself *as* mother—real. I understood that, all those years when I longed for her to let me go, she had been hanging on in order to protect me from feeling this alone.

I remained in the room with my mother's body for three hours. I gazed at her and hummed a few familiar tunes, the best way I could find to comfort myself. *It's over,* I told myself.

•••

As the sky grew marginally lighter, a succession of women began to present themselves at the door before starting their morning shifts. They were the ones who for the past two years had bathed and dressed my mother, combed her hair, fed her, straightened her nightstand and swept under her bed, measured her blood count and oxygen levels, comforted her when she woke in the middle of the night, administered many handfuls of pills. I knew them all by name, but this morning they introduced themselves formally, as if our history together so far had been erased by my mother's death. Accents of the world were unified by the same hushed, reverent tone of voice.

"I am Cecilia. I am sorry your mummy pass away."

"I'm Natasha. I did Mamma's evening care. She was comfortable. She said good night. I think she die peacefully."

"Hello, I am Margaret, I am sorry for your loss."

"Oh dear Hetty! Look, I am crying. I feel a real connection with her. She used to speak to me in Spanish. *'Hola, Juanita!'* she say to me, even the last day. Oh you poor girl, you lost your mamma. God bless you, we will miss our Hetty here."

Sometime later, I became aware of a presence in the doorway and turned to find two enormous men wearing dark suits and stovepipe hats. They were the funeral directors. Dragged from their beds this morning, they had come here through the freezing rain. They stood, sober and silent, at the door, and we stared at one another for a few moments.

"I'm—," but before I could say, "sorry," I imagined my mother's voice behind me: *Oh GOD. What riDICulous hats.* A giggle rose in my throat. "Excuse me," I said, covering my mouth, composing my face into an expression that befitted a grieving daughter. Suppressing the laughter made tears come to my eyes.

"Good morning," the taller man said, extending his hand. "We're from the funeral home."

They had been waiting for me to speak first. As a mourner, it was up to me to initiate the conversation.

"Tell me what to do now," I said.

"Leave her with us, please," the man answered, and I did.

Maria Meindl's *essays, poetry, and fiction have appeared in numerous journals, including the* Literary Review of Canada, Descant, Musicworks, *and* Queen Street Quarterly.

She has made two series for CBC Radio's Ideas: Parent Care (2003) and Remembering Polio (2007). Maria's biography of her grandmother, the poet and broadcaster Mona Gould, is forthcoming from McGill Queen's University Press. She is currently at work on a novel.

Life and Death and 911

CAROLINE BURAU

"It's difficult to quantify what a stranger's death should mean when you're knee deep in it, let alone a hundred miles away," writes 911 dispatcher Caroline Burau. "It's about powerlessness. It's about knowing our place. It's about doing everything humanly possible to keep death from occurring, then letting it go."

Yesterday, three people died on me before my shift was half over. Technically, they didn't die on me, by me, or anywhere *near* me, but they called 911 for help, and I'm the one who answered the phone.

The first was a female cancer patient with an unexplained hemorrhage. In the four minutes before police arrived at her home in North Minneapolis, her husband, screaming and panting, could tell me very little. "It's an arm bleed," I told the paramedics over the radio from my console in the dispatch center, so they weren't going in *completely* blind. The second was a guy in suburban Hennepin County. His wife found him hanging in their tool shed. How long he'd been there, she didn't know. I tried to calm her enough to cut him down, though I'm not sure it would have mattered. When police arrived, they said he was beyond help. The third was a teenager who drank something like seventeen beers and took his Sea-Doo out on a lake after dark. My caller, who had seen the teen crash into a speedboat and hit the water, couldn't get close enough to help him, so I spent the eight minutes before help arrived just making sure we had the right lake and the right boat landing. Location and speed are everything, especially when my caller said the boy wasn't moving. The dispatcher next to me ordered a medical helicopter to the scene, then canceled it when the first responders arrived. The boy was dead; there was no patient to transport by air or by ground.

As an emergency medical dispatcher (EMD), death is part of my job. When you call 911, if you have a medical emergency, the local police dispatcher may transfer you to me. If your husband is choking on a piece of steak, I can use my training and the software at my computer to tell you how to stand behind him, clasp your arms around his abdomen, and catapult that meat right back out of him. If your baby is having a febrile seizure, I can tell you what to do and what not to do and can tell you to calm down. It looks worse than it is. If you're thinking about killing yourself, I'll do my best to keep you on the phone until the police locate you and the paramedics can take you in for help.

I work for a hospital-owned ambulance company in Minneapolis, which has paramedics working all over the metro area and in outstate Minnesota. If you're on my emergency line, we may be five miles from each other or more than a hundred. Depending on the time of day, our living-room-sized dispatch center may be busy and humming with phones and radio traffic, keeping all six of us upright and punching line after line. Or we may be half asleep and bored. But at least once every day, I or a dispatcher sitting next to me will take a phone call from a person in some small, awful scene where someone has died. A bad day is one with a lot of those. An awful day is a death involving a child.

I didn't kill these people, but sometimes that's what we say. It's a joke; as an EMD, it's a way to blow off steam. It's a comment on how little control we actually have over death.

"Joe killed another one," we'll say after an old man keels over while shoveling his driveway (maybe our second or third death that day, depending on the weather.) "I can't believe you killed that 'chest pain.' He sounded fine to me!" Or, before dispatching an ambulance to a stubbed toe that should have just gone to urgent care if not for an overly anxious mother: "Stand by. I have to save a life here."

It's about powerlessness. It's about knowing our place. It's about doing everything possible to keep a death from occurring, then letting go if it does. Maybe I calmed the caller down enough to perform the first few rounds of

CPR. Maybe I got somebody to hold a towel over a gushing head wound at an accident scene. Maybe I sang the national anthem for all anyone would know, since nobody heard a word I said over the screaming and chaos.

Three deaths in just a few hours on the job is a lot, even for someone who's been doing this job for a while. It could be a record, but there's no way to know. We don't keep track of that sort of thing.

When we found out that the lady with the arm bleed had gone into cardiac arrest, we guffawed, let me tell you. "How'd you manage that one?" Linda snorted. "How'd you turn a little bleed into a DOA?"

"I don't know," I replied. "Talent."

In a 911 call center, sarcasm beats grieving every time. It's difficult to quantify what a stranger's death should mean when you're knee deep in it, let alone a hundred miles away from it. Then in just a few short minutes, you're disconnected for good and on the line with someone new.

The alternative is to throw a little funeral every time, for every death. But this doesn't work in a room full of ringing phones, radio chatter, and the constant expectation of that next emergency. Grief is slow. There are too many phone calls to take, emergent and nonemergent, and there are only so many people to take them. We take a break if we can after an emergency, crack a joke if we can't take a break.

None of us wants to admit to one another the reality: that we all fantasize about saving lives. Or at least we used to until we got here and realized how few people can actually be saved, or even need saving. Most of the time, we are talking about broken hips, flu symptoms, hospital-to-hospital transfers . . . a cacophony of calls of the kind you won't ever see on *ER*. Most of the time, we are shuffling people from place to place, and there's no adrenaline rush or drama or even a "thank you." When you add these numbers to the numbers of people who died before anybody ever called, and then divide that sum by the callers who are in a position to administer help, well, you have maybe a baker's dozen you've saved over the course of a career.

It's not what I'd imagined when I left my desk job as a newspaper reporter eight years ago to work at a county 911 center. I wanted to save lives. Three per shift would be great. I like to fantasize about that one great call where I've said everything right, taken the exact right authoritative tone, anticipated every need, and saved a life, two lives, a family!

One call stands out, though. I helped save a choking baby boy on Memorial Day last year. When I told the father how to push on the baby's chest with his two fingers, food popped out, and the baby started breathing.

I was elated that day. I can still hear that baby's gorgeous howl. I can still hear the *whoop!* of the father, the mother sighing and thanking God. When I'd left for work that morning, I had been miffed that I'd be missing a barbecue at my parents' house, that I wouldn't be joining my friend Kellie on her boat, celebrating the holiday with the rest of the "normal" world. Then four hours later, I gave some simple instructions to a panicked father, he followed them, and his baby went from not breathing to breathing. Listening to the baby cry for thirty seconds until the paramedics knocked on their door was joy beyond any missed holiday celebration. It was a trip around the world.

Calls like that will keep a person buzzed for days before the monotony of the daily routine sets back in, which it generally does. Still, it keeps hope alive for the next opportunity. We all want that high of knowing we changed the course of things, that we had power over death just once.

But sooner or later you inevitably let go of the idea that there's glory in this job. We don't get to pull toddlers from burning buildings or lift cars off accident victims. Instead, we have to watch too many lives slip away or, rather, listen to them slip away.

One afternoon later that summer, I took a call from a lady whose six-year-old daughter had just accidentally shot her four-year-old son. Even though ambulances, fire trucks, police squad cars, and one helicopter are all dispatched to her home, I know within a minute of talking to her that her son is beyond help. She describes a head that is no longer a head, but an open wound. She tells me she's holding a body that is no longer moving or breathing. The little boy is dead.

What she tells me about the injury to her son's head is so awful that for a moment, I can't stop imagining it. I picture the kind of devastation that an exploding bullet can wreak on a small, fragile head. I am lost for a moment in blood, biology, and the stillness that comes after the end, when the spirit has left the shell. My eyes move to the back of my day-planner, on which I keep a tiny preschool photo of my four-year-old nephew. The connection between the two boys sends a shock through my system. I shove those thoughts to the back of my mind. I can't let myself care as much about this boy as I do about my nephew, or I won't be able to function.

Because her house is so far into rural farm country, it takes several long minutes for the first helpers to arrive. Until that time, it's just me, this mother, and a terrible, incomprehensible death. I do my best to keep her from going into shock by asking her question after question. Where's the gun? Are there any other adults in the house? Is your house hard to find? I give her things to do. Hold the towel. Open the door. Lock up the dog. At last, the first deputy arrives on scene and I am disconnected.

Nobody will make a joke about this call. When it's over, Lu, a thirty-year veteran with several life-saves, a couple of baby deliveries, and thousands of other calls, comes to my station, puts a hand on my shoulder, and tells me to take a long break.

I step out into the August heat. The parking lot provides neither shade nor a place to sit, but still, it's a refuge from the ringing phones, LCD monitors, and air-conditioning. An ambulance pulls up to the security gate and waits as it slowly opens. The two paramedics wave to me as they drive by and into a large garage. A young couple push a stroller past the security gate; hip-hop music beats faintly from the townhouse complex beyond the privacy fence. If I want to cry, this wouldn't provide much privacy. If I want to scream, somebody would surely hear me—they might even call 911.

I decide to call my husband, Jim, also a 911 dispatcher. He's at work in the county sheriff's department next door and apparently busy, so he doesn't answer his cell phone, which eventually switches over to voice mail. By the time he calls me back on *my* cell phone, my break is over and I'm sitting back down, ready for my next call.

"Everything okay?" Jim asks, but I can't open those floodgates now, so I just tell him I'm having a tough day and leave it at that.

Then my 911 line rings. "Stand by," I tell my husband with equal parts fear, amusement, and hope. "I've got to go save a life."

***Caroline Burau** is author of* Answering 911: Life in the Hot Seat, *a Reader's Digest Editor's Choice and finalist for the Minnesota Book Award. Her work also has been published in the* Chicago Sun Times *and* Mpls.St.Paul Magazine. *Burau works as an emergency medical dispatcher in Minneapolis, Minnesota, where she lives with her husband, daughter, and three cats.*

Snowing in Krakow

MARCIN CHWISTEK

When palliative care physician Marcin Chwistek goes home to visit his dying father in Poland, he comes to realize that, despite his medical experience and training, he's not easily able to talk to his father about death.

In memory of my parents, Anna and Jacek

In the winter of 2004, just weeks before my dad died in an ambulance, en route to the hospital, from what the medical literature calls an "acute catastrophic bleed," I had flown to Poland to talk to him about dying. It would be my third and final visit.

This February visit happened suddenly, so I did not have much time to prepare. M., Dad's wife, had called me in Wisconsin, saying Jacek (my dad) was getting worse. His bone marrow was showing signs of worsening failure, and he was requiring blood and platelet transfusions regularly now. She was worried. I remembered talking to him on the phone just a few days before my arrival; his voice was raspy, distant, and barely audible. He was trying to persuade me not to come, since he was concerned about my leaving work again. He was afraid the trip would jeopardize my green card application and that my partner in my new medical practice would grow tired of covering for me. "I'm fine," he said. "Stay where you are." I bought the first available ticket, canceled my scheduled clinic patients, and one Monday afternoon drove from north-central Wisconsin to Chicago to catch a LOT Polish airlines direct flight to Krakow, Poland.

M. picked me up at the airport the following morning, and we drove directly to L. Rydygier's Regional Specialist Hospital—a huge, ugly rectangular building in Nowa Huta (currently the easternmost district of Krakow). I found my father in his pajamas, in bed, resting. His face, moonlike from high doses of steroids, was more ashen than I remembered. I hugged him strongly. His body felt weak and he was trembling. Sweat on his back came through the cotton of his pajama top, and as I pressed my face to his, a whiff of his body odor reached me, thick and slightly sweet, and I found myself thinking, "Oh my God, he is really sick."

A week later, during the last night of my stay (he agreed I'd spend the night with him, since I had to leave early in the morning for the flight back home), I was lying on a bed in his hospital room. Dad, tired and withdrawn, was stretched out on the bed next to mine. I was fully dressed, with my bags packed and the passport on the night table. If I extended my left arm I could touch him, and yet he seemed to be thousands of miles away, drifting in a country I had no access to. For the past few months I had been trying to accept the fact that he was not going to make it. From a medical point of view, everything was pointing in that direction—his worsening labs, the increased need for transfusions, the episodes of spontaneous bleeding from his gums and skin. And emotionally, I was having a hard time accepting it. Part of the problem, I told myself, was that I lived so far away and had not had a chance to talk to him directly. A long-distance phone conversation from my home in the United States was never really a good option. There was always too much static, literally and figuratively, on the line. This week-long visit, however, had gone by quickly, and despite many opportunities to talk, we still had not had "the conversation." I had imagined we needed to discuss medical facts and then talk about his plans for whatever time remained to him, the need for DNR orders on his chart, and the fact that any efforts at resuscitation were going to be futile (given the status of his bone marrow and his propensity to bleed). I wanted to make sure he was aware of his impending death, and I hoped he would make peace with it. I thought I would be able to reconcile my conflicting perspectives of being a physician and a son. But as in any arranged marriage, perfect on paper and in the minds of those who conceived of it, the reality turned out to be more challenging than I thought.

Death wasn't new to me. After all, I had been practicing medicine for close to ten years by this time. To this day I remember the dark green and swollen face of the first patient I had to pronounce dead after I'd been awakened in the middle of the night during my internship year in the mid-1990s in Krakow. There have been many more since then—a parade of faces. In 2003, a few months before this visit to my father, I had been accepted to a palliative care training program at Memorial Sloan Kettering Cancer Center in New York City. I was scheduled to start in June 2004, and from that time on I would take care of seriously ill and dying patients exclusively. Death would be an immediate threat for all of my patients, palpable and within an arm's reach. And I'd have to learn a new intimacy with it, too. But before I could begin my new job, my own father was going to be my dying patient.

I had once already been the son of a dying parent. My mom had died from metastatic colon cancer when I was a medical student and was unable to be with her. She spent her last night alone in a gloomy building of a regional cancer center in Krakow, confused, in pain, and short of breath. Would I be able to ensure that my dad did not share her fate?

During this week of my visit to my father, I only vaguely remember meeting with Dad's doctors and confused family members, who kept asking, "Is he going to beat this? Is it cancer?" They were flabbergasted by his rapid decline, not understanding that he had a terminal illness. I did my best to explain, but after a few days it became clear that they were expecting to see the popular image of a cancer patient, who declines slowly, over time, and whose ravaged body reflects the struggles of cancer conquering a healthy organism—weight loss, muscle wasting, pale aspect, and sunken eyes. Contrary to this, until now, my dad, in his early sixties and an early retiree from a metallurgical company, had been a robust man, who, just a couple of years before, began, with fresh exuberance, to build his life anew. He was all about the future, and the inexplicable failure of his bone marrow, preceded by cycles of relentless fever, the cause of which was never discovered, set him on an ever-accelerating downward spiral that was coming to an end. No one could imagine this was happening to him. Not even his doctors.

"It all began with a fall from a ladder," he would invariably reply when asked about the origins of his illness. "One afternoon I was hauling long pieces of wood upstairs to finish up the attic, and I lost balance and fell backwards. I must have landed on my heel first. It hurt like hell!" he would exclaim. "I lay on the floor and could not move for a few hours. M. found me there. I didn't want to go, but she took me to a hospital. I fractured my ankle, it turned out."

Dad, newly remarried, was building his new house. The house, the first he'd ever owned, was outside town, on a lot he'd bought from a cousin. This was his master project, his new nest, like his marriage—expanding with possibilities, offering new vistas, alluring with a promise of a new life. His leg was put in a cast, and Dad, frustrated and angry, spent the long weeks sprawled on a sofa in the living room, reading and watching TV—his leg resting on a stool. Six weeks later a surgeon removed the cast, and Dad resumed most of his activities. "I had fully recovered," he would typically finish his story. "Or so I thought."

Weeks later he developed a fever. He did not think much of it, stayed at home and planned just to "sweat it all out." To his surprise, the fever persisted for not just a few days but a week. M. insisted, and he went to see his family doctor, who claimed it must be more than a virus and prescribed an antibiotic. When it failed to cure the fever, his doctor ordered another more powerful, broad spectrum antibiotic. Despite the treatment, each afternoon, Dad's temperature would climb precipitously. His muscles ached and throbbed as the fever ascended, and when it reached 104 degrees Fahrenheit, the pain would resolve and leave him drenched in cold sweat, his pajamas soaked. The fever would appear at exactly the same time each day, and the sequence and timing of his symptoms would repeat with a clocklike precision. There was something premonitory in the way the symptoms manifested, as if orchestrated by a vicious conductor who was executing his plan with the precision of an underground terrorist. As we soon discovered, the fever would occur in cycles, each lasting for months. Each cycle would start and disappear without any logic, at least any logic we could understand. One afternoon he simply would feel the aches and familiar symptoms of cold rising in his body, and a cycle would begin, lasting for weeks. And then suddenly the fever would disappear completely, only to return weeks later, and the process would repeat itself again. When the initial series of antibiotics did not get rid of the fever, my dad was sent on a diagnostic journey. He had labs, X-rays, CT scans, and endoscopies. He was tested for hidden sources of infection, malignancies, connective tissue diseases, and drug reactions. During his second cycle, thanks to the goodwill of a couple of colleagues from my medical school, we succeeded in having him admitted to the university hospital on Skawinska Street in Krakow. A well-respected and internationally known clinician and researcher, professor Andrzej Szczeklik, the same man I had taken classes with during medical school, was overseeing his care now. We were hopeful. The hospital, located in the heart of Kazimierz, the historical Jewish district in Krakow, was funded by the Congregation Israel in 1861. The building was profoundly damaged at the end of the war and remained in very poor condition until 1989, when it was rebuilt and modernized. A new five-story wing was added, including a terrace, accessible to patients and families, that overlooked the historical neighborhood. My dad was mesmerized. He spent long hours there, sipping coffee, reading books, and writing letters. He liked to be there, and M. caught many of those moments on camera. In one of the pictures he is standing at the edge of the terrace. Behind him looms the Wawel Royal Castle and St. Catherine's Church—a large Gothic structure surrounded by the sloped roofs of residential buildings. Dad wears a white cotton bathrobe over his blue hospital-issued pajamas. He holds the tip of his wire-rim glasses in his mouth; he looks tan and happy. If it weren't for the faint patch of white dressing covering an IV line that peeked from underneath his sleeve, you'd never know he was at a hospital. Predicting our bewilderment, he jotted a few lines on the back of the picture that he sent along with a letter. "*So, what are you going to say? This is a therapy! Despite colonoscopy, bone marrow biopsy, endoscopies, fasting, and IV drips the patient is still happy! What is it? Prof. Szczeklik's hospital. The best in the world, because it has terraces and it treats its patients with music and magic.*" A few weeks later, following further consultations with specialists and more tests, my father's exuberant sense of hope and optimism gave way to the crushing frustration and fear that perhaps his stay "in the world's best hospital" was going to end the same way it started. With a fever, but still without a diagnosis.

My dad approached his illness the way one would expect an engineer to react. He attacked it with meticulous scrupulousness. He bought himself a digital thermometer and plotted the curves of his fevers. He wrote down his lab results, descriptions of his radiological studies, and conversations with doctors. He monitored his medications and wrote down the exact time he took them. When meeting with a physician for the first time, he would hand over a thick stack of papers containing his calculations. Each time, without fail, the doctor would take it from him and smile in disbelief at his persistence. I doubt the doctors ever reviewed his many pages of notes. The amount of data he accumulated was staggering. But I knew he collected his observations because he strongly believed that someone eventually would notice a nuance the others had missed, and his case would finally be solved.

During the long course of his illness, I had asked him to send me the copies of his tests, and he did. I felt he did so more out of a sense of humoring me than with real hope that I could help him solve the mystery of his disease. That he valued my opinions, I did not doubt, but he also wanted to shelter me from direct involvement in his case. "You are my son, not my doctor," he once told me. "Besides, you have enough of your own problems," he added, making me only feel guiltier.

As his disease progressed, I tried to do my own research. I called my physician friends and discussed the case with them. We brainstormed, we argued, we speculated. After each of these discussions, I made a list of tests or treatments to consider and called Dad and M. to explain the rationale. They would later discuss all these with his doctors. The process was not easy. My recommendations were not always compatible with the protocols of his doctors. I thought they were not aggressive enough and waited too long to do tests. They felt they had been doing everything there was to do and thought I should relax and trust them more.

One Monday evening in December 2003, just a few months after my second visit to see him, I had had a particularly long clinic day, and by the time I finished dictating my charts, there was no one else left in the building. I was sitting at my desk, surrounded by stacks of papers—Dad's test results and copies of research articles. It was a typical Wisconsin January evening, dark and bitterly cold. I was really tired. I reclined in the chair and looked at the radiological view box on the wall opposite my desk. White fluorescent light seeped from underneath a patient's CT images. I stared at it for a while. Gradually a sense of overwhelming sadness filled me. It was a strange feeling, heavy and dark, and I let it linger, figuring it would disappear the way it emerged. Soon however, I felt like a mantle had surrounded my body; my head was immersed in an impenetrable cloud of heaviness. "What is happening?" The feeling was unusually strong, and I wanted to blame it on fatigue and midwinter blues until I realized I was staring at my dad's images. Of course, I had talked to a radiologist at the hospital earlier that day, and I had put the images up in the view box for a review. I covered my face with my hands, giving in to a feeling of powerlessness; my shoulders quivered uncontrollably.

Later that week my dad made a decision. Overnight, he lost all interest in monitoring his disease and abandoned his journals, graphs, and notebooks, which from that day on lay stacked in disarray on the floor in his bedroom.

"Once upon a time, all fevers were of unknown etiology," Charles Bryan wrote in an editorial published in *Archives of Internal Medicine* in 2003. It wasn't until Carl Reinhold August Wunderlich, a German scientist and father of clinical thermometry, defined the range of normal body temperature (in his book *Das Verhalten der Eigenwarme in Krankenheiten,* published in 1886) that fever lost its cloud of importance and came to be recognized merely as a clinical sign, no longer a disease. "By the mid-20th century, most [fevers] had been unmasked by science, but a few continued to present thorny dilemmas," Bryan continued. Normally most fevers are brief and, in the majority of cases, are caused by minor infections, usually viral. A small subset of fevers, however, persists without an obvious cause. A fever of unknown origin, or FUO, as it is called in the literature, is a term coined and defined by Beeson in his landmark paper "Fever of Unexplained Origin: Report on 100 Cases," published in 1961. Beeson's definition ("fever higher than F 101 on several occasions, persisting without a diagnosis for at least three weeks, including at least one week of investigation in hospital") had remained valid for decades and was modified only recently to reflect the modern change in clinical practice. Today, most investigations can be done on an outpatient basis, and therefore the requirement for "one week of inpatient hospitalization" has lost its validity. My dad certainly met all of Beeson's criteria. With the arrival of modern diagnostic techniques, many persistent fevers are eventually found to be caused by a number of different disorders: hidden malignancies, rare infections, reactions to medications, and systemic diseases like lupus. Surprisingly, however, in a relatively large number of patients with prolonged fever, even twenty-first century medicine can still be powerless. In one study, researchers from Belgium followed a group of 290 patients who had a fever of more than 101 degrees Fahrenheit for at least three weeks. All of these patients were treated in the university hospital in Leuven, Belgium, in the 1990s. In about 34 percent of the cases, a cause of the fever was never found. The authors wrote, "Some prolonged fevers remain enigmatic despite vigorous diagnostic effort. The 8 patients who died in the hospital before a unifying diagnosis exemplify this: the autopsy revealed the cause in only 5. An overview over the last 5 decades of the large FUO series from university-based centers in Western countries shows a clear trend toward an increasing amount of unresolved cases."

In the winter of 2003, I was convinced my dad was going to be one of them.

"Would you like some coffee?" he suddenly asked. We were lying on our beds, not a yard apart in a hot room on the nineteenth floor of the hospital in Nova Huta. Bags of red blood cells and platelets hung on a pole by his bedside. For weeks his blood platelet count had been below 10,000 (normal range is between 150,000 to 350,000 per microliter of blood). His body was covered in maroon-colored spots, signs of superficial skin bleeding. He had had repeated bone marrow biopsies that showed patches of desolate bone marrow, "hypo-cellular . . . with elements of fibrosis," as I read later in the report.

Not waiting for my answer, he got up from his bed and shuffled to the windowsill, where he kept an electric kettle and a jar of instant coffee and cups. His body was profoundly changed. The high dose of steroids he had been given in a desperate attempt to combat his fever caused him to have diabetes, severe heartburn, and weight gain. He felt anxious and wired (from the stimulating effects of the steroids) and spent nights in a steroid daze, unable to sleep, yet deeply tired from his anemia. I watched him move and was devastated seeing his deterioration. My dad, always strong and healthy, seemed broken. *Talk to him*, I heard a voice in my head tell me. *Talk to him*, the voice insisted. *Now.*

I could not have imagined a better opportunity—we were alone in a hospital room with nothing else to do. And yet I found myself paralyzed. I watched him prepare the coffee. I followed his slow, calculated movements—his reach for the white porcelain cups, a spoon in his right hand, the exact measure of finely ground coffee, hot water pouring in. *How are you doing, Dad?* would have been simple enough. He handed me a cup without a word and shuffled back to his bed. He sat down on the mattress, looked at me, and I smiled back. There was complete silence in the room, and I wished he could hear my thoughts. *Talk to me, please, talk to me,* I kept pleading, and when he opened his mouth intently, as if thinking about what he might want to say, I straightened my back and leaned forward with anticipation.

"How about we watch a movie?" he said.

I tried to muffle a moan that nevertheless managed to get out.

Why is it so hard for us to communicate? I thought. We never had had this problem before. *What's stopping us?* Much later, in 2006, I came across James Hallenbeck's article ("High Context of Illness and Dying in a Low Context Medical World") and finally understood what had happened that night in Krakow. The premise of Hallenbeck's paper is based on an idea of anthropologist Edward Hall, who classified communication between people "as being relatively higher or lower in [cultural] context." According to Hallenbeck, my father and I were simply "out of synch." Dad's disease had changed his body, and we both saw it clearly. The body, however, points toward two radically different realities: a biologic process on the one hand (which is what I, being a physician, focused on) and a personal experience unfolding in the context of human relations on the other (which is what he was experiencing). His sense of time was markedly different from mine, and so was his physical space, shrunken to the raw and sterile hospital room. His sense of personhood, severely stunted by his vulnerability, had catapulted him into a different galaxy, and all I could do was to watch him as if from a distance. Clinicians function primarily in the scientific world of medicine; they see illness as a biologic process, and in communication primarily use the low context, that is, precise language of medical terminology. Patients, on the other hand, try to fill the blank page the illness has handed them with their own story. They desperately want to fill it with their own words. Only in rare moments of empathic intimacy can those two radically different universes be reconciled, if only for a moment.

Dad settled into bed, dimmed the lights, and turned up the volume. He was ready. As the movie started, I recognized a typical midwestern landscape: a quintessential main street with a diner and a bar in its center, pickup trucks parked along the curb, and fields of corn, surrounding the town like an ocean. The images would not have meant anything to me a few years before; another American story, I'd have thought. But this night in the hospital, they aroused in me an unexpected feeling of homesickness for my adopted country. I thought of my wife, Marta, and my son, Philip. How strange, I told myself. I am in Krakow, my hometown, next to my dad on the final night of my stay, quite likely the last night I am ever going to spend with him, and we are watching a movie about the Midwest! I looked at him comfortably stretched out in bed, waiting for the movie to start. I got up and put my face against the cold glass pane of the large window in the room and looked outside. "It is snowing," I said, and it made me smile. I felt suspended in the air, flying among extraordinarily large flakes of snow. The city below appeared distant and desolate.

Nowa Huta, a town a few miles outside the city of Krakow, was created by the Communist government in 1949 as an antidote to the artsy and intellectual Krakow, a city the Communists hated. In the summer of 1954, the Vladimir Lenin Steelworks (now T. Sendzimir's Steelworks) was opened, and in less than two decades the factory became the biggest steel mill in Poland. The town grew quickly and was soon filled with a budding mass of ugly apartment buildings built on the promise of a prosperous life for all of its largely blue-collar workers. And yet, despite the government's best efforts, like the acrid smog that filled the air, a sense of doom soon hung over Nowa Huta. The idea for a new and modern hospital serving the local population was conceived sometime in the 1970s. The construction began soon thereafter, but the hospital, a gargantuan and ugly square building erected on a hill, like a glass and aluminum castle, foreign, distant, and overwhelming, stood half finished and empty for years and did not open until the winter of 1993.

The streets far below were completely empty, submerged in whiteness that appeared unreal. I could make out the shadows of people in a mosaic of dark and lit windows in a four-story apartment building across the street. I felt completely removed from their lives.

I had to force myself to watch the movie. Slowly, as the scenes played on the small TV set affixed to the ceiling in the far corner of the room, the movie pulled me in, and for a while I forgot about my dad, his illness, Krakow, the hospital, and my flight back home. I followed Alvin Straight, the main character, and his odyssey to reunite with his estranged brother, Lyle, in Mt. Zion, Wisconsin (a true story). Alvin, played by Richard Farnsworth (who received an Academy Award nomination for best actor for his role in the film and who killed himself one year after the movie was made), is seventy-three, crusty and frail, with bad hips, and in constant pain. His vision has deteriorated, he has lost his driver's license, and yet when one late summer evening a call comes from a relative announcing that Lyle has had a stroke, Alvin quickly decides to make the nearly three-hundred-mile trip on his own. As he explains later in the movie, "We were once very close. . . . I just want to sit with him again and look up at the stars." One day, he climbs onto an old riding lawn mower and sets off on a trip across the flat landscape of the American Midwest at five miles per hour. The movie, *The Straight Story*, was directed by David Lynch, but it bears no resemblance to *Twin Peaks* or *Blue Velvet*. After all, it is a "straight story," without convoluted narratives or lost ears in the field. In one of his interviews while talking about the movie, Lynch said that it was the emotional character of the story that attracted him. Lynch's visual talent, the painter in him, clearly shows in this movie. There is beauty in the most unlikely shots: the identical and perfectly square fields of corn, the long stretches of black highway, the empty one-street towns. The movie is a meditation and, as such, has a slow, poetic rhythm to it. That night in Krakow I gave in to it, letting myself sink into the odorless white hospital sheets, tucked in by the soulful music of Angelo Badalamenti, Lynch's long-term collaborator.

The brothers meet in the final scene of the movie. Alvin arrives on his riding lawn mower at Lyle's decrepit house. He shouts Lyle's name, and after a long moment Lyle responds, emerging from deep darkness.

"Did you ride that thing all the way up here to see me?" he asks.

"I did, Lyle," Alvin responds.

The brothers have not seen each other in ten years, but they don't hug or even shake hands. Alvin silently looks up at the sky, and the movie ends as it started, with a wide shot of a starry night. This time, however, they share it, as they used to, on a farm in Minnesota, decades earlier.

I turned my head to the left and watched my father for a long moment. He was lying on his back, still enthralled by the movie's magic, his left hand tucked under his head. With each exhalation he gave out a loud moan, almost a cry, which he did not seem to notice. How had all the gasping, moaning, and loud breathing become the new norm? I wondered. And yet viscerally I knew that nothing had really changed. Underneath all of these odd noises, and in a body I could hardly recognize, was the same father I had always known. I felt an urge to get up and hug him, and one thing I regret to this day is that I did not act on that impulse right then. I wanted to run my fingers along the contours of his changed body, to feel the coarse texture of his skin, the velvety touch of his palms, the flaccid muscles of his formerly sculptured calves. As I imagined our closeness, I was overtaken by a visceral sense of gratitude, a warmth that filled me then. I was flooded by feelings of compassion—for him and for myself.

The movie ended, and we did not say anything for a long time. We let the credits run, as if we were in the movie theater and wanted to know who designed the set.

The air in the room was dry, and I put a glass of water next to my bed.

"Do you need anything?" I asked quietly.

"I'm fine; sleep," he said. "I will wake you."

I turned toward the window. Lying in bed, I could see only a fragment of the sky, full of heavy clouds threatening to release more snow. Curled up, as if to thwart a sense of loss growing in my chest, the finality of the moment dawning on me, I fell asleep.

As the taxi pulled away from the curb in front of the hospital a few hours later, I looked at the wall of windows in the huge hospital building and located the one in his room. I saw a shadow of a lamp in the sea of blackness, and I knew he was looking out at me. I tried to imagine what he saw: a tiny car moving along roads covered with snow, getting smaller and soon disappearing around the corner. I sat on the backseat with my head turned to the rear window. When the taxi stopped at a red light, I opened the window and stuck out my bare hand. Large snowflakes landed in my palm. I felt the touch of cold, but the sensation dissolved almost immediately into a miniature pool of ice water. I looked back but could no longer see the hospital. I closed my eyes, and as warmth emanating from a sleeping body permeates a bed, I sensed his presence filling the air. I imagined it carried the snowflakes, making them float briefly, only to let them fall onto the ground in spirals of vibration and dance. I watched as they found their way, fell, and disappeared in the snow on the ground.

***Marcin Chwistek** is a physician who specializes in cancer pain management and palliative care. He is a native of Poland and currently practices at Fox Chase Cancer Center in Philadelphia. He has written short stories and magazine articles. He is also a frequent speaker on issues regarding management of cancer pain and end-of-life care. He lives with his wife, Marta, and their two children, Philip and Lena, in the suburbs of Philadelphia.*

Do You Remember?

PATRICIA McCARTHY

Veteran nurse Patricia McCarthy lives with the ghosts of the past—those she could not help, those she fought valiantly for, and those who changed her, helping her to acknowledge when she has failed.

Sometimes, while drinking coffee or browsing through a stack of books in the Ravenswood or Edgewater neighborhoods of Chicago, I'll get stopped by someone who smiles hesitantly, a bit embarrassed and maybe even a little fearful. Or I'll be in line at the Jewel Food Store or at the bar in Galvin's Public House, and they'll approach me and say, "You took care of me. You took care of my mother, my father. You took care of my spouse."

They ask, "Do you remember me? Do you remember my loved one?"

I don't mind being stopped. In fact, I welcome it as a reminder that I must have done something right. But I'm uncomfortable with the questions.

I'm uncomfortable because I see the plea in their eyes—they want me to remember. In my fifteen years of nursing, I have had so many patients, and I have a poor memory for names. But there is something I want to say, something these public moments, with all their rushing and intrusion and noise, prevent me from saying. I want to tell them their loved ones still exist for me, that in quieter moments I can summon them and speak to them.

I admit it. The ER terrified me. I was a new nurse, unused to the bustle and clamor of a big city emergency room. I was lucky to find such a well-paying job right out of school, a position that required me to go wherever I was needed. That afternoon, the nursing office sent me to help in the emergency room, to be an extra pair of hands for the overwhelmed staff. As I passed the curtained trauma rooms and tried to absorb what I was hearing and seeing—the clipped speech of the staff, the flashes of red, the twisted faces and broken bodies—I wondered how I could possibly help anyone there. I passed a soot-covered fireman in a black rubber coat, his helmet still smoking and his arms wrapped around a tiny motionless bundle.

"There's a lady in 6," the charge nurse said, shoving a paper into my hand and motioning the fireman into an empty room. "A nursing home patient. A DNR. No family. Take care of her while we do this, okay?"

I have forgotten the details of your face, but I still see the thin cottony hair, the little bird-claw hands, and your papery skin, thin like an onion's, but soft. A respiratory therapist is at your bedside, but he slips away, relieved of this particular duty, and, with a shake of his shoulders, gathers energy to move on to the next. He can do nothing for you but wait, and now that I have arrived, he can move on to the other patients who need him. Now you and I are alone. I look into your face, into your (blue?) eyes, and I see that you are no longer aware. Your sight is going. I look up at the monitor, and the toothlike complexes, the symbols of life, are still there, but they are widening. I look down at you again. You stare at someplace beyond my shoulder, but I do not turn to look. I hold your hand. I watch your chest as it rises, slow . . . slow. I look up at the monitor again. The complexes are tiny slopes now, a mere wandering line. Your breathing is slowing, faltering. And then, nothing. I grip the side rail. I listen and wait. And wait. And wait.

"Is she gone?" a voice says behind me. The charge nurse is standing in the doorway. "Is she?"

I nod.

She is shuffling a stack of papers and says without looking up, "Can you print a strip of her asystole for her chart?"

I nod again. She looks up from her paperwork and says, "Are you okay?"

"I've never seen anyone die before," I say.

"Oh," she says. She peers over my shoulder and sighs. "Sometimes these poor old folks outlive everyone they love. They're not sad to go." She clears her throat and hands me a slip of paper. "Can you take this new patient?"

"But what about . . . ?"

"Oh, don't worry about her," she says. "The tech will take care of her. Your new patient is already here. Possible stroke. You better hurry. Strokes don't wait."

I am busy for the rest of the shift, and the next time I pass your room it is clean and empty, waiting for another patient.

It is the Wednesday before Thanksgiving, and my sisters and I gather at my parents' house to prepare a sit-down dinner for thirty-five guests. From the sidewalk I gaze at the yellow brick of the Chicago bungalow where we grew up, at the gable where we peered out at the street and called to friends, at the pillared porch where we sat and played together. For the first time in my life, the sight of my childhood home fails to comfort me.

Inside, I can't concentrate. I keep seeing the first time you didn't breathe, that terrible moment of absence. A strange feeling overtakes me, as if I have left something undone or have missed something important. I am chopping vegetables and find myself pausing to look around. While ironing a tablecloth, I strain to hear some far-off sound. While my sisters joke and tease and bustle about, I catch myself standing still and staring off. I am aware that I am waiting for something, but I do not know what I am waiting for.

Thanksgiving dinner drags on and on. The conversation seems silly; the sound is jarring like the raucous chatter of exotic birds. I tune it out, and instead I listen to the silence of the lulls in the conversation. Finally, sick of the smells and heat and noise, I go out into my parents' backyard to be alone. The night is cold, the sky clear enough to see a few stars.

I sit on an old splintered bench and look around. The streetlight behind the garage throws the basketball court into shadow. A few strands of faded gray webbing hang forlornly from the hoop. Just beyond is the withered lilac bush that was planted the year I was born and which, my father has assured me, will die this year or next. I listen and wait.

You had lived eighty-five years, had been a baby, a child, a woman. You had tramped this earth for eighty-five years, such a long time, and when you left, nothing happened. Had I really thought there would be a roll of thunder, a trumpet would sound, and the earth would crack open? No. Yes. *Something*. I had expected something to happen. Not just . . . silence.

I sit outside in the cold and look at the sky for a long time and think about how fragile you were. I think about how you faded from the world without protest or noise. I think about how that world went right on without you. And I know, someday, I too will fade from the world, and the world will keep going on without me.

My assignment sheet provided only the barest information about you. "Jack Smith," it said. "Seventy-two years old. COPD. Lung cancer." If I wanted to, I could find pages of information about your body. A tap of a computer key would produce your weight. With a glance at a page, I could find out the chemical makeup of your blood. There were even color photographs of the inside of your body, but there was no section in your chart with clues on how to help you emotionally. You were so depressed, you stopped speaking, and no one could help you.

I think about you. I think about that January evening, the bitter air so cold it left frost on the inside of your hospital room window. I see you looking at that patch of frost, like lace against the inky black night. I think about writing your name in it. I hear the tempo of your breathing increase, jagged edges to your normally wheezing breath. The cough returns, harsh, barking. The tech comes in. "Time for suction," he says. We nod at each other, and I gather your hands in mine. Then the struggling begins, the flailing arms, the desperate grabbing of your hands and the jerking of your face.

"Stop!" you scream. The tube and the moisture in your throat rattle your vocal chords. "Stop it! Leave me alone!"

Your screams are so feeble. I am tired of hurting people.

I shake my head at the tech, and he leaves.

You gasp and cry. Your face is wet. I get a washcloth and wipe it carefully. You grab my hand, struggle to sit, your mouth works.

"I'm . . . so . . ." You gasp. "I . . . want . . . I want . . . I want . . ."

"You want to die," I say. I don't know how I ever got the courage to say it.

You freeze. Your mouth drops open. With great gusting sobs, all that you have been holding in, unable to say or even to name, breaks apart. But I have said it now, and your face is awash with sorrow and relief and gratitude. "Oh . . . yes . . . yes, I do. I do. I do."

Underneath your sweat-soaked gown, the stringy muscles of your chest strain with every breath. I untie the sodden cloth from your neck and replace it with the softest one I can find. I discard your rumpled bedclothes and cover you with a fresh, cool sheet. I flick off the fluorescent overhead light.

You settle down again, but you are different. Your breathing is easier now. I know you will tell your family what you want.

Just beyond the frost-laced window, I can see Lake Michigan, the diamonds of reflected light from the cars on Lake Shore Drive. A feeble rustling draws my attention back. Your restless fingers scrabble over the fold in the top sheet. I reach down and take them in mine.

We are together in a soft circle of light from the bedside lamp. In silence, we stare at the frost on the window and you squeeze my hand.

My assignment read, "Your objective in this clinical rotation is to obtain a rudimentary understanding of the impact of end-stage illness in the pediatric population. Special attention should be paid to the impact on patients, family, and caregivers."

I was a student and didn't know what to do. I was supposed to be learning from you, assessing you, discussing with your family their impending loss of you, but I felt stupid and inadequate. It felt wrong. So I faked my paperwork for my instructor and played with you all day.

We pretended that the gray tile floor of your room was a vast, bubbling lake and your bed was a tiny boat floating in its center. The unadorned concrete walls became the moving walls of a dungeon, entrapping us until you used the lone, rickety visitor chair as a steel beam, wedging it between them and saving us from certain peril.

In the afternoon, we raced Matchbox cars down the sloping bedrails and across the tray table. I refused to let you win, and you liked that. When you cheated, I play-spanked your hand, and when you won, I ran my toy car over your head, softly, of course, especially over your shunt. You liked that even more.

Your grandpa came just as I was leaving for the day, and you made him get the wagon so you could ride with me to the elevator. I'm glad you didn't see my face when your tiny, wasted legs were revealed from under the sheets.

You didn't say a word when I got into the elevator, but your eyes never left mine, even as the doors closed.

That was eighteen years ago. You would be twenty-three now.

Sometimes I pass the children's hospital. I drive through the Lincoln Park neighborhood of Chicago, where block after block, stone mansions sit behind locked black iron gates. During the day, uniformed nannies push children in strollers as big as shopping carts or drive them about in sleek foreign cars that seem to float down the tree-lined streets.

But at night, the DePaul University students own Lincoln Park. Crowds of young people stream in and out of bars and stores. They are smoking in doorways. They are parading up and down and laughing. They are always laughing. They squeal and grip each other's arms as they race across the busy streets. I search the young faces around me for some familiar feature, an upturned nose or a pale freckled face. Sometimes, a young man will step into the glare of my headlights, and, just briefly, he will meet my eyes through the windshield. I am breathless.

These people are your age, but you are not among them.

The painful truth is that you spent most of your life in cold, tiled rooms and in beds that smelled of bleach and sickness.

I could have come back to visit you. I think you needed someone to relieve the boredom. I think you would have welcomed a person who didn't treat you like a fragile bird. I couldn't come back. I didn't have the strength to watch you go.

You said, "You will take care of her, won't you?"

You stood over me and stared at me until I had to look at you. All day long you followed me from room to room, with little requests. More water. The blinds are stuck. Another blanket. Not this one. It's scratchy. Could I look at a dot on her foot? Her IV looks like it's going to beep.

I wanted to scream at you, *Do you have any idea what I'm up against today? We are three nurses short. We have one nurse's aide. No secretary. I have thirteen,* thirteen *very sick people to take care of today. For God's sake, leave me alone!*

My head snapped up, and I opened my mouth and then closed it.

You were shifting from foot to foot, fiddling with the zipper of your jacket. There was a deep sadness in your eyes. You looked lost.

You said, "We've been married for forty years. She's my girl." (I heard what you didn't say. *She is everything to me. She is all that I have. My world is ending. Please, please take care of her.*)

"I will." I said, "I promise."

Down the hall a patient called, "Nurse? Nurse?"

You shifted from foot to foot for a moment longer, and then you shuffled off. I wanted to follow you.

"Nurse?!"

I planned to check on your wife, but then there was the thud of a heavy object hitting the ground, like a concrete block dropped from a dump truck, and I found a patient on the floor, legs splayed, IV and catheter pulled out, clutching his bleeding nose, astounded. "I was just walking to the bathroom," he said. After I cleaned him up and called the doctor and reinserted the IV and the catheter, I headed toward your wife's room again.

But a woman ran up to me crying, "My mother is having chest pain!" So I slipped a nitro under the patient's tongue and turned up her oxygen. I was informed the EKG tech was in the ER, so I hooked her up and did the EKG myself and drew her labs and called the cardiologist.

I walked back down the hall to check on your wife. This time I was stopped by a patient who shouted at me, "Could I get my insulin any time today?" So I went and drew up the insulin and gave it.

Then the other floor nurse called out, "Help! I need some help!" I followed the sound of her voice to a room at the end of the hall. Inside this room a giant of man, a man so tall and so large he looked like a moving tree, with eyes wild and enraged from Alzheimer's, was clutching her hair, shaking her like a doll. He pushed her to the floor, and the two of us cowered in the corner while he stood over us, whipping the snapped line of his restraint over our heads. The room suddenly filled with blue shirts, and there was shouting and grunting and swearing. When they finally had him pinned to the bed, I left the room. I went into your wife's room and found her gasping amid the hot, twisted sheets. She saw me and held her hand out, in that terrible place beyond words.

I went to the med cart. The call lights were lit down the hall.

"Nurse!"

"Nurse!"

"Nurse!"

I shook my head at them. I didn't even look up. I drew up her morphine and injected it into her line. It didn't even touch her pain. There was too much time between doses. She needed another and another and, still, it wasn't enough.

I want to tell you about the cardinal rules. We have a lot of them. Like: Until proven differently, every chest pain is a heart attack, and every heart attack is a ready grave.

And this: Every fall is a lawsuit.

And this: Stay on top of your diabetics. They go down suddenly.

And this: Safety first.

And the two cardinal rules for pain management: Treat pain before anything else. Never chase pain.

That is, never let patients get to the point where their pain is a thief that robs them of their self-control, of their will, and sometimes even of their sanity. You must never let that thief escape your control, or you will pursue it endlessly in an effort to control it again.

I called the night shift nurse the next morning. They chased your wife's pain all evening and all night long. Nothing they gave her helped. Finally, an anesthesiologist came in the small hours of the morning and ordered a continuous morphine drip and continuous sedation.

"Her husband is at the bedside," the night-shift nurse reported, "but she barely opens her eyes now."

She died later that day.

I want to say: *It was my responsibility but not my fault.* I want to say: *I did the best*

I could. We didn't have enough help. We needed more nurses, more aides, a secretary, and techs. It isn't my fault! Go away!

But you are still there, shifting your feet and thinking about your poor, sweet girl, and your eyes are begging me.

A professor once wrote in a letter to us nursing graduates: "You must always remember that decisions about the delivery of patient care are not always based on what is best for the individual patient. In this climate of health-care-as-a-business, the bottom line will always come into play. You will find yourself in situations where the powers-that-be will make a decision based on that bottom line and not on the needs of the patient. You will find yourself powerless to change this, but your patient's needs are your mandate. You are not excused from your duty."

We fought for you, all of us fought for you.

You cannot possibly know this, and it is not your responsibility to know it, but you should never have come to our medical-surgical unit in the first place. When patients are admitted to the hospital, a determination is made about their condition, and your condition was critical. This means it was recognized that without immediate intervention, you were going to die. A patient in critical condition should always go to the ICU. There, a patient has the benefit of a nurse who can dedicate all her time and all her considerable knowledge and skills and experience to intervention and comfort. The ICU has its own dedicated team of physicians and all the specialized equipment. The care there is seamless and speedy. But you were a DNR—do not resuscitate—and a decision was made that since you were probably going to die, anyway, you should take up less critical and expensive resources. They decided you should go to a medical-surgical unit, where the care is less costly.

We fought for you. First, we fought your admission to our unit. I heard your nurse say, "Are you kidding me? This lady needs to be in ICU. DNR does not mean 'do not treat.' She needs one-to-one nursing care. She needs intensive care. I'm calling the supervisor."

I called the supervisor. "She meets the criterion for ICU, even if she is a DNR.

She needs constant nursing care, and we can't provide that here. Nursing care is NOT nursing care, Susan. That's ridiculous. Think about her as if she were your mother, Susan; would you want her here? Well, then assign her a private nurse. Budget? Oh come on."

So then we redivided the teams, a thing I've seen done on our unit only that one time. We each took patients from Kelly so that you could be her only patient. We moved a patient from your room so you could have some privacy.

When I saw you arrive on our unit, I knew we were right. You were the sickest a person can be and still be alive. Pale. An oxygen mask forcing air into your lungs. You could barely speak from the pain and your hunger for air. The mound of your abdomen protruded like a nine-month gestation. As we slid you, as gently as we could, across the slide board to your bed, my eyes met Kelly's. *This is either a ruptured bowel or a dissecting aortic aneurysm. Either way she's going to die very soon without help.*

We did fight for you. Normally, when a patient comes up from the ER to our unit, the secretary calls the medical service and requests the assigned doctor to come up and write orders. The medical service is assigned to the whole hospital, and for a unit like ours, which provides care for noncritical patients, the doctors come up when they have a chance. It is often an hour or more before they arrive. Not that day. We took turns paging the service every two minutes until the exasperated physician arrived to see what the fuss was about.

Jane stood over the doctor and, with the tip of her pen, jabbed at the page where he was writing your orders. "More pain medicine! More!"

When the surgical resident saw you and wanted to speak to the head of surgery before reserving the OR, Jane reserved it herself, glaring at him, daring him to contradict her. He ordered a portable X-ray, and I paged the tech repeatedly to come up and do it.

But we knew it was coming.

It started with a change in your breathing, a kind of panting. Before, you could barely move, but now, with a look of horror, you thrashed frantically, as if snatched up by a hungry beast. You tried to launch yourself off the bed. You tried to run away from it, but we pressed you back. Your belly grew larger before our eyes. We scrambled for medicine, for equipment. The room was crammed with people who appeared out of nowhere, and you, there, in the center of it, were screaming in agony and fear.

The medical resident shouted your name again and again over the hissing and beeping and clanging and babble. "Mrs. Johnson, we need to know what you would like us to do now. We can take you up right now to the operating room."

"Noooooo." Your breath clouded the mask over your face, "Eeeennnoughhh."

"Give her five of morphine," he said to Jane.

"I'm giving ten slow," Jane announced, and he nodded.

There was nothing to do now but wait with you, and we did.

Usually, in those final moments, it is hard to tell when it is really over. There is a kind of slow ebbing of life, a clock winding down. Not you.

You died midscream, your mouth still open, your eyes wide and shocked.

We ran into the hall, all the nurses. We tore into the hallway at once, bumping into each other like little girls who have witnessed a wretched accident. We were escaping, but there was nowhere to go and nothing to do. We couldn't meet each other's eyes.

A machine was grinding down the hallway, the tech pushing the portable X-ray. We watched it approach. The secretary told the tech the patient had expired.

I didn't know why, not then, but I said, "Shoot it anyway."

The chief resident came out of the room: "I agree."

Everyone nodded firmly. The tech shrugged and stepped into the room.

"What is going on here?" Susan, the supervisor, appeared and stood among us with her hands on her hips. "Please tell me you are not planning on taking an X-ray of a dead patient."

"We want to know what killed her," someone said.

"And what difference does that make? She's already dead. I forbid it." She called over her shoulder, "Leave her in peace."

I might have slapped her if Jane's cool hand hadn't clutched my shoulder.

Mrs. Johnson, I ask myself sometimes, *if you had been in ICU, would you have received better care?* It would have been faster and perhaps more coordinated, less hectic. But, no, it wouldn't have been better. And whether it was a ruptured bowel or a dissecting aneurysm, the hard truth is that very few healthy young people survive those things. You were very old and very sick. Your death was inevitable. We wanted it to be better, though. *Would it have been better, more comfortable, in the ICU?* Again, I don't know.

It was a long time after your death that I realized why we wanted the X-ray. Getting a diagnosis would have been a way of naming you, of saying, *This is Mrs. Johnson, and this is what caused her to die. She mattered.*

That was why we fought for you. You mattered.

When people ask, "Do you remember my loved one? Do you remember me?" this is what I want to say:

I often cannot remember faces and names. But I remember their skin or their hands, their eyes, the fragility of their bodies. You or your husband or wife or lover or child changed me. Their needs forced me to show compassion to them, gave me courage to say words that are so taboo people will do anything, suffer anything, in order not to say them. They forced me to acknowledge when I failed them and forced me to live with my own helplessness and smallness and the inevitability of my own death. They have given me the knowledge that I have not passed through this world without bettering it.

They are with me. You are with me. I say this with the pain of helplessness and guilt. I say this with sorrow. I say this with pride. Above all, I say this with gratitude.

I remember your loved one. I remember you.

Patricia McCarthy *is a registered nurse who resides with her husband and children in Chicago, Illinois. This is her first published work.*

The Business of Grief

JOE PRIMO

Following the death of his grandfather, grief counselor and former hospice chaplain Joe Primo gains some perspective on his personal and professional life. "There are few things we can control; our emotions are not among them."

Some years back, shortly after graduating from divinity school, I joined a few colleagues in the backroom of an Italian restaurant in rural Michigan to discuss formaldehyde and the embalming of babies with a funeral director, a "death midwife," and a couple of "tree-hugging" experts in green burial. We talked for hours—about laying out bodies in living rooms over bags of dry ice, sawing off heads for cryogenics, and alternative funerary practices. At the time, I was a hospice chaplain, and my colleagues at dinner were others in the field who shared my concern about how we care for the dead and grieving. During four years of working at the first hospice in the United States, located just outside New Haven, Connecticut, I had seen plenty of dead patients roughly handled and stuffed into body bags minutes after death. I had witnessed the dead become hostages to outdated laws, such as regulations about who can handle the dead and when and where they can be visited, and common funeral rituals like embalming, which I found bizarre. I saw the separation of the family from the deceased during the first days after the death, a time when touching and seeing the dead can help the reality of death settle in for the survivors and when significant and beneficial grieving can occur. I wanted to work toward changing the ways we handle the dead, the earth, and the grieving. I believed then, and

I still believe now, that funerals, like most rituals, are essential to the mourning process. What is not essential, however, are the merchandise and accoutrements that accompany a funeral. In fact, these are downright wasteful.

It was midspring of 2007 in Michigan, and I had traveled from New Haven, Connecticut, to speak with a farmer who faced bankruptcy because the educational programs he ran at his farm were unattended. But now he'd come up with a new savvy business plan to protect his property from development, a scheme that utilized green burial practices and would replenish the local ecology as well as protect his one hundred acres, a corridor to a state park.

Every ten acres of cemetery has approximately one thousand tons of steel, twenty thousand tons of concrete, and enough wood buried in it to build approximately forty houses—not to mention enough toxic chemicals to embalm a village. Green burial consists of a hole, a biodegradable box, and a nutrient-rich body. In 2007, 2.4 million Americans died, which means it doesn't take long to fill a ten-acre lot. If the farmer could persuade the township to permit him to use his acreage as a green cemetery, it would be a win-win situation for the farmer and for the land, and I went to help him make the pitch and fine-tune his business plan. The visit lasted a week, during which I served as a consultant between the farmer and the Green Burial Council (GBC), which was responsible for bringing me out there. If the farmer had ultimately decided to go the green burial route and if permits had worked out, I could have managed the conversion process and become director of one of the country's first green cemeteries.

The GBC has come a long way in the four years since its inception, but in 2007 it was still a startup, and I was broke and not entirely sure it was the life path I wanted to take. The farmer couldn't compete with the multimillion dollar Catholic cemetery and its marble mausoleums that had just opened in the next town, so he chose to accept his financial struggles for the time being and continue in his efforts to teach children about sustainability. Thus, instead of immersing myself in the green burial movement, I decided to work with grieving children. In a society that is unsure of how to handle death and unable to support a grieving person adequately, especially a grieving child, I felt my earlier experience at hospice provided me with a perspective that might help change the way we support the bereaved.

Grief has been my profession for six years now, but it took root in me when I was fourteen, when I witnessed my great-aunt die of a heart attack at her kitchen table in rural Maine. It took paramedics almost an hour to arrive. Just as the compressions of my uncle's palms forced his wife's heart to beat, I was forced into the direction of grief. I didn't begin my exploration of death with the goal of becoming a professional. Instead, I wanted to talk about the experience and examine life and death, to try to understand them. Since that moment in Maine when I saw my aunt breathe her last, I've witnessed hundreds of people die. Just before they go they're like fish out of water—they gulp and sigh and make suffocating noises and confused faces. Then they go blank. I've held their hands. If it was their time, but they refused to go, I'd say, "It's okay. I'm here. We'll do this together." Sometimes that's all they needed, someone to give them permission to go.

In the fall of 2009, I had a new perspective on personally dealing with grief and dying when my grandfather was diagnosed with stage IV lung cancer and faced imminent death. The disease had had its way with my grandfather's body. I was inconsolable and far from ready to say good-bye to him. When my family gathered around my grandfather's bed in Massachusetts General Hospital in Boston on the last day in September, I refused to let my grandfather's hand go. If I held it to the end, I thought, I could be a companion to him as he moved from life into death. We'll do this together, I thought, as I'd done with countless others. During the many sleepless nights I'd spent in his hospital room that week, I'd been preparing for this moment, imagining his final seconds of life and how I would feel when he died. As the nurses' shift changed, the room darkened, the theater lights dimmed, those of us family members present were quiet with anticipation. We counted the seconds between my grandfather's breaths in the same vein as the nurses had measured milligrams of his urine output to see if his kidneys were working, trying to determine the speed at which death was arriving. After it was clear that my grandfather hadn't breathed in a couple of minutes, my father pronounced him dead.

"He is gone," my father said in a perplexed and relieved voice. Silence surrounded us. Sniffles sporadically filled the air. All eyes were focused on the hospital bed, which was lit only by a dim light overhead, as in a museum. The windows were black, and we could barely see the lights on the gold dome of the state house through the tinted glass. I looked down at my grandfather and saw that his life had left him. His jaw had stiffened, his blood had begun to disperse beneath his skin, leaving the blotchiness people get when they're nervous.

Then, suddenly, his face took on a snarling look—pain-free but almost enraged—and he reached up and grabbed my grandmother, yanking her toward him like a dumbbell, as if to say "There is no way I can leave you."

At the moment of my grandfather's reanimation the sound in the room rose from the hush of angelic choral music to full-out shouting from the sidelines, and I was the coach. Without pause, I pressed my head against his. Head to head, I spoke through my tightened chest, yelping in a baritone that seemed some voice other than my own, "You can do this, Grandpa! You can do this, Grandpa. You just have to let go. Just let go. Come on now, just let go!"

He needed to let go, and so did I. The presence of death was in that room, in its odors and sounds. And then, for the second time, he was dead. His mouth open, his tongue a burnt color, his eyes murky. When my grandmother called out to her dead husband, the grief moved deep inside me. This was my loss, too, not just hers, and I couldn't maintain my professionalism. My skill set was as useless as a hammer in this hospital room.

I walked into the hallway to clear my head and to catch my breath, unable to sit or stand, filled with the need to move while I was transitioning to an emotional numbness, but my father called my cousin and me back to the room, empty now, except for my father and my dead grandfather. He stood over his dead father. "We will wash him," he told us. We raised the hospital bed and filled the washbasins. We stripped my grandfather of his hospital gown. He lay there, a catheter snaked from his groin. My father handed me latex gloves.

"He's your father," I said to my dad. "Take off those gloves and relax. Let's be sure not to rush, this is the most we can do for him right now."

We dipped washrags into the pink basins and worked our way from my grandfather's head to his toe, washing the Gold Bond from his underarm, belly button, penis, and thighs. As I moved my washrag about, I watched my father and myself in the reflection of the massive hospital windows overlooking Boston. Our labor of love was reflected there, and behind those windowpanes were the seas where my grandpa once fished and fed his family. The Italian neighborhood where he grew up was only a few blocks away.

"Look at this body," my father said to my cousin and me. "He's a bull. Can you imagine having this body at eighty-four? He's built like a rock."

As his rag swooshed in the water, my father talked to my grandfather through each move and each rinse. "Okay, Dad, now we're going to clean behind your ears, and put you on your side, and clean up your hair." My cousin slowly pulled the catheter from my grandfather's body. With a little tug it was out. He took out the IV line, and we paused. Grandpa was unattached to anything, machines, places, us. He was simply gone.

We tilted him on his side and untucked the sheet from the bed, pressing it against his back. He was stiffening. We tilted him to his other side and removed the sheets from under him, replacing them with clean sheets. We put a fresh hospital gown over him, and we pulled the sheet up to his waist, placing his hands by his side. We gently combed his hair. I pressed the button at the end of the hospital bed, which lowered it, and the rest of my family reentered the room to say good-bye to him and each other. I remained behind until the nurses came with a large plastic bag and more latex gloves. That was my cue to go. The nurses gave me a look that said, "You're done now and he is ours."

The years I've spent as a grief professional have taken their toll. I've changed in ways both known and unknown to me. Some days I feel as if I'm simply waiting to feel death's sting myself. I'm far more aware of my own impermanence and the impermanence of others. And as I lose the important people in my own life, my perspective is maturing. I know that life is temporary and fragile.

In my days as a hospice chaplain, I told myself I had to persevere. I had to stand at a dying child's bedside because my listening and caring might help. When the demented died, shouting the names of those who didn't visit, I had to be present because it was the right thing to do. When the dead were carted off to the morgue minutes after their death, shuffled away without anyone appearing to acknowledge what had happened, I went into that cold room and blessed them. I stood over them and held their name in my memory, if only for a moment. I said prayers I didn't believe, respecting that many of my patients had a "come to Jesus" moment and had returned to their childhood religiosity. This role asked me to step outside myself and offer whatever the patients needed, whatever comforted them. I once held a hospital curtain over my head because I didn't have proper head covering, a religious protocol for making room for Yahweh, as a widower wailed the Kaddish. I fell to the floor once and sobbed on the night a thirty-five-year-old mother of two died. I had known her for months. My professional boundaries were breached for this friendship. There were no support systems in place for this grieving family, nothing to help her children, and nothing I could do to help.

I did these things because I believed there was meaning in them. I thought maybe my reward might be in heaven or maybe I could somehow circumvent death by being entrenched in it. As I reflected on my work and why it was important to me, I vowed I would be present when the important people in my life died.

The value of what I've learned in my work, especially at hospice, was the ability to listen and be present, to stand in the presence of pain, and to pay attention to the people in my life and the needs of my community. My redemption was in the ability to be present to my grandfather and to connect with him in his final moments, completely aware of his departing and its finality. I was able to grieve at a time when it would have been much easier to be a professional, guarded by boundaries and present to everyone except myself.

I was able to experience the death of my grandfather fully, but I worried about how I would experience his funeral. Two days after my grandfather died we were reunited at a conventional funeral home, a corporate-style building with retro 1950s rugs and morticians around every corner. Because of my brief tenure in the sustainable burial movement, walking into that place felt like dumping batteries in the village creek. As I navigated the hallways, I arrived at my grandfather's viewing room. There he was, in a bluish gray casket that matched his 2005 Honda Accord, apparently a last request. Plastic Pietàs were on all four corners of the casket, and an image of the Last Supper hung from its open lid.

He looked like a doll, made-up with cosmetics, his fingernails painted pink, his mouth sewn shut. He looked like he did twenty years ago, thin lipped.

During my green burial days, just four years before, I had given him a lecture about how our country's mortuary practices are a drain on our natural resources. Embalming fluid is highly carcinogenic, I told him. The complex embalming procedures are mutilation—with draining, probing, slicing, dicing, and even some fine sandpapering. He was sitting in the family room when I decided to enlighten him about these things, despite the fact that we had just finished one of my mother's typical eight-course holiday meals. I walked him through all of the business of death.

"Gramps, they'll throw you into a bag, shove you into a fridge, put you on a table, and then have their way with you. They'll cut you up until you begin to look something like your former self. It's nasty. We can do this so much better if you go organic. We can even decorate your casket and make it cool or something crafty, like you," I said sitting on the floor, looking up at him, hoping I could convince him to plan a green funeral for himself.

Now that I was faced with his casket, staring at him, I wondered if what I'd told him would happen to his body *had* happened to it. When I'd told him the macabre details about preparing dead bodies and old-fashioned funerals after that Easter dinner, he'd responded in a firm, annoyed voice: "This is the American way, and this is how we do things here." His Sicilian friends had told him about the supposed stench in the old country's cemeteries. He would have none of that for himself. He didn't want to rot too quickly; it was important that the crowds come and mourn. This is the way his friends are buried in America, and he liked things to be conventional.

That tacky casket, one that Batesville Caskets warranties for five years with the exception of any "acts of God," presumably including resurrection, is one of thousands used every year. We use enough metal in caskets and underground vaults that we could rebuild the Golden Gate Bridge every January. The embalming fluid they pumped into my grandfather causes a higher incidence of leukemia and brain and colon cancer in funeral directors. The waste from the dead, along with embalming fluids, is pumped into the sewer, draining straight off the embalming table and down the drain, accompanied by the bleach that's used to disinfect the body. This waste goes straight to the water treatment facility and then makes its way back into our drinking water.

This process helps provide future customers to the guy standing at the porcelain table, shoving his trocar into every orifice of the dead, dripping those fluids deeper down the drain. These facts contaminated my thoughts as I stared at my grandpa. The environment of a funeral home is sterile. The dead are on display. There are special pink lights to make the dead glow and lots of distractions, like flowers and pictures. This was the next phase of our good-bye, and my grandfather was the showpiece.

In my early study of death, I learned that the way we care for our dead is a ritual we have maintained since the Civil War, when as a country we were fascinated by the fact that Abe Lincoln's dead body could be trotted around the country for two weeks and not smell like spoiled chicken. And now we've taken the process even further: we have removed the family and inserted a concierge service that controls our grief by constructing an environment that inhibits intimacy. The funeral home is a stage; it bears no resemblance to the places the deceased frequented, despite the pictures we bring and the memorabilia we provide. It is a place where lines form and faces pass through, most of which the bereaved family won't see again during the intense months of grief after the loss. We have constructed a ritual that helps us to distance ourselves from the rawness of grief until the body is "properly disposed of."

When my grandfather's funeral procession arrived in the pouring rain at St. Michael Cemetery, the old Italian burial grounds of Boston, there was the family plot, waiting with a fresh hole, covered by a green canopy. A seven-foot-tall Madonna carved of pink granite marked the spot.

My Lord, Jesus, that hole was deep. To the right you could see the vaults of my uncle and his wife stacked one on top of the other. Straight ahead were my great-grandparents and my other uncle. A marble slab anchored the plot firmly, and at the bottom of the hole was a Monticello vault full of water from the unending rain. My grandparents were married on a rainy day, and my grandfather said he would be buried on one, too. So it happened. We hovered beneath the canvas canopy that covered the hole, and rain poured down from all four sides, pooling on the green turf at our feet.

As the casket was lowered into the ground, the metal clanged against the concrete when it dropped the last foot of its descent, coming to rest, finally in its pool of baptismal waters. A metal contraption was fired up, like an enormous leaf blower. The tractor carried the lid of the vault to the grave and more concrete was added to the already tight hole.

The sacred moment I'd shared with my grandfather two days before, when I'd helped wash and dress him, was gone, wiped away by an industrial burial—metal boxes, Cadillacs, and enough concrete to build a foundation for a bungalow. Rest in peace and carcinogens and concrete and all the shiny metallic stuff you could ever need for the afterlife, Gramps. It was a disappointing ending for a simple man.

And, I wondered about the money we spent, money my grandmother could have used to help her now that she was left a widow with a single income.

I was very much aware of my own emotional needs while my grandfather was dying and during those hours we spent at the funeral home. When I speak with grieving children and families these days, I carry these feelings with me. When I helped my grandmother choose that bluish gray casket, it was her need, not mine. When I listen to a mom tell me about how her son hanged himself, I know it is her need to tell, and I must respect it.

There are a few things about death we can control; our emotions are not among them, though we can control our story and how we share it with others. Death is not a choice, but much of what happens around end-of-life care is about options. We can receive countless expensive treatments for a terminal illness because we want to fight to live. But we also have the choice to surrender. And as our days wind down, we can choose to return our bodies to the earth in a natural, community-minded way, or we can go the traditional route because we want our caskets to match our cars and our friends to be impressed.

Grief, like death, can be engaged or the subject avoided. We can compartmentalize it, project our expectations of what grief should look like onto others, or allow it to be and see where it takes us. Our lack of control over death is probably why we are so interested in the details of dealing with it. Perhaps that is why we maintain some of our thoughtless rituals, despite the consequences.

If we choose to engage grief, what is at the core of caring for bereaved children and the widowed? What is it that my grandmother needed more than anything? I have stood by countless people as they grieved, and others have stood by me. I have heard funeral directors, chaplains, social workers, and death midwives propose many products and beliefs to alleviate grief. I have learned that grief is not like clinical depression, schizophrenia, or anxiety, which can be diagnosed and treated. The grieving need someone to say "I see you, I hear you, I understand you are hurting and you can tell me more." It's a witnessing, as when a playful child demands, "Watch me on the monkey bars." Just watch me do this important thing. Stand there and watch. I may need a little cheering from the sidelines, but just show up and be there for me. Sometimes it takes the bereaved years to surrender to the fact that death has arrived. A true friend will just be present to another's grief, even if that grief seems inconsolable: an empathetic human presence brings comfort, though it might not at the time be apparent. My experiences as hospital chaplain, hospice worker, green practices theoretician, grief counselor, and grieving grandson all tell me this is true.

***Joe Primo** is currently the director of the Good Grief Center for grieving children and teens in New Jersey. He earned his master's of divinity degree at Yale University. Formerly an interfaith chaplain at the Connecticut Hospice and the Hospice of Southeastern Connecticut, he currently serves on the board of directors for the National Alliance for Grieving Children. Primo's essays have been published previously in the* Newark Star Ledger, *where he is also a blogger.*

This Is Blood

SANDELL MORSE

During a visit to her father in his independent care facility, writer Sandell Morse tries to salvage the tatters of their relationship before it's too late.

It is Wednesday, late morning, when I wheel my father to the physical therapy room and wait with him at the Care Center in Lantana, Florida, a small town west of I-95 in Palm Beach County. This was orange grove territory until the last of the groves gave way to development in the early 1990s. Now, traffic is heavy along main roads, all lined with shopping centers, strip malls, trailer parks, and gated communities with watered and manicured lawns, dug ponds, and fountains shooting spray. Some are golfing communities; others are continuing care facilities like this one, where I peer through a single glass pane, watching patients hold on to railings as they struggle to walk up ramps, turn, walk down. A therapist opens the door a crack. "Be right with you," she says. I hear reproof in her voice. I turn to my father and swoop down beside his wheelchair. I'm wearing wide legged linen trousers, tank top, loose-fitting long-sleeved shirt. These corridors are cold.

My father is a tall man, but he looks shrunken, as if something inside of him is sucking on his flesh, leaving behind skin and bone. For years, he and I have expected one last heart attack, but this is the slow decline we all dread. We pray, those of us who believe; those of us who don't believe ask, *Let me go quickly and peacefully into the night.* I am stooping, getting down to his level, making small talk about how well he's doing, telling him he has to keep his good side healthy, work to get his bad side moving again. I don't believe a word I'm saying. The reality of what has happened to him has begun to sink in: the stroke ten days ago that left his left side paralyzed, the heart attack in the emergency room, the second heart attack on the hospital floor. Before I boarded a plane at Logan Airport, in Boston, I knew only about the stroke, and I'd believed then that with rehabilitation he'd be whole—or nearly whole. All of his life, my father has been strong. Defiant. And even at ninety-one, immortal in my eyes.

He pays no attention to my words. He knows a liar when he hears one. That's what I'd like to believe, that he's as sharp as he's always been, that he'll call me out, tell me to *stop talking nonsense,* ask me where my head is; then tell me—*up my ass.*

It is June. A year ago, almost to the day, he boarded a plane in West Palm Beach, flew to Logan, where I picked him up. We drove to my house in Maine. He was tired but talkative, proud of himself for making the trip. "I brought only a small bag," he said to me as I drove north on I-95. "Carried it myself. Wasn't that a good idea. Wonderful flight. Wonderful." He'd come to celebrate my husband's birthday. It was a family gathering, my three sons, my two daughters-in-law, my four grandchildren. My father was the patriarch, sitting on the couch, petting the dogs, my two standard poodles, laughing, cracking jokes, sipping a Scotch on the rocks with "a splash of water." On the other side of the living room windows, beyond the lawn, beyond the rocky shore, the ocean rolled, and on a promontory the family calls Nana's rock, because that's where, four years earlier, we knelt and lowered my mother's ashes into the sea, cormorants sat, spreading their wings wide to dry. At the dining room table, raising his glass, my father offered a toast. This is the man I knew, a man who in spite of his age pulled himself together.

Today, he seems not only lost to the world but also lost to himself. His skin sags, and his head slumps. He blows air through his lips. The neck collar he wears seems useless. He complains. "My rectum. My crotch." Not words the father I know—knew?—would use with his daughter. My father guarded—used to guard?—his privacy.

He still has the damn catheter. His nurse tells me over and over she's waiting for a lab report. I rest my hand, lightly, on his arm. He's taking so many drugs—Colace, Coreg, aspirin, Plavix, Dulcolax, acetaminophen, Ativan,

Imdur, Senokot, Lexapro, Prinivil, Lanoxin, Percocet, nitroglycerin. What are they doing to his brain? to his body? "I'm sorry, Dad." I pause. "About the pain."

Three months earlier on a day in March, we met with a lawyer, then his stockbroker. I'd arranged the meetings, flown down. We drove north on I-95 in my rental car, my father sitting beside me, quiet, taciturn, resigned. He was losing dividend checks, ordering replacements, ordering credit cards, then letting them lie around on dresser tops and table tops. Newspapers piled up. And envelopes, some opened, others not, those free address labels from the VFW, Easter seals, you name it, and because he kept the labels, he felt morally bound to write a check. He lost checkbooks, ordered more. He knew he was failing, knew he needed to make this decision. He'd worked all his life to acquire money, not a lot, but enough, to pass on. This was his legacy. In the lawyer's office, we sat at a round mahogany table. We were in West Palm Beach in a high rise, overlooking a park where children played, a small lake. The lawyer was kind and compassionate, going over each document, answering my father's questions, the same questions over and over, treating my father with patience, preserving his dignity. Hand trembling, my father signed. I couldn't believe it any more than he could. I'd prepared myself for a tirade, his jutting arm, then his hand sweeping the documents to the floor. *I never said I'd sign. What are you nuts, power of attorney, health care surrogate, your name next to mine on the trust?*

Then shoving the papers to the center of the table, he pushed once, then a second time, trying to rise from his chair. He stood on the third try. "Well, that's done," my father said, his words falling like something distasteful from his tongue. I understood, or thought I did. I had no idea, then, how much more life would ask of him.

For much of our lives, my father and I have been adversaries, visiting dutifully but keeping our distance. We didn't get together for Thanksgiving, Christmas, Hanukkah, Passover, or the Fourth of July. I visited mostly when necessary. Then, my mother died, and my father and I reached an uneasy peace. I am an only child. We were what was left. Still, he was mean, calling and speaking angrily into the phone. Where was his check? I took it. Had to be. I was the one in the lawyer's office, the one in the stockbroker's office. Who else? I fumed, *bastard.* Then, calmly, like a mother speaking to a recalcitrant child, I reminded him of the direct deposit.

"No," he screamed. "Nuveen."

"Dad, all of your checks are going directly into your account."

"No, they're not."

"Dad, that's the way we set it up."

"You don't think I tell you everything, do you?"

Gotcha. What a pisser, keeping an account all for himself. Why was I surprised? He was controlling. He was mean. I hear his voice, falling through space. *Don't come here. I don't want to see you.* He'd set himself up, life care, telling me over and over, *I don't need you.* Fine with me, and I vowed I'd leave him wherever he landed, in an apartment, or assisted living, or the Care Center, where I now crouch beside his wheelchair, feeling sorry and sad. What the hell is wrong with me?

"I don't think I can do it," he says.

Physical therapy.

He is a man who speaks in absolutes: I will; I won't. He doesn't consider, qualify, or doubt. No humility. No mistakes. This softness is new—or perhaps old. What has the stroke done to his brain? He wears a pacemaker. No MRI. No clinical diagnosis. Just what I see. Or don't see. Perhaps there is a lesion, a cluster of brain cells the stroke has killed, those mean cells, and I wonder: what was he like as a child? I have a photograph. My father is four, maybe three. Not five, definitely not five. He wears a white hat that looks like a fisherman's foul weather hat, one with a wide brim, soft and turned up. He wears a white shirt that looks like a blouse, short white pants that come to his knees. He wears stockings and lace-up shoes that enclose his ankles. My father was born in 1914. Boys' clothes were feminine then. He's standing in front of an old-fashioned low stool with a wide seat and side handles that he grips. His ankles are crossed. He looks at the photographer, but not directly. There is shyness in the tilt of his head, apprehension in his smile. He looks sweet. Perhaps the stroke has brought that child back.

In this moment, my father is the child in that photograph, and I want to turn his chair, steer him back to his room, his new room where he has a window view. I'll lift him in my arms, settle him peacefully into his bed. I'll take off that damn collar, stretch out his slumping body, his cramped legs. But physical therapy is not only necessary; it also must be continuous. I'm not allowed to choose the days my father will go, the days he will not go, and without physical therapy his care will become custodial. "You don't want that, do you?" the social worker on staff asked me the day I sat in her office discussing my father's care. Hers was a good-sized office, well furnished, with a large wooden desk, upholstered swiveling desk chair, my straight-backed chair, a small sitting area with a love seat, two arm chairs and a coffee table, an area she did not offer. There were the usual landscapes on the walls. She held a pen, looked up from the folder that held my father's records. I didn't like her. She was too blond, too skinny, and too young, maybe in her midtwenties. She had attitude. What did she know? I sat, awkwardly, at the edge of my seat, asked about hospice care.

She crossed her legs, bobbed her right toe. She wore well-tailored slacks, a white blouse, trendy, pointy-toed flats. "Well," she said, "if he goes on hospice care, he won't be eligible for physical therapy."

A conundrum. Or in my father's words, *Damned if you do, damned if you don't.*

I learned, later, that my father could have had physical therapy with hospice. So what was it with the social worker? Was she ignorant? Incompetent? Stupid?

Stupid, that's the one I like. I have attitude, too.

The door to the physical therapy room opens. Same therapist. She has short dark hair, a small head, and square shoulders. She looks like a fire hydrant. She's wary, and I wonder what she sees in my face. What do I see in hers? Some sort of displeasure mixed with resignation. I've overheard talk. In these corridors I'm known as The Daughter: *The Daughter's here . . . The Daughter wants . . . The Daughter says . . .* The tone is not pleasant. I tell myself I don't care, but I do. And I wonder: is my advocacy having an opposite effect? Instead of taking better care of my father, are staff resentful and slower to respond? Is a nurse's sluggish walk intentional? Meant just for me?

Standing, I pump a smile into my voice, greet this woman, then tell her my father is tired. He's in pain. I ask if she thinks the pain is related to the catheter.

I don't tell her that for days I've been waiting for removal, and now, this minute, the waiting seems impossibly long, and my anger, my seething, under-the-skin annoyance, itches like a rash. Can she sense my irritation? See the invisible bumps on my flesh?

She looks past me. "He'll feel better once we get him down on the mat," she says to me. Then, to my father. "Won't you? You'll feel better."

Liar, liar, house on fire. I shock myself. Was I eight? Ten? I didn't know I remembered those words. And I'm there—or is it here—whirling inside a childish fury, confounded by a world I can only partly see. So much is hidden here, whispers among nurses, whispers among aides. Days passed before I figured out the color-coded uniforms: rose, pink, and turquoise print for aides; solid pinks, roses, and blues for nurses; street clothes for doctors and physicians assistants, distinguished from visitors by the stethoscopes dangling from their necks. Doctors, though, are mostly invisible. Mainly, they doctor by phone.

A major hotel corporation owns this complex. Headquarters are far away. Decisions are far away. On a floor above, a head nurse works behind a closed door. I want to speak with her about my father's meal trays. He's on a diet of pureed foods and thickened liquids. If a chunk of meat or lettuce lodges in his windpipe, he'll choke. Liquid makes him cough, then choke. I leave messages. She doesn't return my calls. No wonder I feel like a child, small, shrunken, and powerless inside this hidden world.

Yesterday, at lunch, an aide set my father's tray down on his table. I lifted a plastic lid. Noodle soup. I lifted a second plastic lid, sliced carrots, meatloaf, mashed potatoes with gravy, and in a small glass bowl, cubes of shimmering orange Jell-O. I stared at the Jell-O, those little cubes, sparking in sunlight streaming in my father's window. What if I hadn't been here? What if he'd taken his fork in his one good hand, stabbed that meatloaf, bitten a hunk, chewed, tried to swallow, then choked? Or the Jell-O, so sweet and tempting, turning to liquid in his mouth. How many stroke victims in nursing homes have died that way? How many secret deaths do these places harbor? I looked at my father, his eyes glazed over and staring at the tray. At that moment, he could have been anywhere or nowhere. Or perhaps he'd become the small boy in that photograph, bemused, compliant. "This is the wrong tray, Dad," I said, gently. "I'll have to change it."

I am vigilant, watching every aspect of his care, how often he's turned or lifted from his bed. The lifting takes two workers and a Hoyer lift, a slinglike contraption that moves him from bed to wheelchair, where he hovers while aides position the sling, position the wheelchair. I watch his feet. His toes are red. The undersides of his heels are red. Often his feet jam the footboard. Aides have orders to float his heels, that is, to rest his ankles on a pillow so that the skin on the backs of his heels touches air. Daily, I float his heels. Daily, I call aides to roll him to his side, to lift him higher in his bed when he slips down. I ask to have him moved, bed to wheelchair, wheelchair to bed. His wheelchair has a low back. He needs a chair with a high back, one that will support his neck. I ask for one. His nurse tells me none is available. How can that be?

As the door closes behind my father's wheelchair, I feel an old adrenaline rush. I want to kick in the damn door, send it crashing to the floor. I want to wrest my father from that therapist's hand. I want to scream. I want to rant. But I can't make a scene, can't lose credibility. Do I have credibility? I'm agitated, my body a glass of bubbling soda water. My skin tingles. I stand and stare at the small glass windowpane, seeing nothing. I turn away. The corridor stretches to an intersection where four corridors meet. In the center is the nurses' station. I walk, slowly, passing aides, passing patients holding on to walkers. Outside her door, a woman sits in her wheelchair, pulling an arm through a sleeve of her blouse. She is stripping. She does this everyday. When she gets to her bra, an aide will come. I walk past, each step of my shoes sounding on polished tile. They're stupid shoes for this place, slides that slap my heels, but I brought so little. I hadn't intended to stay. "Stable," the emergency room doctor had said. "He looks good. He's talking fine."

At the nurses' station, I wait for a woman to look up from her computer screen. My focus is arrow thin, the catheter. "Excuse, me," I say. "I'm concerned about my father's catheter. Would you please check to see if the doctor has those results?"

She looks through a file, speaks without glancing up. "Still waiting."

My throat tightens, a little tickle. I will myself not to cough. "Will you please call Dr. Weiss."

Now I have her full attention. A doctor's name will do that, and I feel a weird sense of power. Maybe victory. "Now?" she says.

"Now," I say.

She gives me a look that can kill. "I won't get him."

How does she know? She hasn't made the least effort, and this makes me wonder about the nurse. How many attempts? My voice is unctuous. Obnoxious. "Why don't you try?"

The doctor's number is programmed into the phone. She looks up. It is as if she can't believe what she's telling me. "They're getting him."

I'm not sure I believe, either. This is too simple. Too easy. She hangs up. Dr. Weiss has given the order. A nurse will remove the catheter when my father is finished with physical therapy. Do I feel better? I feel worse, saddened by the failures that are routine here.

Outside, I walk past the "villas," free-standing buildings with four one-story units in each, townhouses, I suppose, stopping, now, at a familiar tree. I love this tree, a dwarf of some kind: pots of orchids hang from its low limbs. Orchids are tenacious plants, growing on air. These bloom, profusely, one yellow with deep burgundy dots in its throat, another snowy white, others in shades of purple and pink. My mother loved orchids; I love orchids. We used to visit a grower here. I think of the rows and rows of blooming orchids, large orchids, flowers bending their stalks, tiny orchids, blossoms clustering. I step closer to the tree, resist the urge to touch a petal, and although the air is heavy with heat, I feel lighter, as if, finally, I can breathe.

Past the villas is a pavilion with an outdoor barbecue. There are palm trees, low-growing palmetto. There is a grassy area. I remember when my parents moved here. They walked me around the grounds, showing me the villas, this brick outdoor fireplace with its cooking grill, its tall chimney, then the picnic tables inside the pavilion. "We'll have cookouts," my father said, "Fourth of July, Memorial Day." A few materialized. It turned out residents preferred eating their hamburgers and their hot dogs in the air-conditioned dining room, and so this place is mostly unused. It reminds me of a house my grandchildren call "the house with a broken heart," because the people who built it rarely visit.

Beyond the pavilion is marshland where a long dock reaches into Lake Osborne, more a canal than a lake. It's narrow. The water is brackish. There are no boats, no swimmers. There is a wooden railing, where I stand watching red-winged blackbirds flit in and out of tall grasses. I love these birds. It is as if their wings hold secrets inside those hidden patches of red, flashing, now, that yellow border, and I wonder: can they lead me through this maze of my father's care? Can they tell me whether the man I see is new or old, a stroke- and drug-induced personality or the child he used to be?

In my father's apartment, I sit at the glass-topped dining table, eating a salad of mesclun greens and roasted vegetables, topped with a sliced hard-boiled egg. I've been to a small natural foods supermarket in a shopping center three miles east of here. I've found the foods I like. I've brought them here, but I'm uneasy. The apartment is airless. My water glass sweats. I've turned off the air conditioner. It's noisy, doesn't really cool the air, and it emits an offensive odor. The apartment itself smells musty, moldy. I've opened windows, opened the door that leads to a small screened balcony. But I can't get rid of the odor inside my nostrils. It is pervasive.

This apartment was my parents' home in their retirement, and the life they lived here was strangely alien to me. Their vocabulary changed. They talked about birthday bashes, decorating for dances on Saturday nights. I felt as if I were talking to old and wrinkled high school kids. Here, in Lakeview, their world grew smaller. They were no longer part of a larger community. There were no parks, no schools, no playgrounds, no shops. They fussed about visiting children, especially in the small indoor pool. They were noisy. Probably, they peed in the water. No dogs, except for a few that had been grandfathered in. Still, my parents had liked their life here, especially my mother, whose cooking and cleaning chores were so much lighter than at any other time in her life.

Alone, my father—never a man to pick up after himself—let debris accumulate, newspapers, those unopened bills and dividend checks. He stopped hanging his clothes, heaped them on the spare bed in his room. He stuck paper plates with unwrapped hunks of cheese in the refrigerator and left them there to grow hard. Milk soured. Soda went flat. Condiments discolored inside jars. Vegetable bins went slimy. Grime and grease coated the toaster oven, the blender he never used. He refused my offers of additional cleaning help. "Hire who you want," he'd say to me. "I won't let them in."

I believed him. I had history, the Medicare nurse I'd sent up. He told her to leave. Then said to me on the phone, "What? Do you think I can't take a pill?"

After the stroke, I cleaned and I cleaned, emptying cabinets under sinks, an accumulation of old patent medicines, makeup that had been Mother's, electrical cords that had lost their appliances, empty bottles of after shave and cologne, boxes of rubber gloves, bedpans, urinals, all of it brought home after hospital stays. I heard his voice playing inside my head. *I paid for it. Why shouldn't I have it?* I hauled bags of trash to the trash room. I scrubbed cabinets. I cleaned mirrors. I washed floors, toilets, the tub, the shower. I cleaned myself to exhaustion, then dragged my body into bed, my mother's bed, a twin near the window in my parents' bedroom, a small room crowded with furniture, an oversized dresser, a tall bureau, twin beds with electric motors that lifted their backs, lifted their legs, a night stand holding a lamp, an alarm clock, newspapers, magazines. This is where I've been sleeping. I needed to clean. Cleaning was cleansing.

Standing now, I scrape what is left of my salad into the sink and grind it up in the disposal. The motor labors. The blades are dull. I'm dull. Exhausted night and day, but I don't know that. I think I'm fine.

At the Care Center, there are too many people in my father's room, all of them looking down toward the tile floor. My father's bed is empty. What's going on? Then, I see him, my father, his face paper white, his body limp and still dressed in his long sleeved shirt, his trousers, clothes he wore to physical therapy, clothes he wore just two weeks earlier to walk from his apartment to the elevator, going to pick up his mail or to meet Gloria, his girlfriend, for dinner. Yes, he had a girlfriend, always a girlfriend. Now, he's lying on a gurney. Why is the gurney so low to the floor? But wait, why is he on a gurney? I crouch down. His breathing is shallow and arduous. His cheek is cool, too cool. He's alive, not dead, looking at me, beseechingly, as if to say, *You have come. You will help me.* A single word passes my lips. "Dad."

And in that word I feel a rush of tenderness. This is my father; this is my infant son. No one in the room speaks, and I believe this is the moment I've feared, expected, dreaded. I lean close, then whisper. "I love you, Dad." And this instant, I do love this difficult, cantankerous old man. His lips pucker, and I kiss those old and crinkled lips, kiss his smell, his foul breath.

A woman steps forward. I've never seen her before. A supervisor. Something I will learn later. She tells me my father has no oxygen level, that his blood pressure has plummeted, that the physical therapists brought him here. She has called 911. "They're on the way."

I live on a dirt road on the coast of Maine. There are wild turkeys, deer, opossums, raccoons, foxes. One late fall day, walking home with my dogs, I watched as they went on high alert, tails erect, fur bristling, nostrils opening wide, quivering and taking in scent. They strained at their leashes. Then, I saw it, a small fox lying in tall dry grass, fur that lovely fox color, a patch of white at its throat, a ring of white on its tail. Dead, I thought. Then, I saw breath moving in its side ever so slowly. I held the dogs on short leashes. They're good dogs, obedient dogs. Sentient. They sat at my sides as I kept vigil, standing and waiting until that small fox took its last breath. Then I said the few Hebrew words of Kaddish I knew.

A strange calm replaces the agitation I felt earlier. My father has a living will, a DNR order. I have power of attorney. I am his health care surrogate. When Dr. Weiss admitted him, we all agreed, my father, Dr. Weiss, and I, no more ambulances, no more ER. Everyone in this room knows this—or should know this. If these are my father's last moments, then he and I will face them our way, not this woman's. I turn my head. "No 911. No hospital."

A hint of tension in her voice. "I can't turn them back. Once they start out, no one can turn them back."

My father has been a distant father, a mean father, a controlling father, a father who confused blind obedience with love. I ran from him; yet, today, I will cover him with my body. With my life. I will fight. I will win. This is blood. "Fine," I say, "let them come. But no one is taking him from this room."

There is a collective holding of breath. The supervisor leaves. I stroke my father's cheek, that high cheekbone. I look into his eyes. He seems calmer. A little more peaceful. The woman returns. I have no idea where she's been, and then it becomes clear. She addresses all of us in the room. "Whatever she says."

Dr. Weiss has kept his word. No more ER. No more hospital beds. And my father survives—for now.

***Sandell Morse** holds master's degrees from Dartmouth College and the University of New Hampshire. She facilitates workshops for the Maine Writers and Publishers Alliance and for the New Hampshire Writers' Project. A fellow at the Vermont Studio Colony and at the Virginia Center for the Creative Arts, she has been a Tennessee Williams Scholar at the Sewanee Writers' Conference. Her writing has appeared in many literary magazines and anthologies and has been nominated for a Pushcart Prize.*

A Figurative Death

CAROL COOLEY

As a physical therapist working in institutionalized elderly care, Carol Cooley knows firsthand that for some of the long-term residents "struggling to live their last years with dignity and purpose," the death of independence precedes the end of life.

When life as we know it ends, what follows is not always a literal death. Those of us who spend our days with the elderly realize that the end of life usually describes a figurative death—the end of life as one has known it and the beginning of something else. Here, independence vanishes, there is no hope it will ever return, and what confronts the aged is an environment telling them there will be no new growth, but rather a drawn-out death in a harsh and unfriendly place. We cannot blame a person living in this state for months or years when he screams from his nursing home wheelchair, "I'd rather be dead." And I do not blame myself for walking by and thinking, "I would too."

I had my first personal experience with institutionalized elderly care when I was in school for physical therapy. As part of our curriculum, we were required to do "clinicals," or fieldwork, in a health care setting. Our professors encouraged us to choose a variety of settings, like a hospital, outpatient clinic, and a nursing home. Nursing homes were not a popular choice. Most students often came back drained from a nursing home clinical, relieved it was over, tossing around words like *depressing.* After following the advice of my mentors to gain a broad range of rehab experience, I decided to take the skills I was learning in the classroom into the nursing home rehab clinic. (While I shared many of the feelings my peers had in this setting, I was questioning the concept of institutionalizing the dependent elderly and found myself asking, "Is this all we can expect when we age?" and "How did this type of care get started?") So, after graduation I began a career as a physical therapist with the institutionalized elderly and ultimately became an advocate for seniors during their drawn-out end-of-life stage.

I met Margaret several years into my work at Westwoods Nursing Home, a one-story orange-brick building with roughly two hundred beds. Near the entrance of a North Carolina suburban neighborhood, the manicured landscape of the facility bloomed with thick-stemmed rose bushes and rows of sturdy crape myrtles, but the plush fescue and perennial gardens only masked the neglect and suffering inside. Westwoods was not unlike other nursing homes where I had worked; there were offices and conference rooms in the lobby area, long railings lined the walls, and a mixture of smells from incontinent residents and cleaning chemicals scented the air. Most long-term residents, as they are called, lived in shared rooms that reminded me of a college dormitory—each side decorated with personal knickknacks, a bedspread from home, and photos of the pets they had to leave behind. Television sets were often blasting in rooms occupied by sleeping residents or no one at all. Residents woke, were cleaned up, and then were lined up in their wheelchairs for meals. I took for granted my ability to leave anytime I wanted—how easy it was to jump into my car, go to a movie, or hike in the woods with my golden retriever.

Margaret was a wife, mother, and grandmother. After retiring from a career in teaching, she began painting and was enjoying her newfound creative outlet. She took a walk every day. No one expected her to have a stroke, but one day her husband found her lying immobilized on the floor of her painting room. She was rushed to the hospital, eventually stabilized, then transferred to inpatient rehab. She did not rehabilitate enough to go back home before her inpatient Medicare ran out, and she was transferred to Westwoods Nursing Home for continued rehab and possible long-term care.

Shortly after Margaret came to Westwoods she was wheeled into the rehab room by one of the aides for an evaluation. Her husband stood next to her with his hand on her shoulder as the couple scanned the windowless room. Corners were cluttered with metal canes, overused walkers, and folded up wheelchairs with missing leg rests. Color-coded ankle weights dangled from hooks, and therapy balls were stashed under desks to keep them from rolling around. In the middle of the room several residents were already in therapy. Some sat in wheelchairs, raising their arms toward the ceiling, while others stood, lifting their knees up and down, as if marching in place. A mild-natured and courteous woman, Margaret spoke just above a whisper. Although she was able to talk, some of her speech and ability to swallow had been compromised, and her food needed to be softened. She was in her eighties and had soft white hair, fair skin, and pale blue eyes. With a smile, she reached out to shake my hand.

Margaret and her family had no idea what to expect at Westwoods. They were still dealing with the trauma of the stroke and confronting the reality that she might never go home again. They frequently asked questions about her rehabilitation, like how long it would take to get her walking again and what would happen if she couldn't regain her mobility. They tried to stay focused on Margaret's rehab instructions but couldn't hide their concern when they walked past the men and women living in Westwoods. Sometimes Margaret's family would stare straight ahead and try to ignore the crying and screaming echoing down the halls. Other times they would offer an awkward smile to a resident with dementia who stopped them by grabbing a coat sleeve. Her family had to wonder if Margaret would fall asleep with her legs hanging off the side of the bed having given up asking for help, or if she would sit in soiled underwear, slouched over and defeated in a wheelchair decorated over months, maybe years, with dribbled sweet potatoes, smashed green vegetables, and pureed meats. And, like many families, they must have struggled with guilt—that Margaret would feel they had dumped her. If she had to be placed in Westwoods long term, she might not understand there were no Medicare resources available to allow her to return home with full-time care.

Margaret's rehab took place daily—a series of exercises on a mat table. I would position her wheelchair next to the table, wrap my arms around her waist, and help her stand-pivot to the mat and lie down. Then, with my assistance, she would move her left arm and leg to strengthen her muscles and keep her extremities flexible, as I instructed her. I'd also have her stand in the parallel bars to try to increase the ability of her left leg to hold her weight while she was upright. She was able to stand a few seconds with support but was unable to take a step with her left leg. She had a tiny amount of strength in her left arm but not nearly enough to wheel herself independently. She often became fatigued after only a few therapeutic exercises. During her physical therapy, I would wheel Margaret into the bars, stabilize her left leg with a brace, and ask her to grab the bar and stand up. Her husband came every day and was eager to participate in her therapy. He would bring Margaret into the rehab room, leave her by the parallel bars, then walk over to me while I was getting Margaret's brace and mat space ready.

"What can I do?" he'd ask me before we got started.

"Talk to her—try to encourage her to stand a few seconds longer than last time," I'd tell him as I put a clean sheet on the mat table.

"Should I move her arm and leg when she's in her room?"

"You can, and ask her to help."

"I just feel like I'm not doing enough." As we walked back to Margaret, who was still in her wheelchair, he repeated the same questions and concerns, searching for ideas to help his wife return to her independence.

Days turned into weeks, and Margaret wasn't progressing. It did not look like this delightful woman would return home unless the family had money for around-the-clock private care. We started the process of admitting her to Westwoods for long-term care, which included many difficult conversations with her family. Eventually, the rehabilitation team and nurses scheduled a meeting in the conference room with Margaret's husband to tell him that Margaret's Medicare limit was approaching and she would not be able to return home without caregiver support. We sat in metal-framed chairs around a long rectangular table. Team members had their copies of notes in front of them, describing the details of Margaret's progress. Unlike most of the residents' section of the nursing home, the family conference room had broad windows allowing ample sunlight to flow through. The interior of this room was professionally designed with tailored curtains, matching carpet, and well-nourished plants—a polished space where administration could freely discuss business matters with families without the distraction of distressed residents.

"I'm so sorry," I said to Margaret's husband. "She is not progressing or tolerating the therapy."

"So, now what?" Margaret's husband looked around the table at each of us.

"Are you able to come together as a family to take care of her at home?" I asked him.

"I don't know how I could. I'm eighty myself, and our children have jobs and are raising their own children."

He needed to make a very hard decision—a decision not to take his wife home with him, to leave her in a small room with a roommate she did not know, and leave behind the life they had known. He was rubbing his hands together repeatedly, taking deep breaths, and shaking his head.

"So now what?" he asked again.

"She'll move to a long-term bed here for ongoing care," one of the nurses said.

"She can't live here. She'll never survive here."

"I wish I knew of another option," I said.

I wished I knew a Medicare program for situations like his where he could've taken his wife home and had all the outside caregivers and equipment he needed. Today, traditional Medicare will pay for some home care, but only temporarily, and this family did not have the funds for private care. I wished I could've told him that, although she couldn't return home, she would be supported and encouraged in what she was still able to do—to continue painting, take day trips to the park, and use her innate gifts as a teacher to nurture other residents. I wished he could have made his decision to leave her in the facility knowing she would receive good care. But I couldn't tell him this. I knew the administration in this facility spent little time focusing on the quality of life of their long-term residents. And, while some facilities might have offered better care or more opportunities, there was still a lack of individualized care and a sense of removal from the outside world in all the nursing homes where I'd worked.

Then it was time to discuss the situation with Margaret. She sat in her wheelchair with her left arm and leg limp. Her name was written on a white label and stuck to the navy blue vinyl on the back of her chair. Her eyes were alert and her voice soft. I couldn't help but think how much her students must have loved her.

"We're trying," I told her, "but your motor control is just not coming back like we'd hoped."

"I just can't do it," she said. "I'm too tired."

"I know you're really trying. How do you feel about staying here for your care?"

"Oh no, I can't live here." Margaret stared straight ahead without any expression.

The message was brutal—if you cannot walk again or get back enough mobility and independence after an illness or injury, you will have to spend the rest of your days lying in bed or sitting in a wheelchair in a facility like this one. There was no discussion of what she still could do. She could still share ideas and stories. She could paint. She could participate in getting herself dressed. She could've also been open to something new. But, this institution, and many like it, did not provide opportunities for Margaret to channel her strengths into something meaningful and purposeful. The *Journal of Aging Studies* published a report in November 2002 titled, "Daily Life in a Nursing Home: Has It Changed in Twenty-five Years?" The study compared its findings with a similar study done in 1974 that reported nursing home residents spent 56 percent of their day doing nothing. The 2002 study found that, although the facility it reported on had a creative activities department, residents there spent 65 percent of their day doing little or nothing, and only 12 percent in a social activity.

It's no secret what life is like in most nursing homes. Visitors come out shaking their heads at seeing the elderly residents with their heads hanging down, drool stains on their clothes, and their hands reaching out while nurses walk right by them. People quickly resume life on the outside and push back thoughts that one day they may be confronted with the same circumstances. I have, too. On another day, I'll imagine living the end of my life in an institution, wondering if I couldn't read, who would read to me? If I couldn't write anymore, what would I do? Who would take me to the woods so I could refresh my connection with nature? And, what about my family and pets—how would I live without the playful energy of children or my dog and the peaceful feeling of my cat kneading and purring on my lap while I'm reading?

Most family members of nursing home residents tend to succumb to the system and eventually stop challenging the aides to have their mother's urine-soaked diaper changed in a timely manner or give up looking for Dad's missing clothes. They might try to find a more aesthetically appealing facility—maybe one with a name like Gentle Winds or Sunny Side that has paisley wallpaper borders, lots of plastic flowers, and classical music playing in the dining room, only to find the quality of care is no different. Some family members are compliant and cooperative to ensure that the aides responsible for personal care don't take any frustration out on their loved ones.

It's not easy to stay positive working in an end-of-life institution where some of the hands-on workers have moods as gray as the cement walls, where nursing assistants stand in the parking lot talking on their cell phones when they should be helping Mrs. Jones to the bathroom, and where aides discuss last night's party while bathing and yanking the limbs of a naked ninety-year-old woman. The aides at Westwoods had supervisors who expected them to perform poorly, vocalizing barbs about them never being on time or being lazy. The employees who genuinely wanted to provide good care couldn't because they were overworked and unsupported.

Margaret's family did the best they could. They came in for regular visits and often found her sitting in her chair lined up with everyone else, becoming less and less responsive to their visits. When they greeted her, she'd pull her head up from looking at the floor and force a smile. Medicine carts stood next to them full of plastic cups, protective gloves, and a medicine crusher. Nurses in powder blue scrubs scurried past them with little time to say hello or give any updates, and residents on each side of Margaret were either asleep or despondent. Her husband would hit an occasional low and come into the rehab room.

"Is there any way we could try rehab again?"

"We have the restorative aides working with her," I said. "Are you seeing a change?"

"No, I just wonder if there's a way to get her walking again. She just wants to stay in bed."

"I'd work with her if I could," I told him. "But Medicare has guidelines about how much rehab a person can get if they're not showing progress."

I had to explain to Margaret's husband that Medicare would pay for ongoing therapy only if a person had "rehab potential." This meant that if a person was not showing progress, she would no longer be covered for services, even if the therapy was beneficial or prevented further decline.

"So you give up on the person or let them get worse?" he challenged.

"It's frustrating for us too," I told him, "but Medicare doesn't cover prevention or efforts to maintain function." I was embarrassed telling him this and wanted to explain that it wasn't *my* law. It was a standard that left everyone feeling victimized and oppressed, yet I kept my emotions under control. Moments like this made me wonder if I was on my way to the work mentality of merely trying to get through the day. I also worried there might come a time when I didn't even notice the irreverent ways some seniors were treated.

Margaret's husband wanted her to walk right out of there, back to her home, where she could gently take her last breath in her painting room, wrapped in an afghan, surrounded by the love of her family. Instead, Margaret was doing her best to adapt to life at Westwoods. Occasionally, she'd smile and try to engage someone in conversation. I saw her watching a man screaming in his wheelchair one day, studying him. She scanned his body, and her eyes widened each time the man reached his loudest pitch. I can't imagine what she was thinking.

Shortly after Margaret was admitted, she began having medical complications. She was transferred in and out of the hospital each time. Her husband stopped in the rehab room after one of her hospital stays.

"How's she doing?" I asked.

"I know her—she's giving up."

Was it the nursing home environment that was causing her to give up? Was this lively spirit—painter, educator, loving wife, mother, and grandmother—saying to herself, "I don't want to live my end-of-life story here." All I know is that she deserved to listen to the sound of a child's voice, to sit in clean pads, and to taste the foods she had always loved, even if they now had to be pureed. She deserved to look forward to something beyond routine care and bland meals.

Margaret's condition deteriorated quickly. She had no strength to get out of bed and was too fatigued to eat. She was discharged again to the hospital and died there. Her husband and children came in one day to pick up her belongings. Margaret's bed was stripped and wiped down, leaving only a bare mattress on metal frame. The cement floor had been mopped and the dark, faux wood bedside table had been cleared of the plastic pink basin, wash cloths, and diapers. They loaded her clothes in Westwoods garbage bags and carried out the few photographs lining the shelf by the window. Her roommate sat in the corner watching TV; she was living a much longer end-of-life story in Westwoods than Margaret had, a story that would include losing countless roommates. The family walked past the employees on their way out—some of whom they felt grateful for, others I'm sure they hoped never to see again. Margaret's husband came into the rehab room before he left.

"I'm so sorry for your loss," I told him.

"Thank you. It's a blessing. Really, we see it as a blessing," he said.

It was a blessing. Margaret did not have to spend more of her days sitting in a wheelchair waiting to die. She was one of the last residents I worked with in the nursing-home setting, and I still wonder if she just gave up. Since that time, I've taken my experience and skills into the home care setting—and now I focus on helping seniors and the disabled stay independent and remain at home as long as possible.

Margaret's story and millions like it are about the struggle in our culture to live the end of our lives with dignity and purpose. Lining up elderly men and women in wheelchairs in a facility with overworked and undercompensated caregivers is not a healthy standard. Allowing men and women who do not have the dependent elderly in their best interest to make decisions over their care is not a healthy standard. Not giving families an option to care for their loved ones at home when they lose their independence is not a healthy standard.

The end of life should not be institutionalized dependency, resulting in loneliness, neglect, and despair. Death is a natural part of life, a time for closure and peaceful reflection on the time spent living, not the beginning of an ongoing struggle for respect.

Margaret might not have been able to walk again, but she still had potential as a human being. She still had a right arm to paint with and a gentle voice to tell stories with. What she didn't have was an environment at the end of her life where those things could be nurtured and used to open up potential for new growth—growth in herself and as a gift to others.

***Carol Cooley** received her bachelor's degree in Health Sciences and master's degree in Physical Therapy from Duquesne University in Pittsburgh, Pennsylvania. She has worked as a physical therapist and advocate for seniors and disabled adults since 1994. She's an active member of the National Patient Advocacy Foundation. Her writing has been published in various journals, and she was named a finalist in the* North Carolina Literary Review*'s 2010 short story competition. She currently works and resides in the Raleigh-Durham, North Carolina, area.*

The Measure of Time

AMANDA J. REDIG

For many patients and physicians time is everything, says medical resident Amanda J. Redig. But it is not the number of our days that matters, but the quality of the time we have left.

There is nothing like medical school—except residency, I am discovering—to make one so acutely aware of the passing of time. There are moments when it slips away unnoticed and others in which each ticking-tock of the clock lasts longer than mere seconds. Yet, like the relentless progression of waves spreading out on the shore, new days keep coming, one after the other. When I stagger out of the OR after a thirty-six-hour shift, there are days I feel ancient, but there are also moments in which the magic of watching a beating heart causes the clock to stop entirely. The linear march of time counts these moments—from the mundane to the exquisite, those that are gone in an instant and those that last a lifetime—with the same measure.

The Greek *χρόνος,* or *chronos,* gives us the etymological root of chronology and chronicle, the meaning behind our word for time. *Chronology* and *chronicle* are fitting words for a hospital, a place where everyone who walks through the door is counting something—for me, usually the number of patients I have to see or the notes I have to write. Yet as I keep track of my "to-do" list for the day, I cannot forget that, for some, counting days means more than measuring time until the next board exam.

"How much time do I have, Doc?" the man in the suit and tie sitting on the exam table asked the minute the door clicked shut behind me. It was February in Chicago. A few days earlier, in the research building next door to the hospital, the pipes had frozen, but beads of sweat perched on the top of his shaved head, and his right foot in its polished black loafer swung back and forth like a metronome. There were just the two of us in the exam room, and I didn't know what to say. I'd seen his imaging. Just hours before, the radiologist at the tumor board pointed out feature after feature of the inoperable mass that had stubbornly resisted all efforts to slow its growth. I turned my head away from the projection screen; snow flurries whipped past the window, and the slate gray sky promised more snow to come.

Now the patient himself was staring at me, and all I could think about were the moments he would miss: holding his wife as they both drifted off to sleep, laughing with his kids at the first snowfall, raising a glass of champagne to toast his retirement, the birth of his first grandchild, a holiday dinner surrounded by family and friends. Right then, in this moment, I could not tell him the unvarnished truth—that he was likely going to die. So I answered his question with the only words I could think to say.

"As much as possible," I said, hearing the hope in my voice despite the heaviness in my heart. "You are going to have as much time as possible." His foot stopped its back-and-forth swing, and he looked away for a moment, staring at the anatomy chart on the wall while taking a deep, shuddering breath. Then he turned to face me again.

"Okay," he said. The corners of his mouth twitched. "Okay."

Time may have blurred the lines of his face in my memory, but I cannot forget his words. He was not ready to die, and I was not ready to admit that he probably would, but beneath our shared resistance to what was happening in his body, we both knew it would happen sooner rather than later. Yet even with the specter of death in the room, he didn't ask if he was going to die. He asked about time.

From the beginning, physicians have an adversarial relationship with death. The pathologists who spend their days surrounded by bits of tissue on glass slides and tumors in bottles of formalin learn to live with death, but that's only because it's part of their job description. For the rest of us, death is the enemy, and though we know we are all destined to lose the battle with death eventually, that doesn't stop us from trying to ignore or defeat the inevitable. Even our lab coats are white, as if the ability to bleach away the stains bestows the added power to make bad things go away with the wave of a stethoscope. In truth, black would be a more appropriate color for our coats. It would hide the stray marks of pen, splashes of blood, and unidentified smears that mar the traditional white. But no one goes to a physician to be reminded of a funeral, so when the white coats get too grubby we replace them with new ones.

Few moments in medicine are more satisfying than the ones in which life happens. Delivering babies is such amazing work, because right there is life at its most primal: a child, slipping and sliding into life without mistakes or regret, a moment that is both timed and timeless. But then life moves forward and becomes the tapestry of events and memories that fill our days, a place from which it is impossible to go back. And whether we are aware of their passing or not, each moment that slips by is one that will not come again, moving us ever closer to the other side of life, the bookend to the birth none of us remembers.

This is the inescapable reality that drives the profession of medicine. We remove tumors, open blocked coronary arteries, counsel our patients on blood pressure and diabetes control, even connect people to machines to help them breathe, all for the same reason—to buy time. I've been in school without break for the last twenty-three years, and I have at least seven more years of postgraduate training to go. An average of five hours of sleep a night is a good week; weekends off are a foreign concept; an exciting Friday night date is falling asleep together on the couch. A daunting investment of time is required to become a physician, but we are also witness to the extraordinary: what it means to be alive. Sometimes this comes in the form of people whose insides we know better than any other part of them, sometimes in the form of people who are unpleasant—like the paraplegic who would purposely throw his dirty diapers at anyone who walked into his room. But there are also moments—when the young woman who was in the ICU on a ventilator for two weeks opened her eyes and smiled around the breathing tube—that take your breath away. In the end, everyone who leaves the hospital is another soul with more time, and that is a victory unto itself.

The catch is this: the time that is measured in the hours of a surgery or weeks between scans is not the only time that counts. It does matter, of course, because time allows a grandfather to attend his granddaughter's wedding or a child to go to Disneyland as the fulfillment of a wish she will not live long enough to outgrow. Yet the *chronos* of time does not give life meaning any more than sitting with a textbook bestows wisdom. Physicians like the language of chronology because everything from the length of our training to the time-course of the drugs we prescribe is charted in this familiar language. But how do we explain the joy of a moment that can last for a lifetime or the pain of decades that is forgiven in a second? This is time that matters. It is not the number of our days but rather their measure that counts in the end.

Chronos is the literal word most familiar in the English lexicon, but the companion idea in the Greek is καιρός, or *kairos,* a word for which there is no direct translation. Like *chronos, kairos* means time, but also something more—it is the right time, the time when something of great importance occurs. There is no *kairos* without *chronos,* but *chronos* matters only because of *kairos.* This truth, that time is not always just time, is one of the most painful yet also the most liberating realizations of living, for the gift of such understanding is this: every moment can matter, whether our allotment of them is as numerous as the grains of sand on the shore or as fleeting as the morning dew.

I have seen death, and I have spent hours talking to those who are facing it. There is sorrow. There is a sense of loss and sometimes anger or bitterness. But inexplicably, there can also be acceptance, peace, and sometimes joy. What explains such drastic differences? As physicians, we are trained to fight death, because every patient who dies is a case we have lost. We want to give more time, and we work at it with the dogged determination of the type A personalities most of us are. But sometimes I think that in chasing the *chronos* that drives our every waking moment, we have forgotten something of even greater value. This is a truth some of our patients know, even when we don't always understand what they are trying to tell us. What value can there be to more time if the *kairos* is lost?

I met Mr. Jackson in the spring. The tulips were blooming on Michigan Ave., a profusion of color so vibrant that my steps would involuntary slow as I passed by on my predawn rush to work. In the beginning, I saw him as another elderly patient with heart failure and pulmonary edema secondary to uncontrolled hypertension. So many of the details fit—his age, his history, his own admission that he didn't always watch his diet. "I do like my french fries and catsup," he said with a sheepish smile, when I asked whether he'd been watching his sodium. Putting it all together with his cough and shortness of breath, I was sure I knew exactly what we were dealing with and what to do next. Pump up the diuretics to get some of the fluid off and relieve the load on the heart, maybe throw in another antihypertensive or two, and this spry eighty-six-year-old would be on his way.

"Sounds good to me, Doc," he said with a bright smile when I told him the plan.

"We're going to get a chest X-ray too," I added, "just to make sure we're not missing anything." As I listened to Mr. Jackson's lungs, I could hear the characteristic crackling and whooshing of fluid accumulating, and in my mind's eye I could almost see his imaging studies.

"Bingo," I thought to myself as I folded my stethoscope and shoved it back into my coat pocket. "Cardiomegaly, batwing edema, probably bilateral pleural effusions," I continued, rattling off the radiographic terms for what I expected to find when the films came back.

But several hours later I was staring at the PACS imaging screen with a sick feeling in the pit of my stomach. Sometimes it takes a radiologist to interpret the subtle shades of gray found on an X-ray but not in this case. I was right: there was fluid in the lungs. The problem was what I had not anticipated, perhaps had not wanted to consider in this World War II veteran who had been smoking something—cigarettes, cigars, a pipe—since 1942. The large mass with its irregular borders and spiculated tendrils occluding the entire upper left lobe of the lung was as visible and as ominous as they come. The biopsy came back squamous cell carcinoma, and all of a sudden instead of a little heart failure and hypertension, the diagnosis was inoperable lung cancer.

Mr. Jackson took the news well, shockingly so, in fact. Wearing his fuzzy navy blue bathrobe and slippers from home, he sat in the chair in his room shaking his head and looking out the window at the unobstructed Chicago skyline.

"I knew I should have stopped smoking that pipe," he said with the same wry smile he'd used when talking about the french fries. "Thanks for telling me," he said. "When can I go home?"

Ultimately, after a few days of intravenous diuretics to dry out his lungs and with a follow-up appointment in the oncology clinic, we did send him home. For the remainder of his days on our service, his demeanor never changed. He was as unfailingly calm and polite as he'd been when we all thought his blood pressure was to blame. He had not a trace of anxiety about his terminal diagnosis, at least that he displayed to our team. Sometimes one wonders whether a patient understands the implications of such grave information, but in this case there was no doubt.

"I guess this tumor will be the end of me," Mr. Jackson said the next morning when I came in to check on him. He was perched in the chair by the window casually eating his eggs. "Oh well," he continued, "that's the way it goes. My Betty had cancer too, and I know."

"Mr. Jackson," I said, once again not entirely sure of the right thing to say under such circumstances. "There are so many new medications now, and I know the oncologists will be talking with you about this," I said, unsure of how long this man had to live but confident in the knowledge that a terminal diagnosis did not mean there was nothing left to do. Two days later we sent Mr. Jackson home, and I could only remind myself that at least his breathing was less labored and he wasn't coughing as much. Had I not run into his oncologist several weeks later, this would have been the last I heard of him.

"Hey, I saw that patient from your team the other day," the physician told me, as we were walking to the auditorium on the third floor of the hospital for grand rounds, the weekly seminar of the Department of Medicine. "Mr. Jackson. Lung cancer. Nice guy."

"That's the one," I said, realizing then how badly I wanted to know how he was doing. Once again, Mr. Jackson surprised me. I listened in disbelief as the oncologist told me Mr. Jackson had listened to his options and then refused even palliative chemotherapy. He didn't want to treat his cancer, even knowing this would hasten his death. At first, his decision was hard for me to understand, in part because it would not have been mine. But the more I thought about it, the more I saw Mr. Jackson in his choice. There was no clouding of judgment, no denial, no fear. Just a calm acceptance and that same slow smile. I don't remember if he had any children or grandchildren, but I know his wife had died some years before. He missed her, that was clear from the wistful tone in his voice when he mentioned her name, but he had lived without her for many years. He had also lived with the memories of a war that continues to cast shadows even now, and from this lifetime of stories, he saw the final chapter of his life and didn't blink.

At first I thought this calm was a function of age. Perhaps time was the secret to facing our own mortality, after all. Yet how many years would it take? Seventy? Eighty? How many was enough? I thought the number must be somewhere between my nearly thirty and Mr. Jackson's nearly ninety.

Then I met Bryan.

Bryan had cancer, too. An inoperable, incurable malignancy that was going to kill him. He had just turned twenty-two, and he had no chance of living to see twenty-three. Death in the aged is sorrow, not tragedy. It is another thing entirely to walk into the room of a dying patient who looks like your baby brother, right down to his sigh of annoyance and the sparse stubble of an unshaven jaw that is more boast than substance. If you can't manage to grow a beard, surely you are too young to die.

Bryan knew his prognosis and the grim details of his medical record, and he wasn't happy about being in the hospital. The only reason he'd reluctantly agreed to come in was because the tumor in his spine was starting to compress his spinal cord. Faced with the possibility of spending his remaining life as a paraplegic, he decided a few lost days for steroid therapy were worth the potential gain. Once he was admitted, everyone on the team felt the weight of watching a young man die. There was something deeply unsettling about the realization that I was more aware of the things Bryan would never live to see than he was; in the years that separated us was a depth of experiences I can't imagine giving up but never knew until they happened to me. How can any of us foresee the joy of building our own independent lives if we never get the chance to do it? In my rare days off, I spent every possible moment outside: shopping along Michigan Avenue, running along the lakefront, wandering the river walk at sunset. I knew what Bryan was missing in the short term, and so did he. But what about everything else? For the senior physician on our team, tasked with supervising the professional development of the fledgling physicians following in his footsteps, this contrast must have been even more marked. For every moment of the years between us that flashed through my mind when I looked at Bryan, how many more did my attending see in the patient who could have been his son?

When Bryan didn't show up for his outpatient oncology appointment two days after discharge, our entire team took it as a personal affront. Didn't he want to take advantage of everyone who was trying to help him? Didn't he want more time? As the person who had the most interaction with him during his hospitalization, I knew he hated what his disease meant, but he had found a way to ignore it in his own mind. Like Mr. Jackson, Bryan wasn't in denial; he knew the end was coming and that no medical options would change that. He could be angry, sullen, and depressed. One morning on rounds I had asked if there was anything he needed, and his reply was swift. "Oh, you mean like a new life?" he answered, rolling over in bed with his hair sticking out in all four directions as though he'd stuck a fork in an electrical socket. "One where I'm not in here listening to you people all the time? One where I'm not dying?"

But there were also times when Bryan would banter with me, the laughter in his voice bubbling under the surface. He would fantasize loudly about the things he planned to eat as soon as he was released from the hospital—double-cheese omelets, bacon, pancakes with whipped cream. "Because," as he quipped, watching my reaction with a glint in his eye, "it's not like the cholesterol's going to kill me, right?" He would talk about having wanted to be a chef ever since he had fallen in love with the white hats as a child, how in order to go to culinary school he'd moved to the city from the farm country of Iowa where he'd grown up, how he'd started waiting tables before being hired as a sous chef. How all of this had happened after he learned he was dying. And for what time he had left, he knew what mattered most. He might have discovered he was a city boy at heart in the last year of his life, but strolling down the sidewalks of the Magnificent Mile, from the river walk and the Gap at one end to Lake Michigan and Louis Vuitton at the other, gave him the strength to live all of the moments that remained. Even though he knew his dream of starting his own restaurant would never happen, he told me he wasn't quitting his job until they fired him.

"My parents want me to come home with them," he told me once, in a rare unguarded moment. "But I just can't," he continued. "I just can't. I need to be here, in my place. You know?" And all of a sudden, I did.

The *chronos* of time is the same for us all. The measure of our days may differ, but the seconds pass by with the same inexorable precision whether we're eight or eighty. Time is time when it comes to chronology. What isn't the same—and never has been—is the meaning of the days we have left. Death is the end of time on this earth, but even when the coming of those last days is upon us, life can still be full of purpose, even when that purpose carries a taste of the bittersweet.

This truth is easily lost amid the machines and technology of medical achievement. The greatest gift we can give our patients and their families is not *chronos* but *kairos,* the opportunity to transform empty moments into those of profound value. Each of us will live a unique life defined by what brings purpose to our days, but we share one universal truth at the end of our lives. Death is greeted with the bitterness of regret only if it brings the realization that our time has had no meaning.

The number of our days is not for any of us to know. But with whatever time is left to me, I have found my *kairos* from those who have shared their moments of living and dying. If I am graced with years enough, I may one day forget the knowledge I will spend a lifetime accumulating. But the one lesson I will never forget is this: what matters is not how we die but rather why we choose to live.

Amanda J. Redig *studied biochemistry and creative writing at the University of Arizona prior to enrolling in the medical scientist training program at Northwestern University. She completed her PhD in cancer biology and graduated from the Feinberg School of Medicine. She is currently a resident in internal medicine at the Brigham and Women's Hospital in Boston. Her writing has appeared on the* Virginia Quarterly Review*'s blog and in the* Journal of the American Medical Association (JAMA) *and* Health Affairs.

The Deep Truth

EUGENIA SMITH

Following the suicide of her seventy-four-year-old mother, Eugenia Smith must restart her own life "on a different plane, a place where the mother-yoke dissolves into filmy scarves of memory."

My mother died lying on a Glad bag—a double layer of industrial-strength plastic she'd spread across the bed to protect her sheets from the mess of her passing. I wasn't there, but I've imagined her final hours in multiple retakes, until the scene is as vivid and real as a home movie, its flickering narrative gaps plugged with random images from stock family footage.

Sometime on Monday night, June 22, 1987, probably after the ten o'clock news, my mother, Ruth, drank a glass or two of Chenin Blanc; bookmarked page 254 of the last book she would ever leave unfinished, *The Prince of Tides;* hoisted herself from her recliner; and shuffled in her floppy pink mules toward the bathroom, where she inspected her wan image in the mirror through rheumy, cataract-clouded eyes. What reflected back was a storied terrain of pouches, ruts, and hollows; thin, chapped lips, their edges puckering downward into commas; baggy, translucent skin mottled by bright capillary sprays—all of it haloed by the white, wispy remains of spent curls, like a dandelion gone to seed.

She ran a tub of warm water, sponged herself with VitaBath, dried herself with a plush, peach-colored towel, slathered lotion on her upper body, dressed in her navy blue pantsuit, sprayed herself with Fiamma, applied fresh blusher and lipstick, and slipped on her silver bouffant wig, the helmet she always wore to meet the world. She probably lingered before the mirror for a moment, regarding one last time the sad, plundered ruins of a face that had once been unreasonably beautiful.

Back in the living room, she kissed Pugsley, her cat, leaving a pale blossom of lipstick between her ears, and swallowed twenty codeine capsules with what remained of the wine. A few minutes later, she opened her bedroom windows to the moonlit night, smoothed a trash bag across her bed, and lay down on it to die. She was seventy-four years old.

This moody, broken woman, whose psyche was so unruly and whose hungers were so extravagant, had always been tidy, even fastidious, in her housekeeping, as if ironing sheets and lining up shoes and shampoo bottles in tight, orderly rows might keep her world from flying apart. This last act was no exception. She left behind shiny faucets, meticulously organized closets, gleaming countertops, and clean, freshly laundered sheets. Her death would leave behind no visible stain.

And so she was gone. In that moment, my own life stopped, only to restart on a different plane, a place where the mother-yoke dissolves into filmy scarves of memory, where pools of grief seep slowly into deep reservoirs, where orphaned daughters join hearts and minds to seek new ways to live in the roiling, twilit aftermath of no good-byes.

Earlier in the evening, she had called me. "This is it. I want to die," she said. "I mean business. I can't take this pain any more. And I'll be damned if I'll hobble around on one leg."

"I'll come and see you tomorrow, Mom," I promised. I felt impatient, exasperated. *Please,* I thought, *not tonight. I've had a lousy day.*

"Don't bother. I'll be dead by tomorrow. You'll be better off without me."

I sighed, told her to try to get a good night's sleep, hung up the phone, and called my sister, Diana. She'd had the same conversation.

Neither of us believed our mother. We'd heard the threat too many times before. We'd spent parallel lifetimes bracing ourselves for service as fragile supports to her rickety psyche. And when the scaffolding collapsed, we were always there to clean up the mess, struggling to reassemble the debris into a makeshift shelter for our tangled lives. This time we stayed away. There would be no more messes to clean up, except what remained in the after-clutter of grief and regret.

When Diana and I arrived the next morning at the modest Edina bungalow where our mother had spent her bleak last years, that force of nature—the maddening, mercurial, tempestuous woman who had twice labored so mightily to deliver daughters into the world, and then to love, care for, and tame what her labors had wrought—was already a few miles away being readied for cremation. From matching chairs flanking the east-facing picture window, we surveyed the sun-struck residue of our homebound mother's life: her weeping fig and several species of philodendron stretching their limbs in luxuriant but orderly profusion into the dense, moist warmth of the living room; bookmarked, annotated books lining the ubiquitous bookshelves; catalogs stacked on the coffee table, the colorful images on their dog-eared pages bearing witness to her vanished dreams and appetites.

On the far wall next to the sofa, wilted peonies shed their frail pink petals onto the mahogany end table. A few graham cracker crumbs from our mother's last meal dusted the immaculate gloom of a TV tray. Deprived of the lap she had nestled into for twelve years, Pugsley crouched and switched her tail in dazed feline bewilderment.

Diana and I spoke of the good times, when we'd sit with our mother on the backyard patio drinking Bloody Marys and tossing peanuts to chipmunks and blue jays, or we'd spirit our mother away to nearby Southdale Center and through the Dayton's perfume department, the three of us giddy with surfeit as we doused ourselves in scents.

As we dawdled in our memories, ducks from the nearby pond showed up at the patio door, quacking earnestly for their daily corn. They would return to the patio day after day and wait for their benefactor, long after all traces of her had vanished.

I would wait, too, for a sign that she wasn't really gone—a page turned in a book, a new stitch in her embroidery, the tired shuffle of her slippers across the floor, the insistent ring of the telephone at midnight, the hoarse, dry dust of her voice sifting through cracks in my ruptured sleep.

The death certificate declared that our mother had died of "advanced atherosclerotic disease." We knew better. The empty pill bottle told the story. Her clogged cardiovascular system and her failing pancreas may have carried her to the brink, but she stepped over the edge on her own steam, while we slept.

More than twenty years later, Ruth's scent rises, faint but redolent, from a perfume bottle I've kept in a dresser drawer. I stare at a photo of her on the dresser, a hand-colored image of a sultry, brooding eighteen-year-old beauty with her life still ahead of her—and I wonder: Where is she now? What remains of that damaged woman who was both the first love and the bane of my life? Could we have stopped her? *Should* we have stopped her?

As for the thoughts she carried to her death bed, they have evaporated with the scent on her skin, scattered with her ashes to Minnesota winds, woods, and meadows and pressed into the rocky soil behind our North Shore cabin among the lupines and fireweed, beside a towering white spruce that she helped plant. There are no good-byes for us to remember, no last words to mull over. No sweet memories of valedictory consolations and endearments, no chance to resolve old grievances and assuage old guilts, not even an exculpatory note—*It's not your fault*—signed "Love, Mom."

If we had really known—believed—what our mother was up to that night, Diana and I would surely have tried to stop her. Or would we? Maybe, in a way, we did know but couldn't rouse ourselves to one more rescue mission. As her diabetic neuropathy had worsened, our mother had talked repeatedly about "ending it all," especially after learning that she might lose a leg. But her threats were too freighted with decades of trauma—panicked, guilt-ridden, just-in-time trips to hospital ERs, false alarms, tears, and recriminations, lives suspended from wobbly support beams between episodes. We were tired. We just didn't want to hear it anymore.

Hindsight is everything—including a whip for self-flagellation. But in truth, maybe we did the right thing by staying away. Maybe she truly did "mean business," and her final phone calls were just good-byes, not cries for help. Maybe we stayed away for her sake, not for ours. Or maybe not.

We'll never know. What we do know is that she was alone when she lay down on that garbage bag. That's the deep and ineluctable truth of our grieving.

Some Years Earlier

Ruth hunkered down in her recliner and took a deep drag of an L&M. She'd just come home from the hospital, her stomach purged of its deadly cocktail of drugs and alcohol. I approached her warily through a fog of tears and smoke.

"You scared me," I said. "I don't know what I did, but I'm sorry . . ."

"If you really gave a damn, you'd treat me better," she accused, waving me away, spurning my solicitude. The chair bucked and squawked against her feeble exertions.

I started to protest, but knowing she'd already won this round, I turned and walked away. A theatrical sob called me back. "What can I—?" I offered, ingratiating.

"Just go. Leave me alone," she snapped. And I did. I knew better than to stay.

I was twelve at the time, or maybe fourteen, or eighteen, or thirty. From where I stand now, in my seventh decade of life, it's all the same. As we replayed this scene over the years, always with the same script, I became hostage to my mother's moods, trapped in her vortex. Even today, those moods live in me, attenuated but insistent.

Our mother's obituary didn't say she'd fought "a courageous battle with a long illness." What she had battled was life itself. And for the last several years of that life, she'd taken on a formidable new adversary, chronic pain—peripheral diabetic neuropathy, the wrack and ruin of poorly managed diabetes. The dying nerves in her legs and feet had risen up to punish her for a lifetime of excess and neglect.

She tried to be a good patient, and she was, in her way. She scrupulously checked her blood sugar, injected herself with insulin twice daily, even kept track of exchanges—fats, starches, fruits, and vegetables. But that regimen couldn't save her. In the end, it wasn't the diabetes that claimed her—not the clogged arteries, blighted organs, or pain-wracked extremities. It wasn't even the pills, not really. It was the collapse of her battered spirit into the gaping maw of her cravings.

Transgression and Retribution

In a culture of commodified health care that fetishizes personal responsibility as the key to a long, healthy, and prosperous life, illness is often framed as a kind of moral failing. Believing thinness and fitness to be the better part of valor, we've come to see many diseases, especially those related to the pleasures of the flesh, as an expression of character flaws, not to mention a drain on the economy and a cause of soaring hospital costs and health insurance premiums.

My mother, at roughly 185 pounds—what she called her "fighting weight"—was a case in point. She ate compulsively, with a kind of exorbitant relish. It would be easy to claim that her illness was her fault. After all, she could never resist a heaping bowl of ice cream or a third helping of pie. I never saw her eat just one of anything.

"The doctor told me I could eat this," she'd say, resisting our attempts to confiscate the contraband sweets. We'd flutter about, wring our hands, and mutter under our breath about how she was killing herself with all that junk. And then we'd walk away. We knew we were powerless to save her from herself. We also knew that as the pain got worse and her failing eyesight and limited mobility kept her increasingly captive in her small house, those sweet treats were about all that gave her pleasure anymore.

"I'm going to die anyway," she'd say, her eyes gleaming with defiance. "So why not enjoy the little time I have left?" She had a point.

Should she have watched her diet and kept her appetites in check? Probably. Was she asking for trouble, as we sometimes alleged? Well, maybe. Was it her fault that she was sick? Not exactly. Was she *morally* culpable? Did she *deserve* to be sick? Absolutely not.

The Physics and Poetry of Pain

Few things have made me feel more useless than watching my mother spiral into the warp of chronic pain. The moaning and cursing, the writhing and grimacing, the tears—that's how my mother's pain expressed itself. But the pain itself was beyond my ken, beyond soothing, even beyond the ken and therapeutic reach of medical science.

Chronic pain is brash, cruel, and uncompromising. And it's crafty. It goes underground periodically, skulking about on padded paws, gathering its forces, then erupting without warning in full fury, sometimes far from the source—as referred pain, like an echo, or reverb, the tsunami miles from the earthquake on the ocean floor, the night terror years removed from the childhood trauma.

Even when it reveals itself, it's perceptible, and describable, only by the person afflicted. And yet, like grief, it's also *in*describable. As the poet Shelley said, "The deep truth is imageless." There are no words for the deep truth of pain, only the cries and moans that rise reflexively from the body's unreachable core of misery.

My mother used to say moaning soothed her pain. I don't understand just how moaning works its magic—maybe by rallying endorphins to action. But I do know the palliative power of pain's operatic sound effects, those exclamations like *argh!* and *yeow!* that scream from word bubbles rising from gaping cartoon mouths. Somewhere in the deepest corridors of my own brain, the walls still echo with the fortissimo high-C wails that once took the edge off my childhood stomachaches and heartaches, their analgesic effects seemingly proportionate to their pitch and volume.

Of course, any relief my mother experienced was transient, a flirty phantom's touch evanescing. Once chronic pain is set in motion, there's no stopping it. All the diets and potions and opiates and fitness regimens in the world won't make it go away. It sleeps with one eye open. Confront it, and it will rise up and mow you down. It might even kill you in the end. Indeed, it probably will.

For most of us, physical pain subsides on its own or with the aid of over-the-counter analgesics. If it persists or gets worse, those of us who can afford health care seek relief from a doctor. First, the doctor asks us to locate the pain, and we report that it's here, or here, or there. We point. We respond to probing fingers with a grimace or sharp inhale. "Hmm," says the doctor. "Does this hurt? How about this?"

Then she asks us to describe the pain. We search for metaphors: *searing, piercing, burning, pounding*. We invoke daggers, needles, hammers. Struggling to convey pain's character and intensity, we become poets.

Finally, words fail. So we quantify the pain, measuring its severity on a scale of 1 to 10, from a pin prick, say, to third-degree burns. My mother reported that her pain mostly hovered around a 10. On a good day, it was a 5 for moments at a time. Sometimes it spiked to a 12, off the charts. That meant it was extreme, severe, wrenching. Excruciating. Unbearable. A full-throttle primal scream. Truly *beyond* words.

I believed her. I'm not sure her doctors did. One doctor even suggested that she had a low pain threshold. How would he know? Relative to what? Had he ever crossed that threshold? He could never know her pain. He could only imagine the agonies that sprouted in the teeming root cellar of her consciousness.

When I try to imagine my mother's pain, I summon the memory of nerves in an abscessed molar, writhing in their death throes. I imagine electric shock. Jagged shards of glass. Molten lava. And I replay in my head the macabre dental health films of my childhood—grainy, crudely drawn cartoons featuring a snaggle-toothed, beady-eyed fiend chipping away with a pickaxe at the ruined teeth of bad children who failed to brush, each blow unleashing lightning bolts of pain.

Thanks to breakthroughs in MRI technology, one thing we do know about pain is that, like joy and love and hunger, it is indeed "in your head." As I understand it, the nutrient-deprived nerves in my mother's legs and feet were, in effect, starving to death—from poor circulation, poor oxygenation. The distress signals emitted by those sick and dying nerves triggered a kind of telecommunications relay, with pain messages traveling as electrical impulses to the brain, where they were processed and signaled back again along elaborate networks of neural pathways.

A friend who knew something about Chinese medicine once suggested acupuncture as a way to intercept the signals. Voodoo, my mother said. Despite everything, she still put her faith in traditional Western medicine. Another friend suggested that she try transcutaneous electrical nerve stimulation (TENS), which delivers electric currents said to short-circuit the relay system.

It seemed to me the principle was more or less the same—just a different delivery mechanism, a machine instead of needles. But in my mother's world, an electronic gadget meant science, and acupuncture, a kind of witchcraft. Come to think of it, maybe there was another reason for her resistance: she just couldn't abide any more needles.

I remember her elation when she announced that she was trying out this new gizmo. I was skeptical but hopeful. And it did work—for a time, for a few moments or hours at a time. And then it stopped. Her pain spiked to a 12. The demon was back, fully armed and invincible. She had no recourse but to numb herself to his blows. So she returned to her pain management arsenal of first and last resort—the ordnance in her medicine chest.

A Long, Slow Death of the Spirit

In her last months, my mother said over and over that she wanted to die. "I just can't take it anymore," she'd say. "It" was both physical and psychic pain. It was the sensation in her legs, to be sure. But it was also the throb of emptiness, the tremors rising from a vast, hollow space where remembered joys should have found a peaceful home that she could amble around in. There were, it seemed, no joys to occupy that imageless space of absence.

Diana and I had heard the same threat for as long as we could remember. And we responded as we always had—with preemptive denials: "Oh, Mom, you're strong as an ox. You'll live forever!" Or with scolding: "Don't be ridiculous!"

"You'll be better off," she'd say. "You'll be glad when I'm gone. Don't think you won't. And don't try to stop me."

Even as we rebuffed her, we heard an urgency we'd never heard before. We heard determination, not surrender. And we understood that somehow this was different from all those other times. The rotting, creaky scaffolding we had so feebly patched together over and over was beginning to give way.

If she couldn't live without pain, we wanted her to be able to die without pain. But what could we do? Assisted suicide was, and still is, illegal in Minnesota, so she would have no help from her doctors. As for hospice care, it was not widely available and had only recently received federal backing. Had it been offered, she would have refused it. "Death with dignity? Ha. I'll go out kicking and screaming," she'd say with bravado, "not strapped to a hospital bed in diapers with tubes up my nose."

She wouldn't have qualified for hospice care in any case, since she wasn't dying in the medical sense; her organs weren't shutting down, and she was not certifiably within six months of death. Hospice care was, and is, available only to those who are so far gone they will soon feel nothing at all.

And so our mother, who couldn't be fixed, also didn't fit the categories or protocols for assisted leaving. Her pain was terminal, but she could not, in her final weeks, drift quietly and painlessly away, attended by a nurse with a morphine drip at the ready, surrounded by her loving family.

In mid-June, a doctor told her she would most certainly lose a leg—first one, then maybe the other. But even that wouldn't relieve the pain, he said. She would experience phantom pain, which would linger long after the offending limb had been severed.

She began making preparations. She had no living will, but she declared in a letter to her daughters that she must never be carted off to the hospital in a stupor and hooked up to machines. She must not be resuscitated if she stopped breathing and her heart stopped. Her daughters were to see that these wishes were carried out. "I'll be watching," she said, watching us.

The Backstory

The pills had always been there—hundreds of them, tablets and capsules counted into small amber bottles, each bearing a different Rx number: narcotics for pain, "happy pills" for the blues, tranquilizers for anxiety, sleeping pills for insomnia; pills for blood sugar management, weight control, high blood pressure, hot flashes, indigestion—all washed down with white wine and Bloody Marys.

No one ever called our mother an addict. Her drugs were prescribed by physicians and purchased from licensed pharmacists. She was under a doctor's care, not shooting up in a dark alley as her pusher slithered away counting his ill-gotten gains and fingering the gun in his pocket.

More times than I can remember, she took too many pills—and she arrived in hospital emergency rooms just in time. Sometimes the overdose was deliberate, sometimes not. Either way, it was a cry for help. Her cries went mostly unheard by her doctors, who routinely silenced them with prescriptions for more pills.

Her stomach pumped and the crisis averted, she was sent home with a scolding, a pat on the back, and a recommendation that she talk to someone. Buck up. Get a grip. Don't do this again. Here's the phone number of a good therapist. Here's a little red capsule to make you feel better. And here's one to curb your appetite.

And she did do it again. And again. And again.

Nothing—not the opiates, not the donuts and hot fudge sundaes, not the love of her daughters and husband, not the spending sprees that gave her a rush but sank her deep into debt—could ever touch her chronic emotional pain, a soul sickness that seemed inbred. If ever a blithe, hopeful spirit had found lodging within her, by the time she married our father in 1940 it had already long since died, leaving her with the worst kind of phantom pain, a profound ache in the core of her being.

Even when she laughed—and she did laugh, often, with gusto and abandon—the laugh was more like keening, a stentorian mezzo-soprano lament. We could always sense just beneath the mirth a ground-note of grief and longing for what was so irrevocably lost.

She very probably suffered from clinical depression, which by all accounts had worsened with the birth of her daughters and redoubled with our adolescence. Rather than seek diagnosis or treatment, she blamed us, our father, and anyone else who failed her. As for us, we saw her condition not as an illness but as a fault line in our household, an ominous crack in the foundation of our lives. Her "spells," as we called them, were unhappy accidents of breeding, temperament, or both, and we were part of the wreckage, always tiptoeing around that crack so as not to tumble into the abyss and be caught in the undertow of lava and quicksand.

Unhappiness defined our mother; it was a *state of being,* her birthright. The chronic physical pain of her later years was something else—not the familiar, gnawing ache of free-floating misery, but an alien thing, a noisy, garish intruder that charged onto her bleak psychic landscape brandishing razor blades, spears, and jackhammers.

I see now that this new pain was a kind of bitter tonic. By distracting her from her deeper, more obscure psychic wounds, it energized her. It gave her life purpose and focus. It even made us closer. For once, we—her daughters—

weren't implicated; this pain wasn't our fault. What's more, it gave her something to hope for, an occasional, if short-lived, remission: "It's better today," she'd say, her eyes brimming, looking to us for confirmation. "Maybe these pills are working. Do you think so?"

Toxic Brew

Our mother's increasing dependence on pills reached a crisis point in 1983, at her seventieth birthday party. We were sure this would be her last birthday. She was visibly addled, staring with woozy incomprehension at the bright march of seventy candles across the sheet cake we'd decorated with whimsical birds and flowers. When we sang "Happy Birthday," about the only sign of life was a single tear that fell from her cloudy right eye, leaving a salty trail I could taste when I kissed her cheek.

For several months, she'd been fading into a disabling incapacity that was both mental and physical. We feared Alzheimer's or maybe a series of small strokes. Doctor X said no, she was just getting old. "You have to expect this sort of thing," he said. After all, she was seventy and diabetic, with plaque-filled arteries and a weakening, overworked heart. What did we expect?

Time for an intervention. We found her a new doctor, who requested an inventory of her medications—ten in all. He said the toxic pharmaceutical brew would surely kill her. And so he took her off the drugs—all except her medication for high blood pressure.

"Cold turkey," he said. "That's the only way." Then, he said, once her body was detoxified, we would see what her body's natural painkillers could do, whether they'd remember how to do their job. Bodies are smart, he assured us. They're wired to remember. But hers was so depleted and frail, he couldn't promise anything.

We were scared. Could pain be worse than a 12? Would those mechanisms be able to switch themselves back on? Or was the circuitry so fouled up that no messages at all would get through, good or bad? Would the angry nerves in her legs start acting up again like fretful children just awakened from a fitful nap?

We watched for signs of withdrawal. At first, we saw little change beyond a slight tremor and some agitation. Within a few days, she was both calmer and more alert. She even seemed to rebound for a time. We had our mother back—feisty and irascible as ever, cursing and fuming, but also laughing that wonderful, gutsy, full-throated laugh that told us she was still a force to be reckoned with.

But there was, finally, no end to the pain, only the usual momentary respite now and then, as if her frayed nerves needed an occasional time-out to get recharged. The cruel promise of those bright but fleeting moments made the pain's return all the more savage. So our mother found a new doctor, and another, and began setting pills aside.

In her final months, the pain kept her awake night after night, rocking, moaning, crying, cursing, sinking ever more deeply into the Ruth-shaped groove in her leather recliner. By June 1987, she had a stash more than big enough to do the job.

The recliner is now at the family cabin. I think of it as a monument to her pain and her tenacity. It fits me perfectly.

Postscript

The day Diana and I cleaned out our mother's house, we rehashed our final mother-daughter conversations and pawed through everything that remained, scavenging for clues, memories, vindication.

I wondered out loud, "Do you think it's our fault? That phone call . . . we should have known. We should have been here." And then: "Do you ever feel relieved that she's gone?" That question hung in the air.

"I thought we were done with all this craziness," Diana said.

"This time is different—isn't it? It wasn't about us."

"It doesn't feel different to me. Except this time she's dead."

In the years since that day, we've replayed our mother's final months and years over and over, editing scenes and imagining interventions. But the reruns are all the same, with the same denouement, the same ending. If she were alive today, and if we knew what we know now, it would all be different. Or would it? Would we try to save her? Did we do right in staying away? Did we stay away for us or for her?

Maybe Diana is right—seeking closure is a fool's errand. As an old friend of mine is fond of saying, "What's done is done. No use thinking about it."

Of course, I'll think about it anyway. And I do know one thing: I'm grateful that our mother was spared the agony of waiting for nature to do its work. And she spared us from ever having to wheedle her into a nursing home, wipe drool from her chin, watch the light of recognition fade from her eyes, or linger by her deathbed for weeks while her body shut down one organ at a time.

But most of us won't have the option she chose. We won't have the stash of pills, or we'll be too sick, feeble, or afraid to act. Or someone will intervene and save us. And unless the laws change, we'll just have to wait it out.

As for me, when it's time, I hope there's an angel-of-mercy-for-hire nearby, wielding a hypodermic. And I hope, without faith or conviction, that I'll see my mother again, so I can tell her I'm sorry, even though I'm not sure what I'm sorry for. And maybe in death she'll take me into her arms as she so rarely could, or did, in life.

For now, I'll drink my green tea and load up on antioxidants, calcium, vitamin D, and organic cruciferous vegetables. And I'll imagine my mother at a celestial spa, eating chocolate-covered cherries, swallowing happy pills, and dancing blamelessly into eternity on lithe, muscular, pain-free legs.

***Eugenia Smith** is a writer of fiction, creative nonfiction, and poetry. She has a BA and an MA in English from the University of Minnesota, where she works in communications. She lives in Minneapolis with her cat, Audrey, and her partner, Kate.*

The Resurrection of Wonder Woman

ELEANOR VINCENT

When her daughter suffers brain death, Eleanor Vincent makes the decision to donate her daughter's organs—and later must balance her fear that she's abandoned her still-breathing child to a macabre death from organ retrieval surgery with the knowledge that she helped save the lives of strangers.

Pink from her bath and aglow with excitement, three-year-old Maya perched on the edge of the bathtub. I stretched out my arms and she jumped, landing in the white terrycloth towel I held out. I set her down on the bath mat and dried beads of water from her skin, wrapping her in the towel. Then I draped a dry towel over my own shoulders and led her into our game.

In our shared imagining, the towels became two white capes. We ran from one end of our apartment to the other as our capes billowed behind us.

Together we called, "Wonder Woman! Wonder Woman!"

Exulting in our superpowers, we extended our arms like wings, grasping the edges of our capes, two beings as one in flight. We imagined we wore magic bracelets on our wrists and golden lariats around our waists, just like our heroine. The fantasy of being all-powerful ended at the side of Maya's bed, where I helped her into her nightgown and tucked her in, a little girl again.

It was the 1970s, and I made a point of reading bedtime stories about exceptional women to her so that Maya would dream of daring and of genius. I hoped one day my daughter would become a woman who embraced her own power.

Sixteen years later, after a daredevil stunt left Maya in a coma, I wished I'd told her more cautionary tales.

•••

I stared out the window in the neuroscience ICU waiting room. Below me, stick figures moved across achingly green lawns. They looked like a cardboard tableau of normal life. Mount Diablo's sawtooth outline cut through a ribbon of clouds. A grandfather of a mountain, its hulking presence loomed above the rolling hills and valleys of Contra Costa County, a collection of suburban towns east of San Francisco. Maya's accident had happened three days earlier on a hot April afternoon in the foothills of Mount Diablo.

She had hiked to a meadow laced with oat grass and wildflowers. A ravine full of scrub oak and laurel trees tumbled down to a dry creek bed. One of her friends dared her to ride bareback on a horse they found there unfenced and unsecured. The animal reared and threw Maya to the ground with such force that she never regained consciousness.

The owner of the horse had sent her minister to the hospital to comfort me. A middle-aged woman with salt-and-pepper hair and a smile that was somehow too sympathetic, she had watery eyes that peered into mine. She had patted my shoulder and assured me her congregation was praying for us.

Now, I looked at my watch, steeling myself to face the double doors that led into the intensive care unit and another ten minutes with my comatose child. I lifted the house phone.

"This is Maya's mom. Can I see her now?"

"Yes," a voice answered. "I'll buzz you in."

I walked toward my daughter's bed, past the curtains surrounding families bent over other silent forms. The walls of the John Muir Medical Center were arctic white. Gleaming fluorescent lights stung my eyes. Antiseptic pricked my nostrils. After seventy-two hours of nursing my hope, willing my daughter to recover, an impossible thought dawned—*Maya might not make it.* When I reached her bedside, I trembled with this new possibility. I took her hand in mine.

"Sweetheart, it's Mom. I've been telling you that you will get well. But maybe that's not right; maybe what I want isn't what matters."

A roar filled my brain. I shook my head, trying to silence my own resistance.

I spoke to my nineteen-year-old daughter, saying out loud what I would never accept in my heart. "You decide, honey. I won't hold you back."

As I stood looking down at the beautiful young woman she had become, I knew I had no magic bracelet, no supernatural powers. Neither did she. Maya's face, inanimate as ice, was rosy-cheeked, bridelike against the stark white sheets.

I leaned into her and whispered the biggest lie of my life, never doubting she could hear me. "I'll be all right, sweetheart, if you need to go."

As my determination dissolved, I wanted to throw myself across her chest and give in to hours of unsuppressed weeping. But then I had a new thought: *If I break down, it will be too hard for her to die. My task now is to let her go.*

I remembered the night two years earlier when Maya had graduated from high school and I returned home alone to prepare for the party. We lived in a modest rented house in Walnut Creek, a middle-class enclave. The olive tree in our front yard dropped silver-gray leaves and shriveled fruit on the front walk. I grabbed a broom and swept the walkway in my suit and high heels. When I went in the house, I glanced at my daughter's senior picture sitting on the mantel, her white-blond hair and the mischief in her brown eyes. I burst into tears, anticipating, for the first time, how empty my life would feel when she left for college in a few months. On that night when I acknowledged that my daughter was moving away from me, I never dreamed that anything more difficult could happen, that any greater surrender might be asked of me.

Maya's chest rose and fell. The ventilator hissed, the monitors beeped, a fiber optic cable snaked into her skull to measure the pressure inside her brain. Over the last three days I had become expert at reading the peaks and valleys on the monitors.

I whispered in her ear, "It's between you and God now, Maya."

I never knew love could be so big, that it could expand enough to allow even this. *God must be mad! I must be mad to say, "Yes, go."*

A few hours later, her temperature soared. The doctor paced at the foot of her bed, thumbing her chart.

"Okay, what next?" I asked, afraid of his answer.

"Routine blood tests to see what kind of bug might be causing this. We have to bring the fever down, or she could go into convulsions."

"Should I spend the night?"

"No, you go home and try to rest. I'll call you if there's any change."

The next afternoon, Maya's brain surgeon, Dr. Carr, asked to speak with us about the results of the cerebral blood flow study he had ordered. One of the nurses gathered us into a windowless conference room where a hospital social worker sat at the opposite end of the conference table, looking grave and sympathetic. Boxes of tissue sprouted from the side tables. Almost a hundred hours had passed since the accident.

Dr. Carr came in, his white coat flapping, and sat down at the head of the table. I sat on his left side, staring at him.

"Did you feel it?" he asked as if he were conducting a pop quiz and we should all know the answer. "Did you feel it coming?" He leaned forward in his chair and said, "Bad news. Bad news."

Why does he say everything twice? I clenched my ice-cold hands in my lap and searched his handsome, dispassionate face with a surge of amazed fury.

"The test we did shows how much blood is flowing to the brain." He spoke to the wall now. "There is none, absolutely none, zero blood flow. I've declared her brain dead."

I could not move or even blink. A collective gasp filled the cramped room. Maya's boyfriend, Dale, groaned. My ex-husband, Dan, put his head in his hands.

"I've called in a second surgeon to confirm the diagnosis of death by neurological criteria," Dr. Carr said. He spoke with exaggerated calm, seemingly oblivious to the emotions swirling around him.

My eleven-year-old daughter, Meghan, leaned against her father and wept. Dale's mother began screaming "NO!" over and over.

I stared at the doctor with absolute hatred. How could he tell such a lie? How could he sit there, so smug, so above it all, so white and clean and antiseptic? Hot tears of disbelief trickled down my cheeks. Of all the people in the room, I was the only one who did not move or cry out. I felt granite-hard, yet sensitive as a tuning fork, paralyzed with grief. The social worker passed out tissues like party favors.

"We did all we could," Dr. Carr said.

I nodded. This was the one thing I *did* believe.

For the first time since he had entered the room, Dr. Carr met my gaze. His eyes were like icy blue marbles. "Would you consider organ donation?"

The question hung in the air for a long moment. In that instant I saw my baby the day she was born, pink and bald, her eyes squinting up at me as if the light might blind her. I saw my diabetic mother plucking at the sheets on her deathbed as her kidneys failed. Then the image of the pink donor sticker pasted on the front of my driver's license. I pictured families in other hospital conference rooms waiting for bad news.

"Yes," I heard myself say.

Dr. Carr nodded. "At least it won't be a total waste," he said. I recoiled.

He waved his hand in the direction of the ICU and all the high-tech gadgetry keeping Maya's heart beating, her lungs pumping, her blood circulating. I could see he meant that all the effort and resources spent on a hopeless case would not be in vain. But my yes was designed to signify something very different. It meant that the love and energy I had poured into my daughter, her very life, must continue. I could no more accept that Maya was truly dead than I could fly to the moon or allow any vital part of her that could save another human being to go to her grave.

Dr. Carr said he would contact the California Transplant Donor Network. Every second counted now, because as long as Maya was supported by the ventilator, the risk of damage to her organs, especially her lungs, increased. People were waiting with desperate patience for what Maya had to offer.

I had made my decision. I had said yes. Now, I trembled uncontrollably. I was about to give my daughter away in pieces. *If I had fought harder, could I have held her here?* I gave Maya ultimate freedom, and she took it.

Across the San Francisco Bay, I later learned, a figure shrouded in white lay on a hospital bed, near death. The man's heart failure was so profound that his fingernails had turned blue. This man, comatose and oxygen-starved, was a blip on the computer screen of the national donor registry. Along with four thousand others on the heart transplant list, he was waiting for someone to die so that he could live.

By his side at the University of California Medical Center in San Francisco on the afternoon of April 6, 1992, his wife stood looking down at the comatose figure of her husband; she knew that even the ventilator could not force air into his lungs much longer. She watched the rise and fall of her husband's chest, the backs of her hands wet with tears she rubbed away without noticing.

Dozens of times in the last ten years she had stood over his crumpled body after the defibrillator implanted in his abdomen knocked him to his knees with a shock powerful enough to restart his failing heart. Her two young children were reading magazines in the waiting room, fidgeting with their candy wrappers—their lives a constant limbo. She turned her back on her husband's bed and prayed for a miracle. She didn't know it, but her prayer had just been answered in another hospital only thirty miles away on the other side of the San Francisco Bay.

Our donor coordinator was a young nurse, not many years older than Maya. She sat across from me at a polished wooden table in a windowless conference room. She read me a list of Maya's vital organs as if they were car parts, asking permission to salvage each one.

"Do you give consent for her corneas?"

"Yes," I answered and then initialed a blank line next to the name of the organ with the pen she had handed me earlier.

The nurse's cheery smile did not mask her discomfort. "Do you give consent for her lungs?" I knew she was only doing her job, but surely she must realize that to a mother this was torture.

By the time she got to the right and left ventricles of Maya's heart, I was ready to reach across the table and slap her.

"Look, I can save us both a lot of agony." I focused my eyes like laser beams. "Just take it—take it all."

She shook her head apprehensively. "The law requires that I must go through each one . . . I know this must be hard for you . . ."

"It is *unbearable,*" I snapped, balling my hands into fists beneath the table. "Do you have any children?"

She shook her head no.

I smiled sardonically. "I am going to initial each of these blanks and sign this form here at the bottom," I said slowly. "Then we are both going to agree that we did this legally. But I am not going to sit here while you read me a list of my daughter's organs."

I pressed through the triplicate form with the ballpoint pen.

"You understand that you are giving consent for them to take bone, skin tissue for grafts, and inner ear bones as well," she said. Her voice quavered.

"Yes," I replied. "You have my permission to take anything that will save lives or reduce pain. Just don't make me stay here another minute."

As a "biomort," or a "beating heart cadaver," Maya was suspended in a nether world between life and death. Her brain would never function again, but with life support, her heart continued to beat and her chest rose and fell, filled with mechanically produced oxygen. When Dr. Carr asked if I would donate Maya's organs, I gave my consent in a state of raw emotion with little knowledge of the ethical fog zone I had just entered. Within minutes, "life support" became "organ support." A few hours later, surgeons began to "harvest" my daughter's organs and tissues, work that continued through the night.

Thank God no one asked me to make the decision to unplug her. I would have left her there, suspended, her brain growing ever more gangrenous, simply to have the illusion of life, to stand next to her bed watching her pink cheeks and her closed eyes, the rhythm of her rising and falling chest, to be able to whisper words of love in my daughter's ear. But tens of thousands of dollars were being spent for her care, and the doctors knew there was no hope she could recover.

In the years since Maya died, I have been to countless donor events where donor families are lionized as heroes. Perhaps we are. But I wonder. Do we really understand the implications of what we have agreed to in a moment of crisis?

Agreeing to donate Maya's organs and tissues without knowing for certain what she would have wanted put me on morally shaky ground. At least the doctors had radioactive dye studies, concrete evidence that her brain would never function again. All I had was an overwhelming desire not to let my daughter die entirely. Donating her organs seemed like the only way to salvage her lost life. My consent was an act of hope, of defiance, a way of keeping my child alive.

Since her death on the afternoon of April 6, 1992, I have lived with the unspoken fear that I abandoned my child to organ retrieval surgery when she was still breathing and her heart was still beating. Rationally, I know that her breath and heartbeat were mechanically induced, but she still looked alive, requiring me to suspend the evidence of life before my own eyes and trust that brain death was also *real* death.

I am not alone in my doubts. Brain death, or death "by neurological criteria," was only recognized in the 1960s, after medical technology had advanced enough to keep people on life support. To this day, according to researchers, a majority of people surveyed do not understand the concept of brain death. Many mistakenly believe that someone who has been declared brain dead can recover.

Interviews conducted by bioethics researcher Vera Kalitzkus with donor families in Germany show how difficult it is for families, parents in particular, to wrestle with the dichotomy of the "living corpse." Kalitzkus interviewed one mother whose two-year-old child was declared brain dead following a car accident. "If the respirator had been turned off, then he really would have died. But the last image I have of my child is that of a breathing child. And that makes it very hard to cope with and go on living," the bereaved mother said.

Now that there are so many shades of gray in what used to be black and white—fifty years ago a person was either dead or not—Kalitzkus argues that we need to acknowledge stages of death. The families of organ donors confront three distinct phases, she writes: *brain death,* when the loved one is in an indeterminate state but is in the process of dying; *actual death,* which takes place after the organ removal; and *final death,* when the transplanted organ dies in or with the body of the organ recipient. She acknowledges this places an additional unbearable burden on donor families: "Organ donation also means to sacrifice the hour of parting, the last moments they share with their dying/dead relative, and surrender this intimate and private moment of life to the necessities and the regime of the transplantation process," she writes.

If I had been one of her subjects, I could have told Ms. Kalitzkus about my surreal parting from Maya and how for years I used to fall to my knees crushed by remorse and beg her forgiveness for what I had allowed doctors to do to her body. But at the time I gave consent, I didn't know exactly what would happen to Maya. All I knew was that her organs could save other lives. Altruism seemed preferable to despair.

At 3:30 that April afternoon, after I had signed the consent papers and pressed them into the donor coordinator's shaking hands, I led the way to my daughter's bedside for the moment of final good-bye. My minister, Rev. Margaret Stortz, stood at Maya's shoulder on one side of the bed; I stood on the other side, facing her, with other loved ones gathered near the foot of the bed. A nurse drew the curtains, and we formed a protective circle around Maya's body.

The ventilator still distended her mouth, but the fiber optic cable that had run from the computer into her bandaged skull was gone. Her cheeks were rosy, and some of the puffiness had left her face. She looked so much like the brand new baby I had held in my arms almost twenty years ago; she had the same swaddled look, the same clean smell. I lifted her warm, limp hand and held it in mine.

The October morning Maya was born they wrapped her in a blanket and gave her to me on the delivery table. I first noticed her fingers—long, thin, strong, with perfect miniature fingernails. I extended my index finger, and she latched on tight with her fist.

"Look, she has piano player fingers. Those hands could straddle an octave," I said to her father, delirious with fatigue and happiness.

At her bedside, it was as if no time had passed since that day in 1972. I slid my right hand under her shoulder and gazed down at her serene young face, playing with her warm fingers, now utterly still.

Rev. Margaret leaned over her. "Maya, this is your graduation from life on earth. We release you with all our love and blessings." She looked at me from across the white mound of sheets covering Maya's body. "Can you let her go, Eleanor?"

The question took my breath away. My chest tightened as if something was squeezing the air from my lungs. I looked down at the pink cheeks, the smooth neck, the slim body. My lovely, lovely girl.

"I love you, Maya," I whispered. "You are as beautiful to me as the day you were born. I'm letting you go now with all my heart, with all my love."

I stroked her cheek again and again.

Margaret's voice startled me. "Eleanor, would you like a few moments alone with her?"

"No." I shook my head mechanically. Tears slid down my cheeks. I was afraid to be left alone with my daughter's body, for fear I would go mad.

I put my head on Maya's chest, resting my cheek against the soft cotton of her gown. The rise and fall of her mechanically powered breath was like a whoosh of ocean tide—in and out, in and out. The steady drumming of her heart filled my senses. At last, I raised my head. There would be no last breath to signal the end. I simply had to walk away and leave her, something I did not have the strength to do on my own.

I looked at the other faces ringing the bed. Without speaking, as if we had planned it beforehand, we each bowed our heads toward Maya's body. Then we walked away from her without speaking, past the nursing station, returning to the waiting room with its hard plastic chairs and TV bolted to the wall. I stared at the blank screen, gathered a stray balloon and a get-well collage made by Maya's girlfriends, and walked away. I could not contemplate what would come next.

I allowed doctors to take a hacksaw to my daughter's chest. They broke open her rib cage to extract her heart, her liver, and her kidneys.

Several days after the surgery I received a bill from the Red Cross for donated blood Maya had been given during the organ retrieval surgery. I called our donor coordinator for an explanation.

"If my daughter was dead, why did she need a transfusion?" I demanded.

She did her best to calm me. "To keep her organs functioning they have to be perfused with fresh blood," she explained, apologizing for the misrouted bill. It should have gone to the California Transplant Donor Network. Later, I learned that Maya had been anesthetized and given muscle relaxant during the surgery to recover her organs. This is done to lessen the chance that the body on the table will move involuntarily. It made me wonder if the operating room staff also questions whether beating heart cadavers are truly dead.

Twelve days after Maya died, I received a letter from our transplant coordinator, the young nurse I had treated so curtly. She told of the miracles that resulted from my decision. Maya's kidneys had been flown across the country to the Boston area, where two patients, one twenty-one and the other forty-seven, had been successfully transplanted. Her liver had gone to a thirty-eight-year-old woman with a rare form of liver disease. She was the mother of a seven-year-old daughter and would have died without the transplant. Maya's corneas had restored sight for two people in the Bay Area. Her skin tissue, tendons, ligaments, cartilage, and inner ear bones would help more than fifty others.

I burst into tears when I reached the paragraph about Maya's heart. It had been given to a fifty-four-year-old Chilean businessman, an import-export specialist who did business in the United States. "He had been waiting for some time for this gift," the letter said. "He is recovering very well after surgery. Without this transplant he could not have survived."

Tucked between the folds of the letter I found a note from his wife. She had not signed her name, but I could hear her voice through her words. "My two children and I want to express how thankful we are to you for the gift of life you as a family have given us as a family. My husband is getting better every day and the children, eight and twelve years old, have another chance to grow up with a father. This was only possible thanks to the decision you made to become part of the donor program. From our hearts—thank you. We will pray for you and your daughter every day." She signed it, "The Receiving Family."

Eighty-six words. During the months that followed I would often pull out that ivory card with its neat, spiky letters and reread it, as if I could balance my grief against another family's joy, as if it were ballast enough.

More than 105,000 people await transplants in the United States today. Each day, on average, eighteen of them die waiting. Some of them are young children. When I think of their parents, I forget my doubts. Yes, my daughter died a more violent death because of my decision. I can look that in the face now, knowing it was the price of altruism. It would have been worth it to save only one life, but Maya's organs and tissues saved or transformed many more.

Indeed, a study conducted in the late 1980s, as transplantation became the treatment of choice for many life-threatening conditions, found that among the general public, saving lives was regarded as the primary motivation for organ donation.

And yet altruism, alone, is not reason enough—at least for me. I chose donation as a way to create meaning from the seemingly senseless death of my child. I also saw it as a way to keep my daughter alive—a fixation, I have since learned, that, in some form, is common among donor families.

The study compared the attitudes of the general public with the attitudes of families of organ donors. When researchers asked what the most important motivations for donation might be, 86 percent of donor families surveyed answered that they wanted something positive to come from their loss.

The researchers, Helen Levine Batten and Jeffery M. Prottas, concluded, "Altruism is the core of the shared motivation of both actual donor families and those among the general public who would agree to donate. What separates the attitudes of these two groups is the far greater concern of donor families for the meaning of donation for their memory of the deceased."

Almost 90 percent of the donor families surveyed by Batten and Prottas said that if they had to make the decision to donate again, they would say yes.

Bioethicists continue to debate the boundary between life and death. Medical anthropologist Margaret Lock argues that death is a social construct, shaped by the values of the culture in which it occurs. She offers Japan as an example. There, only people who have specified in writing that they wish to become donors can be declared brain dead and thus able to donate. "Brain-dead individuals who have not indicated that they want to become donors are not considered legally dead," Lock writes.

Had she died in Japan, Maya could not have become an organ donor. She would have experienced both brain death and actual death, and the four people who received her organs would have waited longer for life-saving transplants or perished before organs became available.

Which is the higher ethical good? Ensuring that my daughter was well and truly dead? Or living with the ambiguity and moral anguish of *not* knowing but giving people in need a second chance at life?

Only 10 percent of donor families ever meet the recipients of their gift. In 1994, two years after Maya's death, I met the man who had received her heart, along with his wife and their two children. We met on a late afternoon in May in the San Francisco offices of the California Transplant Donor Network. By pure coincidence, we had each requested the meeting within days of one another, so the transplant organization granted our wish. As I embraced Fernando and listened to Maya's heart beating in his chest, I had the oddest sensation that she was there, still vital, still alive.

Fernando called Maya *"mi alma,"* my soul. Each time he felt her heart beat in his body, he sensed her soul was one with his. This mystified and disturbed him, yet he formed a close bond with Maya and wanted to know everything about her. When he asked for her picture, I gave him copies of several of my favorite photographs.

In 1996 my younger daughter, Meghan, then sixteen, flew to Santiago as a guest of Fernando and his family. She befriended his son, by then a seventeen-year-old with a drinking problem. He had grown up certain his father would die. I wondered if some part of him could not accept the gift of a dead girl's heart that kept his father alive and his family intact. I later learned that often recipients do not seek contact with the families of their donors because their feelings of guilt—and gratitude—are overwhelming. In our case, Fernando and I both wanted to know more about each other. Neither of us realized how this would affect our children.

Meghan's visit lasted for two weeks. At one point, Fernando asked her to go into his office to retrieve something for him. As she turned to leave the room, she glimpsed a poster-sized picture of Maya displayed on the wall above Fernando's desk. Her sister stared down at her, so lifelike that Meghan gasped. Maya was enshrined in Fernando's heart and his life, so perhaps it is not surprising that he memorialized her this way. It was one more marker of how, in some way, donation had made us kin.

Perhaps Maya was Wonder Woman, after all. She lived long enough to express her daring and genius more than most mortals. Maya was a gifted young actress. The day before her accident, she had learned about her acceptance as a community college transfer student into the UCLA School of Theater, Film, and Television, an honor granted very few. She was offered a full scholarship. She had been out celebrating, riding a strange horse bareback in a remote field.

She flew to the ground with her dreams and her beauty intact and lost consciousness instantly. The last time I spoke with her, as a conscious being, was the morning of the accident. I ruffled her hair on my way out the door.

"I'm so proud of you, honey," I said, my heart practically bursting.

She grinned up at me from the armchair where she was perched, still in pajamas, and gave me a Top Gun–style thumbs up.

"Love you, Mom," she said.

"Love you too," I replied, already out the door, already savoring our future.

Eleanor Vincent *is the author of* Swimming with Maya: A Mother's Story *(Capital Books, 2004). She has won numerous awards for her work, including a Woman of Promise Award from the Feminist Writer's Guild. She lives and works in Oakland, California.*

Twelve Breaths a Minute

GULCHIN A. ERGUN

ICU intern Gulchin A. Ergun has barely learned how to make people better, but now she is being asked to let someone go.

Patients don't show up in the ICU waiting to be admitted. They're transferred from other places: ERs, operating rooms, even other hospitals. They come in a tangle of blankets and wires, hurriedly pushed down hallways with plastic bags fluttering from IV flagpoles. Their things—the pants, wallets, underwear, and shoes—are stuffed into plastic bags with medical center logos and tagged with names and record numbers. But before you ever see them, a hand-off occurs, a separate, private dialogue between the doctor who sends them and the ones who accept them. Descriptions like "seventy-five-year-old man, hypotensive, hypoxic—probable pneumonia" or "eighty-three-year-old woman with diabetes and hypertension coming in with an MI and heart failure." The whole medical history is broken down to a phrase or a sentence, a colorless distillate without the distraction of emotion. Two months into my internship, I'd heard plenty, but when the senior resident called with a voice edged with anxiety, I knew something was up at the hand-off. The same voice earlier that day had been perfunctory, tersely efficient with the business of passing on medical information in the least amount of time.

"We've got Dan Arthurs's mother down here," he said. "She was found down at home. Looks like she's had a big stroke. Neuro's already seen her and talked to the family. I don't think it looks good."

As an intern, your job is to evaluate new admissions, a practice-makes-perfect requirement of training that constitutes almost all you do. It starts with a history, an interview-based assessment to figure out the details of why they've come to the hospital, followed by a laying on of the hands intended to canvass the body for clues to the medical condition. After that you just take care of the patients. Whether that means ordering tests, prescribing medications, or merely watching them, your job is to keep them alive and put them on the road to recovery.

She was already in the unit when I arrived. The room was big and windowless, somewhere near the middle of the hospital. An oversized bed sat wedged next to a column perforated with electrical plugs spraying medical paraphernalia like ophthalmoscopes and stethoscopes. Along a wall stood a flip-down metal commode and a small stainless steel counter sink with disinfectant soap and surgical gloves. The only decoration was a patterned curtain that could be pulled shut, keeping whatever was going on in the room private, since there were no doors, just sliding glass so people inside could be seen at all times. The overhead fluorescence whitewashed the room, and the space was devoid of the usual attempts at personalization. There were no flowers, plants, family photographs, crayon drawings, or get well cards taped to the walls—the things that accumulate the longer a patient is in the hospital. And while a TV was bracketed to the opposite wall, it was off; only the IV pumps and alarms beeped and chirped from inside the room, the background noise of hospitals.

Regular hospital rooms always have chairs where you can sit down and ask questions during an interview, but in the ICU the urgent nature of things doesn't lend itself to sitting, and chairs get in the way during emergencies, so you do everything standing up. As I walked to the head of the bed I was already making my first impression: elderly, pleasantly wrinkled lady with wavy white hair splayed on a pillow, looking like she had just fallen asleep. I bent over the side rail to greet her and introduce myself.

"Hello, Mrs. Arthurs," I said, maybe a little too loudly into her right ear. "I'm Dr. Ergun. I'm going to examine you."

I felt a little silly as the words came out of my mouth, since her placid demeanor was clearly undisturbed by either my voice or the endotracheal tube

I observed emerging from her mouth. The tube was secured to her cheek with tape that had caught a few stray hairs. Maybe haste in placement, I thought, noting the droplets of condensation beginning to collect inside. It didn't look like much: nine inches of clear plastic with numbering on the side, but like an astronaut's hose tethered to a ship in space, this was her lifeline. Connected to the patient with corrugated hoses, this ventilator controlled exactly how much oxygen, humidity, and volume of air she took in with every breath, even the number of sighs. Someone had already chosen the ventilator settings; she was set at twelve breaths per minute—the rate of breath in deep sleep.

I lifted her hospital gown to examine her. She had no obvious injury to her body. No bumps or bruises to suggest a recent fall, no old scars. She looked normal except that she didn't move when I touched her and didn't respond when I pinched her skin or vigorously rubbed my knuckles on her sternum, the intentionally painful stimuli intended to judge levels of consciousness. I pulled her eyelids back with my thumb and saw large black pupils, and I flashed the pen light into her eyes. No reaction. I did it again. Still nothing. Bad sign, I thought to myself. It's a basic reflex that pupils constrict to light. Loss of pupillary reflexes implies significant brain injury.

I stuck a tongue depressor into her mouth, rubbing it across the back of her pharynx to see if she gagged. Nothing. A scrape across the soles of her foot with the handle of my reflex hammer elicited no response as well. How could you look so ordinary on the outside, I thought, with no reflexes on the inside, no signals to do the basic things required for living?

Stuffed into the tan envelope at the foot of the bed were copies of her CAT scan. I took them out of the paper jacket and placed them on the X-ray view box that hung on the wall.

"Edema, midline shift, effacement of the sulci," I said to myself. "Bihemispheric stroke." Even to a new intern, the degree of her injury was obvious. This was catastrophic. The extreme lack of blood flow to both sides of the brain was not something people survived. Worse still, the injury itself would be predicted to cause more damage from the expected swelling that would eventually choke off the remainder of the blood supply.

The family arrived and assembled at her bedside. A woman wearing a camel-colored cable-knit sweater and sensible glasses tenderly adjusted the hair on the patient's forehead, tidying it to the side. Her other hand clutched Mrs. Arthurs's slender, creased fingers, which were calmly arranged on the blanket. A younger gentleman, his brow furrowed in what was either pain or anger, stood next to the sweatered woman but a few steps back from the bed. His hands were jammed into the rumple of his pockets, and I could see the outline of bunched fists alongside his thighs. Given their age and behavior, I gathered they were her children. After a few minutes, the third person in the room and the only one I recognized, Dr. Arthurs, stepped out and asked to speak to me.

Dr. Arthurs was an attending physician at the teaching hospital where I interned. It was impossible not to recognize him. He was a well-known and respected member of the faculty. Doctors like him were part of the reason that I remained in Cleveland after medical school. I stayed where I thought I would get the best education, although I had visited fine programs in New York and Chicago, the big cities where I dreamed of living. He was popular with students and house staff, known for his open and genial manner with patients, as well as trainees, skillful at turning simple points in the history into teaching pearls. Despite the late hour, he was still dressed professionally. With gently receding gray hair and kind eyes, he could have been anyone's uncle or older brother. He was wearing a brown tweed jacket, and the black tubing of his stethoscope peeked out of his right-hand pocket. He reached for my hand, I thought to shake it, but instead grasped it, holding it between his large muscular palms. We stood there in silence, and I waited for him to say something.

"I wish we weren't here," he murmured as he took a deep breath. "We know this isn't good."

I studied his face quietly and waited for him to finish what he was saying.

He then soberly added, "My mother was very clear about her wishes. She didn't want anything heroic. My brother, sister, and I have talked about it, and we would like to turn off the vent."

I stood there silently, nearly motionlessly, taking my cue from him. I tried to appear calm and respectful, meeting his eyes head on, hoping to display some compassion and understanding, but I could barely hear what he was saying. The only thing I heard was turn off the vent, turn OFF the vent. Was he talking to me? I caught myself nodding, suggesting agreement but thinking: I don't know if I can do this.

I had never turned off a ventilator. I had no idea how to do what they were asking of me. In medical school, implicit in every lesson, permeating every choice, was the only Latin I knew, *primum non nocere,* first do no harm. Up to this point, I'd spent more time preparing for my career than anyone else I knew, but I wasn't prepared for this. My education was focused on keeping people alive; how was I supposed to stop doing that? How was I supposed to end a life?

Suddenly I found myself facing the most classic ethical dilemma: was it okay to turn off the ventilator? That it was legal, I knew, but was it wrong? She was brain dead. Of that there was no doubt; no reflexes, no spontaneous breaths. She had had a devastating injury, and no miracle was going to save her, and if she did make it, she would never be who she was. She would probably never talk, walk, or even turn in bed. However, she would be alive, and she could live on a ventilator in a skilled nursing facility with machines to assist her bodily functions. But that would require a surgical tracheostomy for permanent connection to a vent, placement of a gastrostomy tube for nutrition, and a catheter in her bladder to drain her urine. She could expect to get pneumonia and urinary tract infections. What kind of a life was that?

Yet good or bad, it was a life. I didn't want to be responsible for any death, and particularly not hers, the mother of one of my attendings. I could only imagine the sorrow of her family at losing her, but I also imagined the agony they might feel at letting her live, a scrap of what she was. Back and forth this went in my head, always ending with the same thoughts. How was I going to do this and, maybe selfishly, why me?

Fervently hoping that no one noticed the flush sneaking up my ears and cheeks despite the meat locker temperatures that characterized the unit, I discreetly conferred with the ICU attending about what I was supposed to do.

"Yes, I already know about it," he said. "They called me from the ER too. There really isn't anything else that we can do. That's want they want. Just go ahead."

Just go ahead? Go ahead and what? I wanted to leave, step through the double doors and get outside. It didn't matter that it was night and that the closest thing to open space was a strip of weeds by a bicycle stand under an insect-crusted street light on the way to the parking lot. But I couldn't leave the premises any more than I could drag my feet, duck into a call room, and pretend I was too busy. It's not like I could have asked someone else to take care of it. I was it, the intern on call, and I didn't have the luxury of time to figure out the "whether"; I still had to work on the "how." It's not like you take a class on this. There is no "Turning Off the Ventilator 101" in school, and there is no manual in your pocket with an algorithm on how to do this.

Do you write an order for someone to do it, or do you do it yourself? Do you take the endotracheal tube out, or do you leave it in? Maybe you're supposed to turn off the machine, but even that wasn't clear. Didn't most machines in hospitals come with battery support so they wouldn't fail under unexpected circumstances, like electrical failure? There had to be a master on/off switch, right? But with at least ten knobs on the control panel and at least six different dials regulating ventilation, which one was it? Worse, it had to be done without the appearance of confusion, like landing a plane without ever seeing an instrument panel, with all the passengers watching. You have to look competent when you let someone go. You can't cry. If this is medicine, I thought, I'm not sure if I'm cut out for this.

I approached the most sympathetic-looking nurse and asked her what was usually done. Following her explanation I approached Dr. Arthurs.

"I'll take care of it," I said. "I'm so sorry." And I was. Sorry for them and sorry for me.

Reluctantly, I went to the ventilator and searched for the breath frequency dial and turned it down to zero. Then I waited. A peculiar quiet took over the room, broken only by the soft beep-beep coming from a cardiac monitor still detecting her heartbeat. You don't realize how loud the sounds of the ventilator breaths are until they're gone. Her two sons and daughter stood around the bed holding each other and her. They didn't speak or sob out loud, though tears streamed down some of their faces. There was no wailing or thrashing, just a silent ping-pong of serious eyes that moved back and forth from their mother to the screen, still showing green spikes marching erratically across the display.

Why didn't I turn off that monitor? I berated myself. Did anyone need to see the exact moment the heart stopped beating?

I wasn't sure if I was supposed to leave the room or not, so I stayed, staring at my feet, my hands stuffed into my pockets, trying to hide my trembling until it was over. She never took a breath; her heart struggled in a chaos of electricity without air, then finally stopped. I mentally noted when all electrical activity ceased and finally left the room.

"Time of death 0122," I documented in the chart. The rest I don't remember.

I was twenty-six years old. Graduation from medical school had been just seven weeks earlier. I had barely learned how to make people better, but now I'd added "letting someone go" to my list of achievements. Some honor; was there a category for this on your résumé?

Shaking it didn't come easily. I felt guilty and ashamed. Remorse came every time I closed my eyes and saw the three of them standing there around the bed with their eyes glued to the monitor. I tortured myself, dwelling on all the other things I had neglected to do, like offer chairs or call for clergy. I didn't even get them Kleenex; I just stood there.

It was something I couldn't share easily with anyone outside medicine, friends or family. My best confidant was the other intern in the ICU, who didn't mind admitting, "It could have been me. I'm so glad I wasn't on call that night." Weeks, even months later, I would duck into stairwells when I glimpsed Dr. Arthurs. Now a man I had hardly ever seen was everywhere I looked. If I saw him strolling down the hall in my direction, I went the other way. If he sat in the back of the room at grand rounds, I headed for the front. At conferences, I avoided any eye contact, skirting any possible encounter.

When I finished my three years of internship and residency, I chose to specialize. I liked the idea of an action-oriented specialty—one where you could identify a problem, like a bleeding ulcer, then move to stop it. In the beginning I thought gastroenterology was relatively spared from the day-to-day dealings with death, but with training and experience, I was reminded that you cannot avoid end-of-life issues. Rounding lists that didn't include the name of a patient with a poor prognosis were rare. Eventually I became the attending physician, and I was the one families came to when they had to ask the hard questions of what to do.

Many years later, I mingled with other guests at a party at the Smithsonian National Museum of American History. Hors d'oeuvres were still being passed as we prepared to sit down to tables when I noticed an attractive older gentleman making his way toward me.

"I thought that was you," he said, and I recognized Dr. Arthurs. I suppressed a surprisingly powerful but fleeting urge to escape and decided it was time to confess.

"I was sick about the whole thing," I explained. "I didn't know what I was doing. I was so uncomfortable. It was the first time. I didn't know how to help." It all spilled out: how I'd avoided him, the guilt and regret I'd nursed for so long.

"I'm so sorry that you felt that way," he said. He paused and looked me squarely in the eyes. "It wasn't like that at all. You did nothing wrong. We were always grateful at how you handled things. None of us wanted to be there." He cupped my shoulder and steered me away from the crowd. "Come here, I want to show you something," he said, leading me down a hall to a different gallery in the museum. We walked up to an exhibit, and we stood side by side peering into the display.

It was a fourth-grade classroom lined with several rows of old-fashioned, one-piece wooden desks, some with notebooks on them. There was a podium in the front, with a large black chalkboard alongside. About twenty names were written on it, all in the same precise rounded script. At the top was written, *Welcome to my class. Mrs. Arthurs.*

"I wanted to show you something of the person she was," he said. He told me how she had been a dedicated teacher and had devoted most of her adult life to teaching in a poor community in East Cleveland, Ohio. They had lifted the entire classroom, piece by piece, as a representative example of education in American history.

I felt privileged to be shown this, honored he would share this tribute to his mother with me but also comforted and oddly forgiven. But I was also saddened. Saddened, I thought, at how I had changed.

I had carried that guilt for months, maybe years, but if I were faced with the same decision today, I would not struggle the same way. I would not agonize over the choice. Through the lens of retrospection I saw how I had magnified my culpability and that, despite my perceived transgressions, this was still a good death, a painless denouement to a rich life and the facilitation of a patient's last wish. When I dialed down her ventilator, Mrs. Arthurs was already gone. Nothing I could have done would have changed that. Her life was never really in my hands.

Gulchin A. Ergun *is a practicing gastroenterologist in Houston, Texas. She is the clinical service chief of gastroenterology and the medical director of the Digestive Disease Department, Reflux Center, and GI Physiology Lab at the Methodist Hospital in Houston. She is a clinician educator and enjoys teaching trainees and patients, as well as peers. She holds appointments as a clinical associate professor of medicine at Weill Cornell Medical College and Baylor College of Medicine. This is her first publication.*